A
SHORT HISTORY
OF THE
AMERICAN REVOLUTION

Also by James L. Stokesbury

A Short History of the Korean War

Masters of the Art of Command (*with Martin Blumenson*)

A Short History of World War II

A Short History of World War I

Navy and Empire

A Short History of Air Power

A
SHORT HISTORY
OF THE
AMERICAN
REVOLUTION

James L. Stokesbury

William Morrow and Company, Inc.
New York

Library of Congress Cataloging-in-Publication Data

Stokesbury, James L.
   A short history of the American Revolution / James L. Stokesbury.
     p.   cm.
   Includes index.
   ISBN 0-688-08333-1
   1. United States—History—Revolution, 1775-1783. I. Title.
E208.S87   1991   90-29108
973.3—dc20   CIP

Printed in the United States of America

First Edition

1 2 3 4 5 6 7 8 9 10

BOOK DESIGN BY M & M DESIGNS

For Bill and Sandy,
and Laurie and Tom

ACKNOWLEDGMENTS

DURING THE preparation of this work, I was enabled to visit most of the major battlefields of the American Revolution, thanks to a generous grant from the Harvey T. Reid Fund of Acadia University, and it is a pleasure to acknowledge their assistance in this way. As always, members of the History Department of Acadia University, and the staff of the Vaughan Memorial Library of Acadia, have been unfailingly supportive, and I wish to thank my friends and colleagues for their kind interest over the years. None of them, of course, have any responsibility for any errors or facts or interpretation contained herein. My chief thanks go to my wife, Elizabeth.

CONTENTS

MAPS

11

Prologue

Boston lay quiet under an early spring night. But the stillness of spring evenings is illusory, as anyone who lives in the country knows, and in fact the small city was teeming with activity. Lieutenant General Thomas Gage, commander in chief of His Majesty's forces in North America and governor of Massachusetts, had serious business in hand. He had recently received peremptory orders from London; the government at home, finally out of patience with recalcitrant colonials, had ordered Gage to take some decisive action which would reassert royal authority. Gage had decided that the appropriate gesture was to seize military stores the colonials were known to be amassing at the little village of Concord, several miles west of Boston.

To do this he detached sixteen flank companies—eight of grenadiers and eight of light infantry—from their regular regiments, and put them together as a striking force under the command of Lieutenant Colonel Francis Smith of the 10th Foot. At dusk on April 18, 1775, these troops mustered on Boston Common, approximately seven hundred strong, and at full dark they set out on their mission. Boats from the Royal Navy's ships in the harbor took them across to Lechmere Point, on the mainland, where, in the time-honored fashion of military forces, they waited a full two hours for additional rations they did not need before setting out on their march to the west.

In spite of all their precautions, the British were not the only ones awake and about in the night. Just as the countryside was full of loyal subjects who had informed Gage of the presence of stores and colonial leaders in the towns outside Boston, so the capital was full of men who were no friends of the British; a casual word here, a dropped hint there, had been enough for the opposition to have a very good idea of what was going on. The British were closely checked and their moves signaled to watchers across the Charles River and Back Bay. Dr. Joseph Warren in the city had sent William Dawes and Paul Revere out with the warning of British action. Between the two of them, they roused the countryside out as far as Lexington. Revere was later captured by a mounted British patrol, officers sent out along the roads to prevent exactly this sort of thing, but by then his work had been taken up by other riders.

Meanwhile, Colonel Smith and his men plodded along, increasingly aware that they were not alone. At Menotomy, a little more than halfway out to Lexington, Smith halted his troops and called an officers' conference. He decided they were not moving quickly enough, and therefore detached an advance force, commanded by Major John Pitcairn of the Royal Marines. Giving the major six companies of the light infantry, he told him to push ahead and seize control of the bridges at Concord. As the light infantry swung off down the road, Smith also sent a rider back to Boston asking for reinforcements.

Paul Revere had reached Lexington at midnight, while the British were still clambering out of their boats at Lechmere Point. He found there two of the most outspoken Patriot leaders, Samuel Adams and John Hancock, both of Boston; they were finally persuaded to leave, to avoid arrest, about midway through the early morning hours. The commander of the local militia force, Captain John Parker, mustered about 130 men and awaited further developments. He sent several scouts east along the road to Boston, but most of them did not return, and eventually Parker dismissed his company, telling the men to be ready for further action. Many of them drifted off to Buckman Tavern, the only place to keep warm in the cool April night when sensible men were tucked up in their beds.

Parker's scouts failed to return because most of them were scooped up by the point of Pitcairn's advance. Finally one of them, Thaddeus Brown, came in about first light to report that he had just evaded the British, who were only half a mile behind him. Parker hastily recalled his men, but less than half were there on the green, in a ragged line, when Pitcairn led his column into town. The sun was just rising in the east, and the British quickly swung from their marching formation into line. Pitcairn advanced across the green, apparently intending to disarm the American force, which he outnumbered perhaps five to one. Parker, with eminent good sense, was on the point of deciding to withdraw. At that point, a shot rang out, then several more, then a volley from the British, and a smattering of return fire from the Americans. The redcoats charged with the bayonet, the militia broke, and within a couple of minutes it was over. Eight Americans were dead, ten wounded; one British soldier was shot in the leg, and Pitcairn's horse, a better target, had two slight wounds.

By the time Pitcairn had restored some sort of order, Smith and the remainder of the column arrived, and the British soon resumed their march to Concord. They arrived there about seven, to find again that the local militia had turned out. While the grenadiers searched for stores, most of which had already been removed, the light infantry went forward to hold the bridges over the Concord River against interference. At the North Bridge, several hundred militia advanced against three British companies, and this time, having already been blooded at Lexington, there was no hesitation among the redcoats. They opened fire as soon as the Americans came within range, and after a short but spirited exchange, they then fell back into town.

Smith had now done all that it seemed he could, so he began his return march to Boston about noon. By now everyone felt that it had been a pretty sorry day's work, but few could realize how much worse it was to become. About a mile back down the road from Concord, at Meriam's Farm, the British were ambushed by American militia companies who had swung around from the North Bridge. Now from all the towns that flanked the British route the militia had mustered, and the British were forced to run a gauntlet all the way back to Boston.

Wherever the ground offered any sort of cover, the Americans came up singly or in small groups and fired on the British column. Smith sent out patrols of light infantry to keep the Americans at a distance, and many were killed when taken unawares. But equally many, operating in their own loose, undisciplined way, filtered in close enough for shots at the redcoats. It was near midafternoon when the head of the column reached Lexington.

Here the British encountered at last their supporting force, commanded by Earl Percy. About fourteen hundred strong, this unit had left Boston at nine in the morning; even before Smith's request for reinforcements arrived, Gage had directed such a movement for 4:30, but orders had been mislaid or not delivered, so Percy was a good five hours behind schedule. His arrival probably saved the original column from annihilation, and he took over command from Smith, who had already been wounded.

The British left Lexington soon after three, and reached Charlestown Neck as the day was ending. All along the way they were attacked by ever-increasing militia arrivals, from Framingham and Sudbury, Danvers and Woburn. The fighting became nastier as the British, frustrated and enraged, burned houses sheltering snipers, and shot or bayoneted anyone in arms they were able to catch.

By the night of April 19, the stars had altered in their courses. A political disagreement among members of the same family had become instead a blood feud. Things could never be the same again. The word of fighting was running like flashes of lightning through New England; while Percy's men were still being harried back to Boston, militia were turning out as far away as New Hampshire and Connecticut, and overnight little groups of men, the genesis of squads and companies, were stuffing rations in pockets, filling ammunition pouches, kissing wives good-bye for the indefinite future, and coalescing on the roads to Boston. It was an astounding display of the militia's ability to respond to a local crisis, a display that has haunted American military preconceptions ever since. By the morning of April 20, Boston was effectively besieged.

For Thomas Gage, sitting in his headquarters, sifting the reports of what had happened, counting his losses—about 250 killed, wounded, or missing—the day's events were astounding. He knew Americans; he had served in the colonies for much of his career; he was married to an American lady. These people were friends and relatives; they might call themselves Americans, but they were loyal British subjects—weren't they? How on earth had such a thing, such a tragic collision, come to happen?

CHAPTER ONE

The Causes of the War

THE SMOKE of Lexington and Concord had hardly cleared before both sides appealed to public opinion. General Gage immediately sent his dispatches to London, while the Americans, with a well-developed sense of political propaganda, set up investigatory committees and took a series of depositions, all with the aim of discovering who had fired the first shot and proving that it was not they who had done it. As it happened, their reports were sent after Gage's, but went on a faster ship, so the American version of events reached Britain before the official report did.

Though probably more ink has been spilled over it than there was blood shed at Lexington, the question of the first shot was a meaningless one, to which no definitive answer has ever been produced. The actual fact far transcended the details, and the fact was simply the logical culmination of events that had been in train ever since the founding of the colonies two centuries earlier. In the nature of human affairs, the relation between mother country and offspring was bound to change over time; for the later, second, British Empire, that change would be evolutionary, but that was because of the lessons learned in losing the first empire. Barring evolution, there was instead revolution.

Some historians have argued that ultimate separation was almost inherent in the founding of the colonies to begin with, that metropolitan and colonial British were two different peoples within the single society, and that from the earliest stages they viewed themselves as different. Those who left and went abroad saw the stay-at-homes as docile and spineless, willing to put up with injustices or lack of opportunity, or whatever else had driven the emigrants out; they saw themselves as the members of society who were willing to put principle into practice, who had the initiative to seek and make new opportunities, to suffer hardship and privation, all to create better lives for their families and subsequent generations. In this view, as it might be later mythologized, all the colonists were of the Puritan, Pilgrim, or Virginia tidewater aristocracy types, holding a monopoly on truth and virtue.

The opposite view, as it might be held by the metropolitan Briton, was that the colonists represented the exportable surplus of Englishmen, people who could or would not fit into society at home; religious cranks like the Pilgrims; down-at-heels gentry such as those who went to Virginia and starved rather than worked; men and women at the extreme end, of whom England might well be rid, such as paupers, indentured servants, and transported criminals. Such views are too overstated to make the argument, but emigration, by its very nature, is an act of rejection of some sort, and however much the colonists might have thought of themselves as British for however many generations, the potential for eventual separation was always there.

By the third quarter of the eighteenth century, the British Empire was the chief world power. Great Britain itself was small in population compared to some of the other states of Europe. There were perhaps eleven million people in England, Wales, Scotland, and Ireland, altogether about half of the population of France or the German states. Yet thanks to a largely homogeneous society, and the accidents of history and ge-

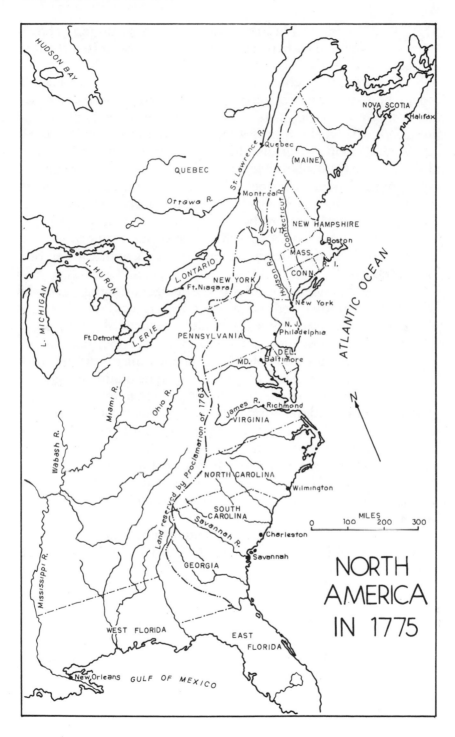

HUDSON BAY

NOVA SCOTIA
Halifax

St. Lawrence R.
Quebec
(MAINE)

QUEBEC

Ottawa R.
Montreal

NEW HAMPSHIRE
(VT)

Connecticut R.

Boston
MASS.
R.I.
CONN.

L. ONTARIO
NEW YORK
Ft. Niagara

Hudson R.

New York

L. HURON

L. MICHIGAN

L. ERIE

Ft. Detroit

N.J.
PENNSYLVANIA
Philadelphia

DEL.
MD.
Baltimore

Miami R.

Ohio R.

Wabash R.

Land reserved by Proclamation of 1763

James R. Richmond
VIRGINIA

N

NORTH CAROLINA
Wilmington

SOUTH
CAROLINA
Savannah R.

Charleston

MILES
0   100   200   300

GEORGIA

Savannah

NORTH
AMERICA
IN 1775

Mississippi R.

WEST FLORIDA

EAST
FLORIDA

New Orleans   GULF OF MEXICO

ATLANTIC OCEAN

ography, Britain had built an empire that was the envy of all the other states. The bedrock of that empire, and its ultimate reason for existence, was trade.

The operative economic theory of the period was a set of ideas known as mercantilism, or, after their foremost practitioner, Colbertism. In this view, there was a fixed amount of wealth in the world, represented by gold and silver; it was all allotted: the king of France had a share, the king of England had a share, and so did the Mogul emperor in India or the chief of the Iroquois. If one person or society was to get more, someone else had to have less. Trade therefore became a kind of war, and wealth might be pursued by what we would consider legitimate trade, or by force of arms. Sometimes, especially outside the borders of Europe, it was hard to tell one from the other.

To profit and expand in this scheme of things, a well-developed empire needed several components, which could be worked out almost mathematically. First of all, the system must have a strong mother country in Europe, capable of taking and holding the colonies it needed, of providing military and naval support, of producing manufactured goods, and of holding the whole thing together. Then, in lesser order, the empire needed different types of colonies: tropical, to produce the materials not provided by the climate of the home country; African slave stations, to send labor to the tropical colonies where Europeans found it difficult to work and survive; and last of all, temperate colonies, to provide whatever residue of materials the home country could not grow for itself.

All of these elements were held together by the mother country, and the whole was in competition with other empires. The ultimate aim for any given system was to produce a surplus of goods, which would then be exported to other, less efficient systems, bringing bullion back into one's own empire, making it rich, and powerful, and ultimately impoverishing one's neighbors, rivals, and enemies. The needs and perceptions of the mother country were absolutely paramount, and the growth, development, or perhaps ambitions of any of the lesser component parts had to be subordinated to the central direction.

This was all a theoretical construction, and in practice it never worked out as neatly as the statesmen and imperial administrators in London, or Paris, or Madrid, would have liked it to. Things were always slipping out of balance, and any one empire always had some things that it did not need, and lacked some things it did. In the British Empire, the construction of the edifice had been very informal. The French, beginning in the seventeenth century, had attempted to build an empire on logic, and a whole series of first ministers had sponsored companies, for the Indies, for the fur trade, for India. The Dutch had put together an empire that was a unique blend of private enterprise and state support and direction. But the British Empire had just grown, more or less by happenstance, without a great deal of central control. By good luck as much as by good management, the British had created an empire that conformed roughly to the mercantilist dictates of the day. They had a foothold in India, they had sugar islands in the Caribbean, they had slaving stations along the African coast, and they had the temperate colonies of the North American seaboard.

In terms of what they contributed to the imperial scheme, these last colonies were useful but not crucial. The view from London was different from the view from Philadelphia. The former is best illustrated by the famous speech of William Pitt condemning the government at the end of the Seven Years' War in 1763. Why on earth, he asked, had the ministry been stupid enough to keep Canada, a few thousand acres of barren wilderness, when it could have had the rich sugar island of Martinique instead?

Indeed, the marginal nature of the American colonies in the empire was exacerbated by their phenomenal recent growth. In 1700 the colonial population was only about 250,000, but three quarters of a century later, by the outbreak of the Revolution, it had increased ten times, to 2,500,000. New colonies had been founded—Georgia in 1732 was the last of the "thirteen"—or added, most notably Canada in 1763. None of this growth was planned by government, and only belatedly was it realized in London that the colonial situation had gotten somewhat out of hand. That realization came at the end of the Seven Years' War.

* * *

The Anglo-French struggle for primacy in western Europe, and for empire overseas, was one of the main features of world history for two hundred years. It began in 1689, when the Protestant champion, William of Orange, seized the English throne from his father-in-law, James II, in the Glorious Revolution. William was actually Dutch, and he rather disliked Englishmen, but he wanted their money to pursue his lifelong struggle against the growing power of Louis XIV's France. The conflict thus begun ended only in 1815, in the carnage of Waterloo; Napoleon's final defeat also ended the French attempt to gain hegemony over Europe. The next aspirants for that position would be from east of the Rhine.

The period from 1689 to 1815 has been called a "second Hundred Years' War," and during it British and French, and each other's allies or satellites, fought a series of wars, all having similar characteristics. In each of them, Great Britain acted as paymaster, guiding spirit, and organizer. The British repeatedly created anti-French coalitions, sent small armies to the Continent to assist their allies, and always dominated the seas and picked up colonies abroad to offset defeats on land. The French invariably divided their efforts between campaigns along their land frontiers, either the Low Countries, the Rhineland, northern Italy, or the Pyrenees, and secondary naval and colonial attempts, which, in spite of occasional successes, were in the long run failures. So they fought the War of the League of Augsburg, of the Spanish Succession, the Austrian Succession, and the Seven Years' War. Then they fought the War of the American Revolution, and finally the French Revolutionary and Napoleonic Wars.

The simple listing of these contests suggests that the nature of warfare was different in the eighteenth century from the twentieth, and that was blessedly true. The twentieth century has seen near-total war, in which the aim has been to destroy the enemy utterly, or come as close to that as a modern, nationalistic, industrialized society could manage to do. In the eighteenth century, England did not expect to destroy France, or vice versa. In all the wars of the period, the only sovereign state which really disappeared was Poland, and that was as much the Poles' own fault—the unwillingness of their nobility to accept a workable constitution—as it was their neighbors' greed. States expected rather to gain advantage, a small accession of territory, a colony overseas, an important trading privilege, the accession of a relative to a vacant throne. It was a society which throve on blood sports, and war was the sport of kings. The Tory poet Robert Southey summed it up in a famous phrase by saying that in that period men fought "because their betters fell out."

It was not simply benign inclination that kept these wars from being more decisive; indeed, they could be nasty enough at times, and territories were ravaged and people slaughtered repeatedly throughout the course of the fighting. But all of the states of the day labored under severe limitations both of technology and of national organization, which militated against decisive conclusions. The Americans had already found this out during the colonial wars, and were to discover it even more during the Revolution.

As the French had founded and built up colonies along the St. Lawrence gateway to North America at the same time as the English were settling the Atlantic seaboard, the European struggle was transported overseas from the earliest days. Each of the wars on the Continent had its equivalent in North America, where they were called by different names. To Americans, the War of the League of Augsburg was King William's War; the Spanish Succession was Queen Anne's War; the Austrian Succession King George's War; and the Seven Years' War was thoroughly misnamed as the French and Indian War, and by the time of the Revolution, it was commonly referred to as "the Old French War." Beginning in the 1690's, small parties of militia, Indians, and local or regular troops had ranged back and forth between the two nations' colonies, raiding and ambushing, occasionally besieging a small frontier post, and fighting also at sea. Northern New England, New York, and the Ohio Valley saw repeated clashes, and the Americans, who rapidly outnumbered the French, tried several times to take Quebec; their failures were more often of organization and resources than actual military defeat.

By King George's War—that of the Austrian Succession, fought from 1740 to 1748—the British colonies were slowly but perceptibly becoming dominant. During that war the New

Englanders took the great French fortress of Louisburg, on Cape Breton Island at the mouth of the St. Lawrence, and this could have been the beginning of the end for New France. Unfortunately, to the intense disgust of New England, the British government ceded Louisburg back to France in 1748 at the peace conference, in return for Madras, which Britain had lost in India.

But during the French and Indian War British policy finally came together under the guiding genius of William Pitt, one of the great war leaders of history. He subsidized allies on the Continent, Frederick the Great of Prussia, and used British resources to destroy the distracted French empire. The French Navy was blockaded in port or beaten at sea, Bengal was secured in India, French islands were seized in the West Indies. In North America, Pitt sent for the first time substantial numbers of regular British soldiers to help the colonials in their struggle. British professionals took a rather dim view of colonial military talents. Louisburg fell in 1758, and the Ohio Valley was secured. The next year a combined expedition took Quebec itself, and with that, the French threat was removed from North America. By the time the war ended in 1763, the British Empire stood supreme; among other things, it was now certain that North America was going to be English and not French. It had been a very expensive war, but it had been well worth it—or so it looked at the time.

Partly because of the successes the British enjoyed, and more because of the expenses incurred in achieving them, the government in London spent the next several years trying to rationalize and regulate its empire. This attempt was what brought it into increasing conflict with the American colonies. To understand why, it is necessary to look briefly at the British system of government and the constitution of the empire, as they existed in the eighteenth century, for they bear little relation to the present British system, and less to the American.

The most important single fact about the British constitution is that it does not really exist. In the United States, as it eventually became, the written Constitution was probably the supreme political expression of the Age of Reason; it is right there, everyone can read it, and periodically it has been subject to amendment, wisely or not. This idea, and the reverence the document inspires, is quite foreign to the British. To them the constitution is, and was, a rather vague collection of statutes and usages that go all the way back to the Magna Carta of 1215; but even among British scholars, no two would produce the same list of what statutes actually made up "the constitution." Certain late medieval documents might be included, others would be left out; some statutes contradict earlier ones. In modern times, for example, the British have had to call elections every three years, or every five years, or every seven years; the most famous of all prime ministers, Winston Churchill, was not ever elected as such, and in fact the office of prime minister does not even exist constitutionally—it is simply a convenient usage that developed during the early eighteenth century.

Thus the constitution of Great Britain, or of the British Empire, is whatever thinking persons generally agree it is at any particular time. In the 1760's, that meant what a few hundred leading, political families, and a few thousand electors thought, because they were the only people concerned with the question.

The governing body of the empire, Parliament, was unreformed, unrepresentative, and responsible not to the people but to the Crown. Electoral reform and some degree of proportional representation both had to wait for the nineteenth century. There were usually about 560 members of Parliament in the House of Commons, of whom slightly fewer than 100 came from the counties, 4 from the two universities of Oxford and Cambridge, 45 from Scotland (a block added in 1707), and the rest from towns, or as they were known, boroughs. Very few of these were sent up as a result of real elections. Most of the seats, even in the boroughs, were controlled by the great landowning families; they posted the candidate they wanted, and their tenants elected him. Some boroughs had no electors at all. William Pitt, for example, sat for a borough that was actually no more than a pile of moss-covered stones. Some families had controlled parliamentary seats for centuries, and the Scots could usually be delivered en masse by some of the great landlords; but in any case, all these non-elective seats were known as pocket boroughs, for they were figuratively in someone's pocket. Elections were more choices than contests, and not once in the entire eighteenth century did a sitting government lose an election.

If there were not really elections, there were not really parties, either. The British political classes grouped themselves loosely into Whigs and Tories, or very roughly liberals and conservatives, but neither of the terms strictly translates into modern ideas. Generally the Whigs saw themselves as Low Church, business, urban, and possibly internationalist in outlook, while the Tories were seen as High Church, rural, agricultural, and less interested in foreign alliances, but there were so many variations as to make such classification virtually useless. What happened instead was that a charismatic figure such as Pitt, or a power broker with important friends such as Thomas Pelham-Holles, the Duke of Newcastle, would attract and control a block of members and therefore votes. Alliances and interests constantly shifted, ministers were regularly undermined, driven out of office, and then reappointed, as the tides of political opinion shifted. There were not elections producing clear parties with stated platforms; there were instead shifting coalitions, as men who could deliver parliamentary support combined with other such men to form ministries, and policies had to be trimmed to suit the composition of the government. Some men might be so antagonistic to others as to refuse to serve with them, but it was always possible to find someone to form a government. This was especially and unfortunately true in the period from 1763 to 1783. It was once remarked that Britain in these twenty years suffered from a brain famine, but that could hardly be farther from the mark. If anything, there were too many intelligent and ambitious men about; they were simply not organized properly.

Part of that was the fault of His Majesty King George III, the man who played what was still by far the most vital role in the running of the British government. George has been damned as a villain, and, less often, praised as a hero; he was neither. He was a profoundly unfortunate man in an enormously difficult situation. His concept of his position is central to the whole story.

*   *   *

George III was twenty-two in 1760 when he succeeded his grandfather on the throne of England. He was shy, immature, insecure, and extremely naive politically. His father, Frederick, the Prince of Wales, had died in 1751; like all the Hanoverians, Frederick had hated his own father, George II, and young George had been brought up in the same tradition. He distrusted his grandfather and despised his ministers as a pack of political scoundrels. His mother had constantly reminded him of his destiny: "Be a king, George," and he intended to do just that. He wanted to cleanse the Augean stable of British politics; unfortunately he did not understand that the King himself was necessarily the chief politician in Britain.

George's job was actually to run the government, to make policies and to see them carried through. He had certain fixed ideas, the most important of which was his determination to preserve the constitution as he understood it. For example, he vigorously resisted any lifting of the punitive laws on Catholics, for he had taken an oath to defend the Church of England. He would equally resist what he perceived as an attempt by his American subjects to alter the political complexion of empire.

Because a large number of members of Parliament were automatically loyal to the Crown, and another large number were placemen, who sat because they held offices at the Crown's pleasure, George could control a substantial block of votes. He could therefore usually get what he wanted through Parliament, and a combination of the Crown, plus the other vote deliverers, actually produced the government of Britain. George recognized that occasionally his policies might be unpopular, and if they were simply minor questions and not what he regarded as matters of principle, he would drop them. If, however, he considered them crucial, he would cling to them with all the strength of a drowning man clutching a lifeline. He also acknowledged that at some times, his choice of ministers might be unacceptable, and he would then dismiss the men in question. But because he had to give up one man, or set of men, it did not mean he had to appoint another; there were always plenty of cliques available to choose from, and George could usually put in office men he found personally agreeable. The government was very much His Majesty's government, and the policies carried out were His Majesty's policies.

This role was but dimly perceived in Great Britain, and totally misunderstood in America. Even after the war began, most Americans considered themselves as loyal subjects of King George III; they believed not that he was at fault, but that he was being ill-advised, and that his powers were being usurped by his ministers. They directed their anger and their complaints not at the King, but at Parliament and the King's ministers. Their prewar protests and their early war propaganda habitually referred to abuses of parliamentary power, ministerial injustice, and even, in 1775, to "the ministerial army." It dawned on them only slowly that George III was their real foe, and in the end, he was their last one. Long after Britain, and even the government ministers, had sickened of the war and given up heart, George kept them at the task of trying to subdue his rebellious subjects. He, after all, had taken the oath.

In an address to Parliament, soon after his accession to the throne, George III had referred to the Seven Years' War as "this bloody and expensive war." This did not endear him to the ministers who were even then bringing it to a victorious conclusion. As soon as he could manage to do so, George both got rid of the ministers and got out of the war. After the Peace of Paris in 1763, the new British government set about putting its house in order, and getting life back to normal. The thing that bothered them most was the debt left over from the war years. That debt was minuscule by our standards, but heavy by theirs, and they decided that their priorities must be both to reduce the debt and to rationalize the empire. The one should assist in the other; bringing the empire under closer central control and direction ought also to improve the collection of taxes.

The burden of both these new policies would rest most heavily upon the American colonies, but that was only fair. Much of the expense of the war had been incurred on their behalf; they had received grants to help defend themselves, and the British had waged substantial, and very expensive, military campaigns in America to remove the French menace. In a longer view, the Americans really had been left alone to do as they pleased, a policy or lack thereof known as "salutary neglect," and now those days were over. It was, in short, time for the empire to shape up; every unit must be made to pay its share for benefits that all enjoyed.

In the twelve years from 1763 to 1775, the American colonies grew increasingly restive under British attempts to control and tax them; in other words, the policies developed in London had precisely the opposite effect from what was intended. It can even be argued that these years actually constituted the American Revolution, for it was during them that antagonisms hardened, that the colonists discovered they were becoming Americans rather than British, and that the government determined to bring its fractious children to heel, whatever it might take. The years saw a progression of moves by Britain, and an escalation of reaction in the colonies.

George Grenville was the first of a series of ministers who tried to deal with the American problem. Appropriately enough, he took office on April 1, 1763, a domineering, businesslike, and altogether rather pedestrian politician. He decided that he would rigorously enforce the Navigation Acts, the laws governing imperial trade. In plain language, that meant he intended to prevent American smuggling, for much colonial trade was carried on with places such as the French West Indies, in violation of the mercantile system and its principles. He also proposed to tax the colonies directly, and use the money to maintain the British military establishment in America. His government passed the Sugar Act, to raise revenue and rationalize tax collection, and the Colonial Currency Act, to prevent the colonies from paying off their debts in depreciated currency.

Every one of these acts violated some segment of colonial sensibility. Smuggling and sugar were both vital to the economy of New England, both in its carrying trade and distilling business, which made up a large part of New England's already narrow profit margin. Americans did not see any further need for a large military force in North America, now that New France was gone, and they resented paying for it. They were already short, chronically so, of specie to conduct their business, and thus saw the government denying them money at the same time it was asking them to produce more of it for taxes.

Grenville plowed ahead. In 1765 the Stamp Act required a stamp, that is, a tax, on legal documents, newspapers, playing cards, and dice. It antagonized the most potentially difficult kind of opposition—lawyers, writers, and gamblers. The howl was easily heard across the Atlantic. Next a Quartering Act allowed the billeting of soldiers in private establishments.

Opposition began to coalesce, and this was the real importance of this sequence, for it forced the Americans to act together, to bury their perpetual internecine quarrels and jealousies, and to act as a whole. In Virginia, a lawyer named Patrick Henry introduced resolutions in the colonial assembly that were close to treasonous. Massachusetts called all the colonies to a Stamp Act Congress which met in New York in October. Only nine colonies sent representatives, but they adopted a Declaration of Rights and Liberties and protested their position to London.

The British then backed off. They repealed the Stamp Act, but as they did not wish to appear as if they were bowing to pressure—which of course they were—they then passed a Declaratory Act, pointing out that they had the right to legislate for the colonies when they chose to do so. A couple of conciliatory schemes came to naught, Grenville then went out of office as the result of a domestic squabble, and the task of running the colonies fell to Charles Townshend. In 1767 he imposed duties on a whole series of goods, including tea, with the idea that the money raised would pay the salaries of royal officials appointed to the colonies. The colonists refused to pay the duties, and they did not want a class of financially independent royal officials anyway. Boston passed a nonimportation agreement; and when a sloop belonging to a merchant named John Hancock was seized for evading duties, the citizens rioted. Massachusetts petitioned the King and protested against the arbitrary actions of his ministers. By late 1768, the government sent troops to Boston to enforce its edicts; the town refused to quarter them.

Neither side could or would understand the other. Slowly

antagonisms hardened into settled positions. The center of
the storm appeared to be Boston. The British saw Massachusetts and its capital as consisting of stiff-necked, hot-headed
radicals determined to have a fight. The New Englanders saw
themselves as people trying to survive within the imperial
system, and hindered on all sides by a bunch of distant bu-
reaucrats who had no conception of or sympathy with their
difficulties. In March of 1770 a gang of Boston loiterers got
into a fight with off-duty British soldiers. Troops were called
out, shots fired, and three Americans were killed and two
fatally wounded. The unfortunate but essentially minor incident was seized upon with glee by some of the more radical
American leaders—there were in fact some charges that the
whole affair was staged by one of them, Samuel Adams—and
went down as "the Boston massacre." The fact that the guard
commander and most of the soldiers involved were tried and
acquitted, after being defended by John Adams, was far less
important than the propaganda effect of the matter.

There was then a backing off. Yet another new British
government, now under Lord North, an amiable, unexcep-
tional man whose chief quality for office was his friendship
with King George, rescinded all the Townshend Duties except
that on tea, and the merchants of the colonies adopted a more
conciliatory tone. Things in the north were quiet for almost
two years. In the south, however, there was endemic factional
strife between different segments of society, and some groups
of dissidents known as Regulators virtually replaced royal government in parts of the Carolinas, where there was practically
a civil war for several months. Then in 1772 in Rhode Island,
the revenue cutter *Gaspée* ran aground, and was boarded and
burned by Rhode Islanders. Later in the year the towns of
Massachusetts formed committees of correspondence, to keep
each other informed of developments in the antigovernment
struggle, and early in the new year Virginia did the same on
a provincial level, inviting other colonies to follow its lead.
Within a year all but Pennsylvania had complied. Gradually
the colonies were being pressured into a common front. Finally, at the end of 1773, there came the penultimate straw
as far as the government was concerned—the Boston Tea
Party.

*   *   *

The events of December 16, 1773, figure fondly in American memory—thumbing a nose at authority, a successful college prank recalled years later at a reunion: colonists thinly disguised as Indians, the lovely odor of tea wafting over the clear night air of Boston Harbor; it is always looked on as good harmless fun.

In fact it was the chief turning point in the progression toward revolution. More sensible Americans regretted the action, and even offered to pay damages, which were close to a hundred thousand dollars. They were prevented by the radical elements, led by Samuel Adams, who had also organized the Tea Party, and who figures as the Iago of the whole revolutionary movement. In London, when the outrage was reported there, the British decided that they had at last had enough. Here they had devised a scheme that should have made everyone happy; it would have bailed the East India Company out of serious financial difficulties, provided the government with considerable revenues, and still given the Americans cheaper tea than they had had before—and look at the result. There was simply no satisfying these people. It was time to get serious.

So they did. The Boston Port Bill closed off the city's commerce. The Administration of Justice Act removed royal officials from colonial legal jurisdiction; the Massachusetts Government Act practically overturned the colony's ancient charter. The Quartering Act was extended, and at about the same time, the passage of the separate Quebec Act extended royal jurisdiction west of the Alleghenies, guaranteed the Roman Catholic religion to French Canadians, and retained a legal system there that the Americans found unacceptable. In the colonies, the whole set was lumped together as "the Intolerable Acts."

Once again, the British had succeeded in pushing the opposition together. The immediate response to the Intolerable Acts was a widespread call for a meeting, and in September 1774, all the colonies but Georgia sent delegations to the First Continental Congress in Philadelphia. There was near unanimity; the only real question was how vigorous the protests should be. In the end, the Americans declared that thir-

teen of the British government's acts since 1763 were illegal;
they set forth their rights as they saw them, drafted a petition
to the King, decided on economic sanctions and nonimportation of British goods, and finally agreed to meet again in
May of the following year if their demands had not been met.

By the late fall of 1774, then, the situation was at an
impasse. General Gage had moved his headquarters from New
York to Boston, the garrison of that city was being increased
almost daily, with regiments brought in from Britain, Quebec,
and Newfoundland, and ships of the Royal Navy were congregating in the harbor. Royal government throughout the
colonies had come to a practical halt; the colonies had always
governed themselves locally, and by now their assemblies were
simply ignoring any royal officials who happened to be about.
Most of these either sat nervously and did nothing, or sought
convenient excuses to be around British troops. For all intents
and purposes, the country was in a state of rebellion long
before the shots were fired at Lexington and Concord.

The tragedy was that both sides started with the same
concept—the seventeenth-century social contract as enunciated by John Locke—and were moving toward the same goal,
the democratic polity that both reached in the twentieth century. But they went by divergent paths, looking in different
directions. The British interpreted the social contract in a
conservative, familial way, and the Americans in a liberal,
egalitarian way. British revolutions—and they have been
more revolutionary than anyone since the classical Greeks—
invariably harked back to the past; whenever they introduced
some startling political innovation they explained it away as
restoring a mythical past balance that had somehow become
upset. They saw society as an ordered hierarchy, in which all
men might be free, but in which some were still lords, or
commoners, or kings, and always would be. The Americans
saw a society in which all men were indeed born equal, and
were free to rise as far and as fast as they were able to do.
They did not of course carry it to its logical conclusion—not
for two hundred years would "all men" include women and
blacks, for example, but their ultimate inclusion was inherent
in American thinking. The paths had begun to diverge with
the first generations of Americans, people born in a wilderness

and forced to work out their own salvation, people who learned their lessons of government in the local town meeting, where the poorest taxpayer had as much right to be heard as the richest. Now, when the British government for practically the first time had sought to impose its view of empire, and order, and society, on its offspring, the paths had come into collision. Blood had been shed, and that always makes all the difference. What lay ahead was hard to see, and frightful to contemplate, but it had to be faced.

CHAPTER TWO

Decision and Indecision

THREE WEEKS after the battles of Lexington and Concord, the Second Continental Congress convened in Philadelphia. Its task was far different from whatever had been envisaged the previous year. Then there was protest, couched in respectful terms, to the King. Now there was war. The delegates, again from all the colonies except Georgia, began the creation of a national government. In all of this, the most important and immediate question was what to do about the army before Boston. Other elements might wait, indeed had to wait, but there could be no delay on that score. John Adams moved that the Congress adopt the troops around Boston as a Continental Army, and a committee sketched in the bare bones of an administration for it. Congress voted to raise companies of riflemen in Pennsylvania, Maryland, and Virginia, and to send them north to Boston. But the thorniest question was that of command.

There were plenty of men in the colonies with military experience, though relatively few of them had handled any large-scale operations before. And this was also an era when some knowledge of war, at least on the theoretical side, was part of the mental baggage of a gentleman. Everyone who was educated had read the classics, and a man who knew his Caesar or had studied the career of Alexander the Great might well imagine himself a potential general. Leaders in peacetime society and business tended to step into similar roles in war. Sir William Pepperrell in Maine had been a businessman before he led the colonial troops in the capture of Louisburg in 1745. Around Boston itself, already with the army, were several men who might aspire to command, such as Artemas Ward or Israel Putnam. The former, as a Massachusetts militia general, had taken command of the troops gathering after Lexington. The latter, a brigadier general among the Connecticut troops, was given to drawing the long bow over a pot of rum, but had a great deal of catch-as-catch-can experience in the old colonial wars.

Congress needed something more than that, however, and found it among the Virginia delegation, in the person of George Washington. The forty-three-year-old planter and politician was a leading figure in his colony's resistance to the Crown, and more importantly, he had had substantial military experience on the frontier in the Old French War. In 1754 he had been surrounded by the French and forced to surrender a little post named Fort Necessity; in 1755 he had been aide-de-camp to General Edward Braddock in the disaster of that year. For two years he had commanded the militia of Virginia, and tried to hold the frontiers of the colony, and he had also been on the successful Forbes expedition to Fort Duquesne in 1758. So he actually had more command experience than almost any American around, as well as the social standing thought necessary for leadership in the period, and the correct politics. In addition, his appointment demonstrated the national character of the resistance, so far largely confined to New England, and when John Adams nominated him on June 15, he was unanimously elected. The new commander in chief, conscious of the enormity of his task, set about organizing his advisers and a rudimentary staff, or military family, as it was then called. Before he left Philadelphia, rumors filtered through of a great battle up around Boston.

* * *

Through April and May, Boston had been besieged by New England. Connecticut, Rhode Island, and New Hampshire had all sent troops to support those raised by Massachusetts, though the former two colonies kept their own command structure, and merely cooperated with Massachusetts General Ward. None of the colonies succeeded in raising as many men as they actually voted, but by the end of May, there were about 15,000 men in a loose ring around the city, from Roxbury in the south up to the Mystic River in the north.

Boston in 1775 had a population of some 16,000; it was confined almost entirely to a roughly tadpole-shaped peninsula connected to the mainland by a narrow strip called Boston Neck. West of it lay Back Bay and the Charles River, while to the north lay another peninsula on which was the small village of Charlestown. This peninsula was dominated by a hill, called Bunker, and connected to the mainland by another narrow strip, Charlestown Neck. Boston was therefore both an easy position to besiege, and an easy one to defend.

After his troops had been driven back in disarray on April 19, General Gage seems to have been totally at a loss what to do. He therefore did very little, aside from disarming the citizens of Boston, and he refused even to proclaim martial law; one authority has characterized him as "the weak link of empire." The government in London, which had gradually lost confidence in him over the preceding winter, did not help. Instead of firm orders, or a statement of real policy—of which they had none—it sent him reinforcements and the worst possible support: three more generals, John Burgoyne, Sir Henry Clinton, and Sir William Howe. Any one of these might well be Gage's relief, and he knew it. Winston Churchill, notorious for letting his generals hang in the wind, was once told, "Back him or sack him!" This was now Gage's situation.

Eventually they got around to declaring martial law—in a bombastic piece written by Burgoyne, who had literary pretensions—and finally they decided to take some action, to seize and fortify Dorchester Heights on the mainland to the south, which might serve as a preliminary to rolling up the American line. This decision was taken on June 13, to be acted on five days later.

The Americans immediately heard of this; Boston might be disarmed, but the British could keep no secrets there. The rebels moved first. On the evening of June 16 they sent about 1,200 men across Charlestown Neck with instructions to fortify Bunker Hill. The troops were mostly Massachusetts men under the overall command of Colonel William Prescott. At the Neck, they met Israel Putnam with some Connecticut troops detailed as a working party. They crossed the Neck, passed Bunker Hill, and went as far as Breed's Hill, only half the height of Bunker, where the soldiers lay on the grass waiting while the officers spent two hours discussing their orders. Eventually they agreed to fortify Breed's Hill and then to prepare fallback positions on Bunker.

Whatever else might be said of the Yankee soldier at this stage of the war, he was a great digger. Between midnight and first light, the troops dug up a square earthwork, about forty-five yards on a side; they fortified a breastwork running northeast from the redoubt about halfway to the water. A quarter mile behind that, they scooped up positions along a stone wall and rail fence that ran the rest of the way down to the shore. Finally, along the shoreline itself, they later built another breastwork between a low bluff and the waterline. Tactically, the whole position was sheer genius; strategically, it was something less than that.

Came dawn, and the British generals in Boston were awakened by the sound of gunfire. The sloop *Lively* had opened fire on the rebel positions, and this was taken up by several British ships in the Charles River, including the frigate *Glasgow* and the 68-gun *Somerset*, a small ship of the line. All of these made a great deal of noise and did almost no damage.

Obviously the colonials had stolen a march, and must be driven off. The logical thing to do would have been to send ships to interdict passage across Charlestown Neck, land troops there in the rear of the Americans, cut them off, and handily and painlessly put the 3,000 or so now on the peninsula safely in jail. Several small ships did in fact move in and fire across the Neck, but that was as far as the British got. Looking at all they could see from Boston, the generals chose instead to land right across the Charles, in front of the American position but out of range. They then would attack the redoubt frontally, to pin its occupants, while sending troops around to the right, the Americans' left, over open ground, to come up on the redoubt from the rear. There was nothing wrong with this as long as the rebels had not covered that left flank, and as far as the British could see, they had not done so. The British just had time to get their troops organized and across the Charles in ships' boats and barges before the tide turned against them. They set the landing for one in the afternoon; high tide was an hour later.

The British plan, which has been as much derided by amateur military buffs as has the American position on the peninsula, has been defended by professionals as the best they could do in the time available, and on the basis of the information they had, which was what they could actually see. On the other hand, the British had eight hours between hearing the *Lively*'s guns and actually doing anything, and in that time three miles out and back in a dory—two hours' work at most—would have shown someone that the American position was not as completely stupid as it looked. Most military men might have thought reconnaissance was a good idea.

For better or worse, the stage was now set for one of the crucial battles of the entire Revolution. Gage gave tactical command of the operation to Sir William Howe, and soon after noon he landed with about 1,200 men on the peninsula. The Americans had also been reinforced during the morning; eventually, about 1,500 American troops and some 2,500 British actually took part in the fighting.

Once they had landed, the British officers could see that the basis of their plan was faulty: the Americans had fortified the space between the redoubt and the northern shore. But to regular British troops and their officers, this could not have looked too impressive; they were generally contemptuous of American fighting abilities, and a gaggle of farmers behind a low stone wall topped with rails and hay would hardly have given them pause. So far Americans had demonstrated no great ability to shoot, and they certainly would not stand to receive a bayonet charge. Howe directed Brigadier General Robert Pigot and two regiments against the redoubt, and he sent several companies of light infantry along the shoreline below the bluff. He himself, leading two regiments and several grenadier companies, moved out toward the rail fence. The British had brought along some light cannon for direct artillery support, but these had the wrong size ammunition with them, and therefore remained useless. No one expected to need them anyway.

Here was a classic confrontation; the British infantry was universally regarded as the best in Europe, which meant the finest in the world, and these were highly trained professionals commanded by good officers. Howe had led the forlorn hope when James Wolfe took Quebec back in '59, and Pigot had fought at Fontenoy in 1745, one of the bloodiest battles of the whole century. For these people, it was all in a day's work. Most of the New Englanders had never been in a fight before, and certainly had never faced anything like this; this was not a matter of shooting deer or partridge on the farm back home. But there was a surprise element here; there were enough men leading the Yankees who had seen battle to know the effect of massed fire at close range, and to know that even British soldiers could be stopped if the right men went about it in the right way.

An eighteenth century battle was a mathematical equation. The muzzle-loading musket could be fired only so fast, and had only a short effective range. If the attacker could get enough troops, in sufficient order, through the very narrow killing zone of the musket, if he could charge with the bayonet, he would probably win. Few soldiers anywhere would stay in place to receive a bayonet charge; so the trick was to get through that killing zone.

The red ranks came closer and closer, ominously silent and ordered, drums tapping out the step and the sergeants grunting to keep the files closed up. The American officers paced up and down behind their nervous men, cautioning them to hold their fire, to make every shot count, to aim low because soldiers always fire high downhill, to go for the officers, the men wearing the little gold gorgets on their breasts.

The light infantry along the shoreline made contact first. Advancing on a narrow front, the British came within fifty yards of the breastwork held by Colonel John Stark and his New Hampshire troops. Formed in three ranks, the Yankees poured in unceasing volleys, and simply blew away the head of the column. The first company, of the Royal Welch Fusiliers, was wiped out. The King's Own and the 10th Foot charged successively and gallantly through the wreckage and met the same result. With nearly a hundred dead in the first moments, the British gave up.

On the left, Pigot fared no better; his assault was driven off by concentrated musket fire from the redoubt. And in the center, Howe led his men against the rail fence. The grenadiers leading the assault became disordered crossing some earlier fences, paused at fifty yards to fire at the Americans, contrary to their orders, and got mixed up with their supports. Then the Yankees opened up with devastating fire, and shot the heart out of the attack. After vainly trying to stand, the British rolled back down the hill.

It took a mere quarter of an hour for Howe to organize a second attack. The beach was left alone, and the light infantry headed for the rail fence while Howe and Pigot both converged on the redoubt. The second attack met the same fate as the first one; again the Americans stood fast, held fire until the last moment, and then absolutely decimated the attackers; once more the red waves broke and washed back down the hill.

By the third try the British really meant business. The soldiers stripped off their packs—more than a hundred pounds of useless equipment they had twice carried up that fatal hill. Sir Henry Clinton came over from Boston to organize stragglers milling around on the beach, another regiment arrived, as well as some companies of marines, and, finally, some proper ammunition for the artillery pieces. It was obvious by now that something had gone terribly awry, and this time they intended to do it right.

Things were going the opposite way on the American side. So far they had done everything correctly, but now the day began to fall apart. Units ordered across the Neck as reinforcements refused to march, and only a few volunteers came forward. In spite of the fact that there had so far been remarkably few casualties, the Americans faced an even more serious deficiency: they were running out of ammunition.

This time the British concentrated almost everything against the redoubt. Their field guns swept the rail fence, driving off its defenders, some of whom went to the rear, while others took shelter in the redoubt. Against that the British advanced in column, taking fairly heavy losses, then deployed into line as the American fire dwindled. With a final cheer the British swept up to and over the walls of the earthwork. The Americans, with few bayonets, fought back with rocks, fists, and clubbed muskets. There was a rough melee for a few moments, then the rebels broke to the rear, leaving about thirty dead behind them. There was little panic, and the Yankees moved back from fence to fence, holding the British at bay with their remaining ammunition as they went. The dog-tired British followed them only as far as Bunker Hill, where they gave up the pursuit and sank to the ground, exhausted.

By the official standards of the day, Bunker Hill, as the battle was soon miscalled and known ever after, was a British victory; the side that remained in possession of the ground was considered the winner. The real results were far different. The American casualties were about 450, of whom a third were killed, the other two thirds wounded. Given that about 1,500 took some part in the battle, that is a casualty rate of thirty percent. The British eventually employed about 2,500, and their generally accepted casualty figure is 1,150, of whom about 225 were killed, a casualty rate of very close to fifty percent. The British might well have echoed Pyrrhus: another such victory and we are lost. But even that was not the whole tale, for the real American victory was over the minds of their enemies. In seven years of actual fighting, and twenty more or less major battles, one eighth of British officer deaths, and one sixth of wounds, were sustained at Bunker Hill. There are valid grounds for arguing that the British Army, and especially Sir William Howe, did not recover from the shock of that gory afternoon. In Parliament former officers might harrumph that with a thousand men they could sweep the entire continent, but they had not gone up that red slope. Those who had knew that they were in for a fight.

A fortnight after Bunker Hill, the newly appointed commander in chief of the Continental Army, George Washington, arrived to take up his active post. He was apparently awaited with curiosity tinged with resentment; after all, the New En-

glanders had done the work so far, and saw little reason to
have a commander imported from Virginia. Fortunately, the
day of his arrival was a Sunday, so New England's rigid re-
ligiosity was an excuse to have no ceremony. The next day
there was a review of the troops, and they and their new chief
got a look at each other. Washington was an impressive figure,
and one of the most noted horsemen of his day, so he looked
good. The troops, by and large, were neither uniformed nor
well drilled; they remained basically raw material to be
molded into an army.

The difficulties Washington faced over the next several
months were truly monumental; Congress was little help to
him, for it had its own problems, and he was forced, virtually
single-handedly, to keep together an army that constantly
threatened to fall apart. It is fair to say that George Washington was the one indispensable man of the American Revolution, and that without him, there were several times when the
whole enterprise would probably have collapsed. But he was
also a human being, early biographers to the contrary, and it
is equally fair to say that he and the New Englanders never
really understood each other. He was always the Virginia aristocrat, admired and respected, loved by some, but somewhat
distant and aloof. He did not care for the leveling tendencies
of the Yankees, and their cantankerous egalitarianism. A mod-
erately rich man, he had difficulty sympathizing with what he
considered the northerners' obsession to leave the service and
get home again. In many respects, he was psychologically
closer to the British than he was to his own northern troops,
and his letters during this period reflect his frustrations. Those
were certainly real enough, but it would be unjust both to
Washington and his soldiers to take his exasperation too seriously.

The basic problem was that his army was no sooner built
up than it began melting away. In October Congress authorized an army of 20,370 men. By November Washington had
approximately 17,000 under his command. But these were
largely short-term enlistments and embodied militia formations. His problem was to transform the men from part-time
soldiers into regulars serving for the duration, and most men
simply would not, could not, make that commitment. The

militia enlistments were up at the end of the year; in fact, most of the Connecticut troops intended to leave even earlier, on December 10, arguing that their enlistments were for lunar months rather than calendar ones, a barracks lawyer's trick that did nothing to endear them to the general. By the end of November, less than 4,000 men had enlisted for long service, and to get them, the officers had to offer extensive furloughs. By the new year, only about 8,200 had enlisted, and of them, 3,000 were on leave. The gaps were filled by calling out militia for a month at a time, but that of course could not have improved the army's efficiency. There was little to be done about it; Washington wrote begging letters to Congress, tried to keep supplied what few men he had, and hoped for the best. The British in Boston were the least of his worries.

Inside Boston General Gage was at his wits' end to know what to do, but he was hardly alone in that. The entire British government was in the same quandary. Lord North's ministry remained basically undistinguished, and the brightest minds were in opposition. William Pitt, now the Earl of Chatham, spoke vehemently on behalf of the colonists, and Edmund Burke, one of the greatest orators ever to sit in the House of Commons, was all for conciliation; indeed, in a brilliant speech he enunciated the ideas that would later infuse the British Commonwealth. But all this was too little, too late. The weak gesture of good will that North did make was simply an attempt to put the clock back, and that was not good enough. In the colonies, conservatives among the Congress succeeded in creating the Olive Branch Petition, which still protested loyalty to the King while asking for redress of grievances. This was adopted on July 5 and reached London, carried by the Loyalist Richard Penn, in mid-August. But the King refused to see Penn, or even to receive the petition. He had made up his mind, and nobody can be as stubborn as a weak man whose mind is fixed. The colonists were rebels, and that was all there was to it, and rebellion against constituted authority was one of the mortal sins of the eighteenth century. They must be put down by whatever force was necessary.

It was simple enough for His Majesty to decide that; it was another matter to get it done. The ministry itself was divided; several members left, and only slowly did what would become the war cabinet take shape: Lord North as First lord of the treasury and prime minister, Lord George Germain as secretary of state for the American colonies, the Earl of Sandwich as first lord of the admiralty, and Viscount Barrington as secretary at war. There were actually about eighteen or twenty offices that made up the cabinet, but these four were those who held the primary responsibility for the conduct of the war. Unfortunately, they all disagreed on policy. North wanted as little war as possible, and to keep expenses down. Barrington, responsible for the army and conscious of its weakness, wanted to defeat the Americans by naval blockade, but Sandwich, responsible for the navy, feared war with France more than with America, and wanted to keep the navy at home. That left Germain, and he was the stormy petrel of the government.

His real name was Lord George Sackville, and he had taken the name Germain when Lady Elizabeth Germain died and left him a fortune in 1770. Previous to that he had been more or less notorious in the British Army and in political life. He had a good military record, but was a very haughty and difficult subordinate, and in 1760 he had been dismissed from the service after he had refused an order for the cavalry he commanded to make a charge during the battle of Minden. In Parliament he had gravitated to the opposition, fought occasional duels, and then gradually made his way into power. He was a meddling and energetic minister, constantly at odds with successive military commanders, with whom he really should have had little to do. His dominance in cabinet was a measure of its essential mediocrity, of the fact that the primary qualification for office was acceptance by the King. And like the King, Germain was for coercion.

Public opinion in the country was still split, even after Bunker Hill. Many of the people who counted sided with the ill-organized opposition and hoped to avoid a war. The commercial classes did a great deal of business with the colonies, and did not want to see that disrupted. The government was not successful in promoting its views through the country at large, but finally the Americans did that for them. Ironically, it was the attempt of the rebels to export their war to Canada that made British opinion swing toward force. Once the rebellion could be perceived as an offensive movement rather than an arguably just protest against government impositions, then reluctantly Britain fell into line. The opposition was discredited, and the ministry gained more votes in Parliament. Through the winter of 1775, less was heard about conciliation, more about coercion.

But for General Gage and his garrison in Boston, this did not translate into action. Gage grumbled that the Americans showed more spirit against the British than they had ever shown against the French, and he damned Boston—"I wish this Cursed place was burned"—but he did not act. Instead he was relieved; officially he was called home for consultations, but he was never really employed again. Sir William Howe took his place in Boston, and as commander in chief of His Majesty's forces in America. Howe did nothing either. The British government sent reinforcements over to Boston, and they did nothing. While Washington's army melted away and was rebuilt, the British huddled in the city, trying to keep warm. They burned up all the firewood, then they burned all the fenceposts, then they stripped the doors and interiors of houses abandoned by the rebel sympathizers. Boston was a trap, a pit, and the British realized it. Howe soon decided, with every other British military and political observer, that Boston had been a mere accident; the real key to the continent was New York. So the winter wore slowly on.

CHAPTER THREE

Action and Inaction

Boston was the epicenter of the crisis, but it was hardly the only place where there was action. There were Loyalist factions assembling in both the Carolinas and in Virginia, and appealing to the government in London for assistance. Throughout British North America men were being forced into hard choices. One now thinks of the thirteen original colonies as a unit; at the time, however, there were actually sixteen areas of British control, and the way they ended up was a decision of the Revolution itself.

For example, Newfoundland belonged to Great Britain; it was a barren, sparsely settled island, subsisting on the fishing off the Grand Banks, with a largely seasonal population. It remained an outpost of the empire. Nova Scotia had originally been settled by French, the Acadians of Longfellow's stories, and then taken over by Britain during the colonial wars. In the French and Indian War the Acadians had been expelled and their lands settled by New Englanders, mostly from Connecticut and Massachusetts. There were also a couple of settlements, especially Halifax, that had been initiated from Britain. Nova Scotia at this time looked more to New England than Old for its attitudes, and which way it might go was up in the air. The present-day state of Maine was then a district of Massachusetts, and modern Vermont was something of a no-man's-land between New Hampshire, New York, and Canada.

Finally this last, which was in 1775 for practical purposes the strip of Quebec along the St. Lawrence River, would be a major acquisition for the Americans, if they could get it. The city of Quebec, largely French in population, was the seat of British government for the whole area, but the town of Montreal, up river, had seen in the years since the conquest a substantial influx of English merchants, particularly from New York, and these influential people might well side with their southern cousins. The French population was anybody's guess. They had no love for the English, whom they still saw as unwelcome occupiers. On the other hand, they had even less love for the Americans, their primary enemies for a century and a half. The Quebec Act, which to the Americans was one of the "Intolerable Acts," was seen in Quebec itself as a piece of real statesmanship. The Roman Church, protected by the act, was well-disposed to the British, and there could hardly be an adult in the province who did not know that Quebec and its religion had been roundly damned in New England pulpits for a hundred years. To the Yankees, Quebec was practically the seat of the Antichrist. None of which stopped the Americans from thinking that Quebec would probably join eagerly in their rebellion. In fact, the American Congress addressed an open letter to Quebec, inviting the French to join them, and pointing out that the protection of their religion depended solely upon an unrepresentative and factious Parliament. Rather foolishly, they then also wrote to the British an open letter in which they condemned the establishment in Canada of a "sanguinary and impious" religion. From Quebec's point of view, the British devil they did not know looked better than the American devil they knew all too well.

The classic route of war between Quebec and the English colonies was the Lake Champlain–Hudson River route; for seventy-five years, the French had tried to come down it, and

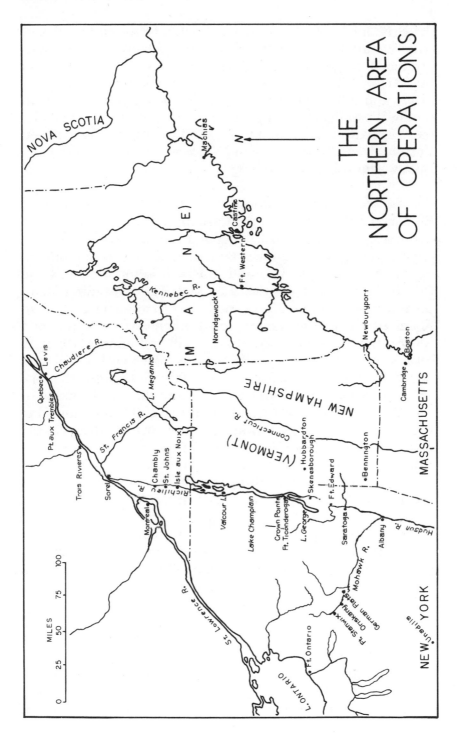

THE
NORTHERN AREA
OF OPERATIONS

the British had tried to go up it. Some of the great battles of empire had been fought there. Sir William Howe's older brother, George, had been killed leading a British attack on Fort Ticonderoga, near the southern end of Lake Champlain, in 1758, and New England had subscribed to a monument to him in Westminster Abbey. Since the end of the French wars, the area had subsided into peace, and the frontier had moved westward, and Ticonderoga in 1775 was a backwater garrison. But all that might soon change.

As soon as the Revolution began, both New York and New England began thinking about Canada, and incidentally about Ticonderoga as well. In Connecticut, an ambitious and energetic young officer named Benedict Arnold got a commission from both that state and Massachusetts to occupy the fort; in the Vermont district, a band of Patriots calling themselves Green Mountain Boys and led by their own man, Ethan Allen, also had designs on the post. Allen was gathering men for the operation when Arnold arrived, and on May 10, early on a stormy and rain-swept morning, the two leaders with about 200 men crossed Lake Champlain and rushed the fort. Opposition was almost nonexistent, and the actual taking of the place consisted largely of shouting and haranguing between the American leaders and the two British officers in the post, which was held by a mere 48 men, most of them pensioners, or Invalids as they were then called.

The most important thing about the fort was that it was a major storehouse of guns and ammunition, of which the Americans were chronically short. Bronze cannon in those days did not become obsolete, and guns cast in 1705 were as good as ones cast in 1775; the Americans took more than eighty guns of one type or another, plus thousands of balls and other military stores. It was a very substantial coup. They followed it up by taking the lesser post up the lake at Crown Point, and they then raided all the way north as far as St. Johns across the Canadian border, which they even tried, unsuccessfully, to hold.

Naturally, the Americans were not the only ones aware of the value of this area, and the British governor of Quebec, Sir Guy Carleton, also had his eyes on it. In fact, twenty of

the men taken at Ticonderoga were the advance guard of reinforcements he had sent hurriedly down the lake as soon as
he heard news of the fighting in Massachusetts. Carleton was
highly popular in Quebec, and some authorities give him virtually complete credit for holding Canada for the Crown. He
did make the mistake of thinking that his personal good relations with the French meant they would fight for Britain,
so he sent off much of his small garrison to support Gage in
Boston. When the American invasion did come, then, he was
very poorly prepared to withstand it.

Arnold's and Allen's business on Lake Champlain was but
a preliminary to greater things. In early June Congress decided
not to attempt to capture Quebec, but it soon changed its
mind, and at the end of the month directed that Canada be
invaded. It gave the task to New York's man on the list of
American major generals, Philip Schuyler. A rich landowner
from the Anglo-Dutch New York establishment, Schuyler had
considerable experience in military supply and administration. Unfortunately, as would shortly be shown, he was happier and more effective behind a desk than leading troops in
the field. He was also, because of both his aristocratic manner
and his role as a boundary commissioner before the war, very
unpopular with the New England troops who made up a good
portion of his field forces. Finally, he was wracked by gout
and rheumatism, and he soon left the actual leading of men
to his subordinate, Richard Montgomery. Happily, this turned
out to be an excellent choice, for Montgomery was one of the
brilliant younger men the Revolution produced. Irish-born, a
professional British soldier, he had recently married well and
settled in New York. A strong supporter of the Revolution, he
threw himself into the preparations for the march north,
trying desperately to instill order and discipline into his few
hundred soldiers while Schuyler tried equally desperately to
arm, equip, and supply them. It was late August before the
expedition got under way, an unpropitious time, one might
think, to invade Canada.

Lake Champlain was not the only route to Canada,
however, or Montgomery the only man going there. The Revolution had scarcely begun when Colonel Jonathan Brewer

suggested invading Canada by the well-known, if little-traveled, route that led north from Maine to Quebec City. General Washington, after arriving in Massachusetts, picked up the idea and began to develop it. This route had actually been surveyed by the British and occasionally traveled by the French and Indians. It led up the Kennebec River, across the Great Carrying Place to the Dead River, up that to the Height of Land, and from there to Lake Megantic and then to the Chaudière River, which flowed into the St. Lawrence, a mere four or five miles from Quebec City. On paper it looked easy. Washington, who had considerable wilderness experience, after all, thought it had real possibilities. A two-pronged invasion of Canada, with forces heading for both Montreal and Quebec City, would force the British to split their already depleted garrison, and surely one or the other, or more probably both, attacks would succeed.

When Benedict Arnold showed up at the Boston siege, still itching to do something, Washington offered him command of the expedition. Arnold accepted eagerly, and began putting things in order. Boats were ordered to be built at the Kennebec, troops detailed, and supplies gathered. On September 6, Arnold mustered his command, about 1,050 strong, at Cambridge. Most were naturally New England troops, but there were as well three companies of riflemen, two from Pennsylvania and one, led by Captain Daniel Morgan, from Virginia; the New Englanders were supposed to be woodsmen, but were actually farmers, which turned out to be rather a different thing.

The troops marched from Cambridge to Newburyport at the mouth of the Merrimac, where they boarded ships for Maine. They sailed up the Kennebec to near modern Augusta, where they picked up their small boats, bateaux hastily built of green lumber, and on September 25 they started up the river.

The next month and a half was an epic tale of abject misery. It rained most of the time; boats were wrecked, provisions lost, the men constantly wet, hungry, and generally wretched. Several detachments left the expedition and straggled back; day after day the soldiers floundered on, usually waist deep in cold October water. The Kennebec system has now been largely dammed, but the area is still a center for whitewater rafting. For Arnold and his men, it was more torture than adventure. On November 9, with about 700 hungry troops, Arnold reached Pointe Levi, across the St. Lawrence from Quebec. He immediately gathered up whatever boats he could find, was delayed several days by a gale, but then pushed across the river, encamped on the famous Plains of Abraham, and laid siege to a walled city whose defenders outnumbered him about two to one.

While Arnold struggled through the swamps of Maine, General Montgomery had run into a small hornet's nest at St. Johns, on the Richelieu River about twenty miles from Montreal. Here a determined little British garrison, reinforced with odds and ends that Carleton could scrape up and send forward, delayed the skittish Americans for more than a month. Most of the regular troops then available to Carleton were lost when the post finally surrendered, but they bought sufficient time to force the Americans into a winter campaign, and they may thereby have saved Canada for the Crown. Montreal fell with no resistance on November 13, and Montgomery began his move downstream to Quebec City.

By December 5 Arnold and Montgomery had united their forces, now only about a thousand strong, and closely invested the city. Inside, Carleton had a scratch force of perhaps 1,200 men, but this included 300 French and 200 British militia, both considered somewhat undependable; their best group was probably some 350 sailors from the British ships in the river. Neither side felt strong enough to do much against the other, but the British were snug behind their walls, and could afford to wait. It was Arnold and Montgomery who had to act.

And soon. For if their little army did not dissolve before the blast of the Canadian winter, it would self-destruct with the end of the year anyway: the American enlistments expired then. Under these circumstances, the American leaders came up with a plan both desperate and heroic; on the first bad night, they would storm the city.

Quebec, then as now, consisted of two parts. The upper town was walled and protected by the Citadel atop a steep bluff; the older, lower town huddled along a narrow shore at the bottom of the cliff. There was no chance of getting directly into the upper town, so the attackers decided to force the lower one, Montgomery from the western end, and Arnold around the point from the eastern side. Unfortunately for them, Carleton had also foreseen that this was the only approach, and had fortified both spots.

Dirty weather did not arrive until the night of December 31, and virtually every writer on the event has commented on what a supreme act of leadership it was to carry men into a life-and-death assault on such a position when their enlistments were up the next day. In the middle of a blizzard the Americans formed up and moved out. Montgomery's little column painfully made its way among the huge ice blocks that littered the narrow shore. Reaching the western end of the lower town, the troops tried to rush the fortifications at Cape Diamond. But the British were awake and waiting for them, and the head of Montgomery's column was blown away by the first British volley. Richard Montgomery went with it, killed in the first moment of the attack. That was almost the end of it as well. The heart went out of the attackers with his death, and they retreated back they way they had come.

Arnold's men did slightly better. About 600 strong, they quietly made their way through some suburbs to the eastern end of the lower town, and broke into the Sault aux Matelots (Sailors' Street), before being discovered. The street is still there, a dingy, twisting, working-district street beyond the usual tourist area. Fired at from loopholes on both sides of the narrow way, the Americans rushed along, over a couple of barricades. Arnold took a wound in the leg and collapsed; Daniel Morgan seized the lead and roared ahead. Before a last barricade, ironically all but undefended, he halted, listening to the fears of his officers, and the moment was lost. The route was cut behind them, the Americans were hemmed in, and finally, exhausted, they surrendered. A few scattered survivors escaped, but the invasion of Canada was finished. With a loss of five killed and thirteen wounded, Carleton had inflicted nearly 500 casualties on the invaders, five sixths of them captured. And he had kept Canada for Britain.

That was not immediately obvious. The Americans retreated upstream, but they sullenly held on. The convalescent

Arnold implored Congress for reinforcements, and as spring came on, he actually got them. But there were too few Americans at the end of too long a line of communications. Carleton sat smugly behind his walls and waited. Inevitably, when the ice went out of the river in the spring breakup, there was the Royal Navy, there were reinforcements from Britain, and the whole overambitious enterprise had to be given up. Back to Lake Champlain the Americans went, wracked with smallpox, malaria, and dysentery. The illusion of Canada would linger long, but for the immediate future, the Americans were hard-pressed to defend themselves, let alone conquer anyone else.

While Canada was being held for the Crown, the southern colonies were being lost for it. In a series of small but significant actions the rebels, or Patriots, managed to secure control of Virginia and the Carolinas, an accession of enormous ultimate importance, for these areas might have gone either way.

Of all the southern colonies, Virginia had been foremost in opposition to the Crown. Its House of Burgesses had produced the most inflammatory statements of the American position, and its leaders, men such as Patrick Henry and Thomas Jefferson, represented the intellectual spearpoint of resistance. As early as 1773, the Royal governor, Lord Dunmore, had dissolved the assembly when it wished to form a committee of correspondence with the other colonies; he had done so again the next year when it declared a day of mourning over the closing of the port of Boston.

Dunmore had actually been a fairly popular governor, but when the rebellion broke out, he embarked on several rash actions, intended to hold the colony for the Crown and to rally Loyalist sentiment, of which there was considerable; unfortunately for him and his cause, he did more harm than good. In March 1775, after Patrick Henry had delivered his famous "Give me liberty or give me death!" speech, Dunmore had decided to move. In April, he seized the provincial gunpowder stores at Williamsburg, then reversed himself and gave them back, then reversed himself again and outlawed Patrick Henry. By June he had fled aboard a British ship, and during the summer the situation further deteriorated. With Dunmore cruising futilely offshore, hurling verbal bombardment at Virginia, the colonists went their own way, establishing a government that for practical purposes was totally independent of royal authority.

Late in October, after the Americans had destroyed a British vessel that ran aground, Dunmore took action. He sent a naval expedition to burn the town of Hampton. Several small vessels cannonaded the town, but when they sent boats in to burn it, the sailors were driven off by the local militia; the next day the ships moved in closer, but made the mistake of coming within range of the Virginia riflemen. The gun crews were cut down, and when the British tried to move out of range, they were shot out of the rigging. Two ships drifted ashore and were captured; five were sunk; it was an utterly humiliating experience.

Dunmore now declared martial law, considered freeing the slaves, and called on loyal Englishmen to rally to the Crown. He was then forced out of Norfolk by Patriot pressure, in December, and he responded in January by bombarding and destroying the town, which effectively destroyed also any lingering Loyalist sympathies in the area. He fell back to an island in Chesapeake Bay, and was driven from that in midsummer of 1776. Eventually he gave up and sailed for the West Indies, trailing a forlorn little band of loyal subjects.

In North Carolina, the situation was somewhat different. The royal governor there, Josiah Martin, was a former soldier. He seems to have been a fairly sensible man, but even before the rebellion broke out, he, like his colleagues elsewhere, was at odds with the local assembly. Nonetheless, he initially thought he could hold the colony. He was mistaken, and at the end of May 1775, he had been forced to flee to Cape Fear, and from there, in July, to take refuge aboard ship. There was, however, some substantial reason for Martin to think the colony might be saved. North Carolina was seriously divided; the tidewater area was pretty solidly in rebellion, but the back country was different. It had been settled by large numbers of Scottish Highlanders, who had emigrated from home after the uprising of 1745. These people had come out for Bonnie

Prince Charlie, and paid the price for failure in confiscation and exile. Now they came out again, this time for King George.

Martin and the other southern governors had reported home that the south could be held, prompting the British to send an expedition to the area. The expected arrival of this relief brought the North Carolinian Loyalists into the field, though many authorities insist they were as antagonistic to the domination of the old tidewater colonists as they were loyal to their King. In any case, early in February 1776, the Scots gathered, with kilts, bagpipes, targets and broadswords, and visions of the good old days dancing in their heads. From modern Fayetteville they headed toward Wilmington.

There was not a great deal in their way, as most of the colony's newly formed regular forces had gone off to help Virginia against Governor Dunmore. But the rebel militia coalesced around them, and some regular troops barred their advance. The two sides finally met at Moore's Creek Bridge, about fifteen miles northeast of Wilmington. The Americans took up their position behind the stream, entrenched, and also took up the planks across the bridge. Later reports say they also greased the stringers on the bridge, just in case. On February 27 the Highlanders came up to the position, tried to rush it, and were beaten back disastrously. The Americans then counterattacked, quickly replacing the planks on the bridge, and drove the Loyalists back toward Cross Creek, where they were hit by other militia units. Several hundred prisoners were taken, as well as most of their military stores. At a cost of one man wounded and one dead, the Americans secured North Carolina. If and when the British should arrive, they would find little help waiting for them there.

The same sort of confusion prevailed in South Carolina. In the fall of 1775 both Patriot and Loyalist militia had taken the field, especially in the western part of the colony around the little frontier post of Ninety-Six; in November some 600 rebels had been briefly besieged there by about three times as many Loyalists, but there had been little actual fighting. Within a month the Patriots had raised their forces to sufficient strength that the Loyalists, choosing to bide their time, simply collapsed and remained quiescent.

Georgia went the same way, so the end result was that the four southern colonies all sided with the rebellion. Their governors, however, were convinced they could be readily regained, and through the summer of 1775, while the matter still was undecided, the British government at home accepted the view and advice of its men on the spot. Officials driven out of their territory invariably think they are the victims of a small cabal, and that popular support will rally to them if only given the opportunity to do so.

Through the following winter Washington, on the one side, and Sir William Howe, on the other side, from their Boston bases, sat and stared each other down. The Americans could not get in, the British could not get out. Washington was almost totally absorbed in the effort to keep his army in being, but he still wanted desperately to bring about some sort of action that would change the status quo. For Howe's part, there was little to do but wait—for orders, for reinforcements, for spring, for the Royal Navy, for something to happen. He might indeed have waited a little more vigorously, but since the government at home was only slowly reaching decisions on what it wanted to do, there was little sense in Sir William's rushing things.

What either general needed was a lever to shift the balance of the siege. Washington found it first, in the person of a large, good-natured Boston bookseller named Henry Knox. A gifted amateur and avid reader of military classics, Knox had served General Ward as a volunteer and had been at Bunker Hill. He impressed Washington sufficiently that the commander in chief named him colonel of the Continental Regiment of Artillery; the title was largely honorary, for at the time the Americans possessed hardly any artillery worthy of the name, and certainly none of the heavy pieces that would constitute a siege train, as opposed to smaller field pieces. The taking of Ticonderoga changed that, however; all that was needed now was somehow to get sixty tons of bronze and iron the three hundred miles from Lake Champlain to Boston. As winter came on, Knox conceived the idea of hauling it on sledges.

So he did. He arrived at Ticonderoga in early December, chose fifty-odd cannon and mortars, got sledges built for them, and hired local contractors and oxen to get them moving. It was early January before he had moved the guns the thirty-five miles to the southern end of Lake George; from there they went south to Saratoga, through Albany, and down to the little town of Claverack, before turning east. Across the Massachusetts line, and through the hills of the Berkshires, the sledges slipped, the oxen strained, Knox cursed. But in fact they made amazingly good time; Knox himself got back to Cambridge and Washington's headquarters on January 18, and a week later he was proudly displaying his "noble train of artillery" to his general, his face wreathed in smiles, and blushing under the well-deserved congratulations showered on him.

While Knox was still hauling his guns eastward, Washington was trying to develop a way to attack the British. His first ideas took shape by early February, for an assault across the ice of Back Bay; he thought the British would be surprised by this, that they were at the moment outnumbered by his new militia regiments, and that therefore something might be done. Fortunately, the senior officers with whom he discussed the plan were all against it; it was far too risky, and they thought instead that there should be some sort of artillery bombardment. They now had the guns for that, and were busily trying to find sufficient powder and shot to use them. What they favored was a replay of Bunker Hill: seize a strong position, and force the British to come and attack them. The obvious choice for this was Dorchester Heights, east of the American positions and just south of the Boston peninsula. As the ground was now frozen, Yankee ingenuity was put to work, and the troops were employed constructing portable fortifications. These could be set up on the ground, filled with bundles of wood called *fascines*, and bales of hay, and then made solid as the troops laboriously dug through the frost. Barrels of earth were also got ready to be used as a semi-portable barricade, and to roll down the hill at the advancing British.

The American operation opened with a preliminary covering bombardment. On the night of March 4–5, the troops moved onto the heights and began hammering the frozen ground, under cover of the noise of the guns. Twelve hundred Yankees with picks, shovels, and crowbars could do a lot of

work in the course of a night. British officers heard them, but
did not bother to do anything about it. So with the dawn,
there were the fortifications crowning the heights, and Sir
William and his miserable band stood agape. Howe reported
home that at least 12,000 men must have been working on
the position; his chief engineer thought it would have needed
20,000. There must be a great horde of rebels about if they
could do that.

Even more serious than this indication of numbers was
the fact that Howe was now caught. His own guns could not
elevate sufficiently to reach the Americans, and his naval officers were telling him they must move their ships out of harbor. Howe decided to attack and take the position with a night
attack with the bayonet, but then, presumably with visions of
Bunker Hill stirring in his head, he called it off. The next night
there was a huge storm which did a great deal of damage to
the British shipping, and by then Howe was concluding that
it was time to go.

It took him another ten days, but on March 17 the British
garrison went aboard ship; they blew up Castle William out
in the harbor, but they left the town pretty well alone, except
for a good deal of casual looting. They also left behind some
welcome military stores for the Americans, material they
could not carry off for shortage of shipping, that did not get
destroyed in the confusion of departure. All in all, about
11,000 troops and sailors, and another 1,000 Loyalists, left
with Howe. For ten days the fleet of British vessels sat out in
Boston Roads, then on March 27 they set sail and disappeared
over the horizon. No one knew where they were going, but
the betting was on New York.

With the war almost a year old and operations at something of a period, it was time to take stock. The spring of 1776
for both sides gave pause. The Americans had slightly more
than held their own to this point. The colonies from New
England to Georgia supported the Patriot cause; on the other
side, the Americans had demonstrated their inability to extend
their revolution to Canada, so while they claimed the eastern
seaboard, the British firmly controlled the St. Lawrence gateway to the continent. The southern colonies were still a bit of

a question mark, and though they were temporarily in American possession, that might not last. Or at least such was the British perception of the matter.

The situation was peculiar in that, although it was the Americans who sought to alter their status, it was the British who had the initiative. The Americans, like the Confederacy in the Civil War, simply had to sit pat and survive. The onus was on the other side to do something to restore the prewar equilibrium. In that sense, politically, the Revolution was already an established fact; yet militarily, it was a fact the British had yet to accept. It was therefore up to them to deny the fact by destroying it, and to do that, they would have to reconquer America. William Pitt said they could not do it. George III and his ministers were determined to try.

So they had ordered an expedition to the south, to rescue their supporters and reclaim the country there. They ordered Governor Carleton to move south from Canada by way of Lake Champlain, and they directed Sir William Howe to what they perceived as the commercial and financial heart of the colonies, New York. They had had enough of sitting and waiting for the Americans to come to their senses; this would now be real war.

Both sides would have a hard time waging it.

CHAPTER FOUR

Creating States
and Armies

T HE BRITISH in the winter of 1775–76 might decide to attack New York and South Carolina, and the Americans might recognize that this was what they would do, but for either side to carry those perceptions into action presented huge problems. The twentieth century is accustomed to thinking of government as all-pervasive, and nearly all-powerful; if a problem exists, the application of sufficient energy by government, whether that energy be in the form of money, time, expertise, or other human resources, ought to resolve it. But the eighteenth century thought and acted differently. Government was small, it did not do a great deal, and what it did do, it did not do very well. This was a matter both of ideology and technology.

For the first, men saw government not as the answer to difficulties, but as a necessary evil that had to be tolerated. There was in fact an increase in governmental functions throughout Europe in the later eighteenth century, as society became more complex, and the different classes developed conflicting interests and ambitions. But thinking people did not particularly approve of this. The foremost school of French political thinkers, known as Physiocrats, took as their slogan, "To govern better, govern less!" In Britain, the greatest writer on political economy of the period, Adam Smith, was producing his doctrines of free trade, and it is always remarked that *The Wealth of Nations* was published in the same year as the American Declaration of Independence. In London, this antigovernment attitude, as well as more particular opposition to the ministry's handling of the American war, was summed up in the famous Dunning Resolution of 1780: "Resolved, that the power of the Crown has increased, is increasing, and ought to be diminished."

In such a climate of opinion, governments expected to do little. They voted taxes, which provided for the royal establishment and a small central government, they raised and maintained armed forces, and they indulged in war and diplomacy. The civil service bureaucracy was meager, consisting of the clerks and government servants in the capital, and customs and revenue officers throughout the country. There was no health, education, or highway service in most countries, though the French, highly innovative, had built military roads and canals under the aegis of government, and the Prussians were experimenting with primary education. By contrast, though, most governments did not even possess police forces. Local government, especially in Britain, was almost exclusively in the hands of the great landed families, so the connection between local and central government was familial and informal rather than a legally established network.

The level of technology also militated against any close control, or excessive exercise of power, by a central government. It was simply impossible, when communication went at the speed of a horse or a wind-powered ship, to provide quick answers and directions to problems arising at a distance. The classic example of this difficulty was the Spanish American empire, in which the Royal and Supreme Council of the Indies, in Spain, tried to provide close supervision of its South American empire—and totally failed to do so. For a government in London, trying to deal with a crisis in America, there was always the knowledge that situations changed far more rapidly than ministers could respond to them, and orders always had to be conditional, and were usually far out of date by the time they arrived. But the Revolutionary government was almost equally hampered by the distances and the difficulties of communication in America, especially with the British blockading the coast. To send a message several hundred miles by land was a formidable undertaking, and Congress in Philadelphia was often nearly as far behind events as the ministry in London. Things were bad enough in summer; in winter, between Atlantic gales and North American snowstorms, it might be impossible to move or communicate at all. Such general conditions naturally affected everyone; nonetheless, as they were magnified by distance, they disadvantaged the British somewhat more than they did the Americans. To us it appears as if great affairs of state proceeded by inexplicable fits and starts, but that was simply the logical inertia of a preindustrial society, for whom the natural order was a state of rest rather than, as for us, a state of constant motion.

Both sides also faced difficulties peculiar to themselves, and since the Americans were just starting out, their problems in this area were especially onerous. Probably the greatest political liability was the disinclination of the separate colonies to unite for general purposes. Their attitude is typified by the term they soon adopted for themselves—"states"; other countries had provinces, or counties, but the American colonies called themselves states, because a state is a sovereign power, an entity, by definition, over which there can be no greater power. Only slowly and reluctantly did they accept the truth of Benjamin Franklin's aphorism that "We must all hang together, or assuredly we shall all hang separately," for the tradition of intercolonial cooperation was a young one, while that of dislike and rivalry was as old as the colonies themselves. New Englanders and New Yorkers cordially detested each other, New Jersey disliked New York, and everybody scorned Pennsylvania, whose Quaker-dominated government was generally seen as willing to profit from a war, but not partake in it. And all the northern colonies distrusted all the southern ones. The British government, conscious through the earlier wars of the difficulty of effecting colonial unity, in the end counted too much on this divisive attitude.

And indeed the American central government was certainly hampered by it. It had almost no coercive power; it could not tax, it lacked any bureaucratic structure of its own to see its wishes carried out, and it was throughout the war dependent upon the acquiescence of the states to get things done. If, for example, Congress wanted to raise troops, it must let the states do the actual work of it. It could print money, but it had no central treasury or bank to back its bills, and it was therefore perpetually threatened with bankruptcy, as the traditional phrase "not worth a continental" testifies. It is customary to deride the Continental Congress for its ineffectiveness, and the small-mindedness of some of its members; considering the difficulties it labored under, the wonder is rather that so many good men stayed with it, and that they accomplished as much as they did. After all, if one had to choose between the American Congress in Philadelphia, trying to make the states work together for the common goal, and Lord North and company in London, trying to juggle the King and the Parliament, Congress obviously did the better job: it won.

One of the major problems for both sides was the very basic one of figuring out what they actually had to work with. Just who wanted the Revolution, and who was for it or against it? Neither side was ever entirely sure, and historians, who have argued the matter for two hundred years, have ranged widely on this, as on every other question of the period. The general estimates are that perhaps one third of the population were active supporters of the Revolution, or Patriots; and one third were actively for the King, or Loyalists or Tories; with the other third wanting to be left alone as much as possible; or, that one quarter took either active position, and as much as one half formed the amorphous and neutral middle. What really matters is less the figures than what actually happened, that the Patriots seized control of colonial and local, and then of an incipient national, government, so that they actually had the government in being, while the Loyalists, disorganized and aloof, saw legitimacy slip from their hands. The British were therefore already faced with an accomplished fact by the time they tried to subdue the rebellion. A second important point is that the government in London never really realized this; they listened, as in the case of governors Martin or Dunmore, to their own officials and supporters, and thus they were always convinced that they faced not a true mass movement, but rather a plot by a few power-hungry radicals, such as Samuel Adams actually was and they perceived Washington to be. They were thus always hopeful that if they simply showed up in an area, say upper New York State or the southern colonies, the true majority would rally around them. To borrow the phraseology of another war, they were sure the silent majority was with them—and they were wrong. Of all the mistakes they made, this one cost them especially dear.

Both sides faced a major problem of raising and maintaining an army, so that the war could actually be fought, and they found radically different solutions to it. American troops initially belonged to the colonies or states, as there was, of course, at that point no real central government. The army that gathered around Boston to besiege the British consisted of militia regiments furnished by the northern colonies. At the same time that it appointed Washington as commander in chief, the Congress adopted these troops, and their formations, as a national army. In fact, the first troops it raised specifically as national troops were the Pennsylvania and Virginia rifle companies that it soon sent north. When it subsequently authorized the 20,370-man army that its commander recommended, as a result of a visit to Boston by a committee from Philadelphia, it was seeking to build up, and formalize, a regular standing army on the European model, and it proposed that these men be organized in twenty-six single-battalion regiments. If realized, this plan would have given Washington and the Americans a small but presumably efficient force with which he could meet the British on their own terms.

The general firmly believed that this was the only way to wage the war, and much of his, and Congress's, efforts on this score, throughout the entire course of the conflict, were directed toward obtaining men, and turning them from local temporary soldiers into regulars. These Continental troops thus were to form the backbone of the American effort. The battalions were apportioned to the various states, in accordance with their populations, and the state governments were asked to raise and forward the units. During the first year of the war, about 27,500 men were officially carried on the national rolls.

For 1776 Congress authorized twenty-seven regiments, then later in the year it upped the number to eighty-eight, and tried to enlist men for the duration of the war, rather than simply for the year. Then, at the very end of the year, it voted to raise another sixteen, as well as cavalry and artillery formations. In fact, authorized strength was never reached, in spite of the offering of enlistment bounties either of hard money or future land grants, and there were fewer troops under arms in 1777 than the year before, and fewer still in 1778. For 1779, recognizing both reality and the diminution of activity, the figures were adjusted downward, back to eighty battalions, and for the last two years of the war, down again to a mere fifty-eight.

Figures compiled soon after the war showed that there had been some 232,000 enlistments in the Continental Army; many of these were reenlistments, so it is estimated that they represent perhaps 150,000 men, though one historian puts the number as low as 100,000.

In addition to the regulars, and often in competition with them, there existed the militia. Their record was very uneven, and is still a subject of dispute, though indeed, it remains a major influence in the American military tradition. Every able-bodied man was officially part of the militia, and subject to call-up in an emergency. There were, however, severe limitations on the availability of such formations. They could only be required to serve for certain periods of time, and in certain locales and situations. It was up to the government of the separate states, for example, to determine when these forces should be called out, and whether they should be sent beyond their own borders. They might be called out for as much as a year, or, in dire conditions, for a few days, though usually they were called for at least a month. There were times when Washington was reduced to begging militias to stay with him for another week, or to leave the border of one state to cross into another. They tended at times to be poorly disciplined and commanded. On the other hand, they were occasionally capable of excellent work; it was for all practical purposes militiamen who fought the entire campaign around Boston, who did much of the work of the Lake Champlain area, and who also did effective fighting in the south. Some generals, such as Horatio Gates, understood and got good results with them. Washington hated having to rely on them, but often had little choice. The figures for militia service are far less reliable than for the Continentals, but there seem to have been about 145,000 periods of service under militia auspices.

Taking regulars and militia together, the total would be about 377,000 enlistments, which still settles down to probably a range of 175,000 to 225,000 men serving in the armed forces of the American Revolution. Critics have scorned this as not very many to fight for independence, but that seems hardly fair. It would represent roughly eight to ten percent of the population, a population which of course included women, children, and aged people (though there were at times boys as young as twelve and men as old as sixty in the ranks, even of the regulars) and in fact that percentage is as high as most modern states have been able to mobilize for a war effort. When it is considered that these men came out of a subsistence, still largely frontier society, not all of whose people were in favor of the war, it is actually fairly impressive. It becomes even more so when to the number is added the women, wives or sweethearts, who must have at least acquiesced in their men being away, and finally, when one remembers that these people were volunteers, for the states had no power to conscript, except in the peculiar circumstances of calling out the militia for emergencies.

How many men were actually available at any given moment is a far different matter. The peak strength for a year was 89,000 in 1776, and half of those were militiamen. The highest strength of the Continental Army came in 1778, at 35,000, and Washington never commanded more than 17,000 troops, regulars and militiamen together, at any one time. So the impressive total has to be projected over several long years of war. For any specific operation, there never seem to have been enough troops, and manpower remained a constant worry for the Americans throughout the war.

*   *   *

Ironically, manpower was an equal worry for the British, because they faced difficulties similar to those of their opponents. Britain was the only major power which had no conscription for military service, so British forces had to be raised voluntarily, just as American did. The British Army of the period was an excellent one, but small by European standards, and the traditional way of waging war for Britain was to subsidize allies, and support them with her small army, rather than to raise a large one herself. It was a policy that had worked well in the past, and continued to do so until World War I. But the American war was so different in character that it negated previous patterns. It was fought not against a nearby European enemy, but overseas at the end of a long line of communications. It also came at a period when Britain was temporarily friendless in Europe, the result of too much success achieved at the hands of both allies and enemies in the last generation of wars. The British were therefore forced to rely initially on their own forces, and their own resources, and they proved inadequate to the task.

In the period from the end of the Seven Years' War to the American Revolution, the British Army was reduced to a strength of some 45,000 men, in seventy regiments of infantry and seventeen of cavalry. These were stationed in the United Kingdom itself, in outposts of empire such as Gibraltar and Minorca, and, some 10,000 of them, in North America. Such a number was hardly sufficient for the peacetime needs of the empire, and as soon as serious trouble began, the government attempted to increase its troop strength. This proved difficult to do; military service was largely a last resort in British life, and most people did not do it if they could do something else. It happened at that particular time that Ireland, the most fertile source of recruits, was enjoying one of its occasional periods of prosperity. Service was bad enough in peacetime —stultifying drill, heavy punishments, few amenities—but it was worse in war, and especially in a war which did not have a great deal of public support. Young men could usually be found to go off and fight the French, and Britain's traditional wars had a certain panache and element of patriotic gore to them. Indeed, once France entered the war on the American side, recruiting in Britain improved noticeably. But not many young men wanted to enlist to go to America, to fight against people perceived as their distant cousins in a war that half the country opposed anyway.

The government therefore resorted to a standard device of the period, the employment of foreign units. The profession of mercenary soldier now carries a stigma with it, but in the eighteenth century, before the concept of nationality had fully developed, and when military service was thought the only honorable work for a gentleman, there was nothing amiss in hiring out to a foreign power. Most governments maintained units of foreign troops, often, indeed, as household troops, that is, in positions of trust around the sovereign himself. Thus, in the French Army one of the most famous bodies of troops was the king's Swiss Guards, and the French also had Irish, German, Italian, and Polish regiments in the line. The Spanish had Irish troops, the Dutch had Swiss, and on and on. Even some of the oldest British regiments had a century ago been hired out to the Dutch. To the British ministry, then, it was perfectly logical to hire foreign troops, though their doing so was a measure of how little they actually understood what they were up against.

In western Germany there were several independent states whose rulers were happy to rent regiments to Great Britain; several of the states had been allied with England in the Seven Years' War anyway, and hiring out bodies was a good way to increase revenues. Eventually six principalities made deals; the most important of them was Hesse-Cassel, which provided almost 17,000 men. The others ranged from some 5,700 Brunswickers down to 1,200 from little Anhalt-Zerbst. All told, almost 30,000 Germans fought in America. Because their overall commanders were always from Hesse, and because Hesse supplied most of them, they became generically known as Hessians. Good troops drilled in the Prussian fashion of the day, they were known initially for their ferocity, but they did not, as a general rule, do well in America, and their overall record was mediocre. For their rulers, it was simple blood money; for the poor troops, conscripted and given little choice in their futures, it was something less. And of course, their introduction into the American theater had an intensely negative impact on American opinion; it was hard to retain some lingering fiction of loyalty to one's king when he brought in foreign mercenaries to fight. Even though the Americans considered the same recourse, and were busily soliciting help from France or anyplace else they might get it, American propagandists still had a field day with the Hessians.

A totally different source of manpower for the British was seriously underemployed. That was the Loyalists. Far more than is generally realized, the war was a civil war, and in spite of British neglect, many Loyalist formations fought in the war. It is estimated that about 50,000 Americans actually fought for the British side, either as militiamen or in regularly formed units. Something close to seventy Loyalist formations existed, though most of them never got very far; nonetheless, there were about twenty units that fought long and well for the Crown, earning both enviable military records and the bitter hatred of the Patriots they often faced. Many of these were drawn from the frontier areas, especially of the southern colonies or of New York State, where several men, such as Sir William Johnson, were influential and powerful. The soldiers they developed were skilled fighters and bitter men, and they waged war seriously; units such as Butler's Rangers, the Queen's Rangers, or Johnson's Loyal Greens were formidable fighters who gave, and received, little mercy.

The British, at the same time that they allowed their strategy to be unduly influenced by their delusions of Loyalist strength, neglected this resource to a considerable degree. Perhaps their attitude stemmed from the general metropolitan sense of superiority over the colonials, but whatever the cause, money that would have been well spent on encouraging Loyalist forces went instead to hire Germans. Many times potential Loyalist forces were dismissed or forced to disperse for lack of support. Yet New York, an extreme case, supplied almost as many men to the British forces as it did to the American. It was ultimately refugee Loyalists, unable to keep America for the King, who turned Canada from a once-French into a future British territory.

Next to finding the men to fight, maintaining them while they did so was the greatest problem; indeed, sometimes it was the worse of the two, as Washington's starving soldiers found to their dismay. The British were infinitely better off than their enemies in this regard. They had behind them an established system, and even though it was occasionally inefficient, and functioned over great distances, they still did reasonably well. Britain at the time was entering the early stages of the Industrial Revolution, and was already the greatest producer in the world; for years its industries had supplied not only British forces, but allies as well, and often even sold to its enemies too.

In addition to the national infrastructure for the waging of a war, the British had two other advantages: they could afford to pay in hard cash for local supplies of all kinds, from food to forage to transport; and they also, through most of the war, held the strategic initiative. This meant that during the winter lulls, while Americans were forced to starve at Valley Forge or Morristown, the British could sit snugly in Philadelphia or New York, whiling away the winter months with gambling, amateur theatricals, or the company of well-disposed local society. Eighteenth-century warfare was often strenuous, and occasionally actually risky, but life went on, after all.

For the Americans, however, everything had to be done the hard way. The colonies largely lacked the manufacturing element that would have supplied armies for war, partly because the mercantile system of the empire discouraged colonial production of finished products, partly because labor had been so expensive that it was cheaper and easier to import goods from Britain. There was no real arms industry, in spite of the excellence of some gunsmiths; most cloth was produced by women simply for familial consumption. In other words, this was still a subsistence society, and war requires more than that; it requires a society that has surplus goods and money to divert to its waging. The Americans lacked both.

They did have available, eventually, three sources. First, there was the small amount of war material that they themselves did manage to produce. Secondly, there was what they captured from the British; the guns of Ticonderoga were an early example of this, and before the war was many weeks old, American privateers and cruisers were at sea, snapping up British supply ships as prizes—in fact, one of the things the rebels did possess in abundance was a shipping industry. Finally and most important, they had the assistance of the French. Actual alliance, and overt military intervention, had to wait until the Americans had shown they were likely to succeed, but aid around the edges started early. There was no love for England across the Channel, and a trickle of French volunteers, and far more importantly, supplies, was soon flowing westward. It happened that in 1776–77 the French Army introduced a new model of musket, and as they switched over, much of the surplus was turned over to thinly disguised firms, such as the famous Hortalez and Company, which were fronting for American suppliers. The French also had a well-developed clothing industry, and it turned out most of the uniforms the Americans ever had.

Uniforms, indeed, provide one of the indices of how well the American cause was prospering at any moment. The more uniforms they had available, the better they were doing. At the start of the war, there was little standardization at all. The army around Boston wore mostly civilian clothing, which was all it had. A few militia units, mostly from the larger towns or cities, had managed to develop sufficient spirit, and funds, to obtain uniforms; the Governor General's Foot Guard of Connecticut, for example, wore uniforms so closely resembling those of British grenadiers that they were dangerous. The riflemen sent north by Congress were told to get their own clothing, and they showed up in thigh-length frocks with fringes along the seams, known as hunting shirts. The fringes, incidentally, were not merely decorative; they carried water away from the seams and kept the wearer dry. These were so useful, and available, that Washington suggested their adoption for the entire army, but they were presumably not thought sufficiently military looking.

Colonial formations during the empire's wars had often been in blue, again when they actually had uniforms, and Washington appeared in Congress in the blue and buff of the Virginia militia; Maryland troops wore blue faced with red; however, shades of brown or gray, both of which colors were readily obtainable for local dyes, were actually more prevalent. In New York in 1775, the 1st Regiment wore blue faced with dark red, the 2nd brown faced blue, the 3rd gray faced green, and the 4th brown faced with scarlet. The facings referred to the distinctive colors worn on collars, cuffs, and lapels, which marked off one regiment from another.

In fact, though these colors might be officially designated, usually only officers managed to obtain them, and only a few of them. Most officers wore their civilian clothing, with some mark of military distinction, such as a sash or epaulet, and of course the sword carried by every gentleman anyway. Private soldiers wore whatever they could get, and were often barefoot, ragged, out at knees and elbows. By 1777 uniforms were so scarce, and so varied, that Washington decreed that American soldiers should wear a sprig of green leaf or evergreen in their hats as a distinguishing badge; there could hardly be an emblem more symbolic of the material bankruptcy of the American cause.

Washington, however, was always concerned to make his men look like soldiers, both for their own morale and well-being and to impress their allies and enemies, and he never stopped trying to create a uniform appearance for the army. In 1779 he promulgated a general order setting out a code for uniforms: New England regiments were to wear blue faced white; New York and New Jersey blue faced buff; Pennsylvania, Maryland, Delaware and Virginia blue with red; and the Carolina and Georgia regiments blue faced light blue with a white edge and buttonhole lace. Another peculiar distinction of the period was the color of the cockade, the bit of lace or ribbon worn on the hat. Hitherto the Americans had worn black, the Hanoverian cockade for King George, and it was now changed to black with a bit of white ribbon, as a compliment to France. Since this was one item of uniform that could actually be obtained, most American soldiers ironically fought the end of the war under the colors of the Elector of Hanover/King of England and the Bourbon dynasty of France. Even at that late date, however, most of this was an expression of intent or hope rather than a reality. Nonetheless, these uniform regulations of 1779 were the ones most commonly followed, and gradually, as more and more assistance from France arrived, and also as the army shrank in size toward the later stages of the war, some regiments actually did get to wear uniforms. These form the picture that has come down through the years, and in patriotic imagination, Washington's lean soldiers are better dressed than ever they were in reality.

A man could fight without a uniform; he could hardly do so without weapons or food. Throughout the war the Americans remained chronically short of weapons and accoutrements. One reason Americans would seldom stand to receive a bayonet charge—aside from the sensible fact that few men are foolish enough to do so anyway—was that they usually did not have bayonets. Congress early on organized both a quartermaster general's office and a commissary general's office, to provide for supply, transport, provisioning, and all the other unsung services that are never noticed until they go wrong. But it was very heavy going. They did all right until the disasters around New York City, and the heavy losses of supplies incurred there. They then virtually collapsed, and for much of the war after that, the army lived a hand-to-mouth existence, finding what it could, buying where possible, then begging, and occasionally stealing. Here again, Washington was determined to have a regular army and to have it behave itself, but on rapid marches, especially retreats, the men often went hungry, and in winter quarters they soon stripped bare the immediate area of their cantonments. The great propagandist of the American cause, Tom Paine, once wrote about "summer soldiers," men who were not there when things got bad. To serve in the Patriot army, even at the best of times, let alone the worst, one had to be a winter soldier. Gradually even the British gave them a grudging admiration.

There was, finally, the problem of commanding armies. On both sides, there were men above and below the ostensible commanders who thought they knew more about war than those charged with winning it. From above, larger political considerations always obtruded; from below, personal politics and ambitions did the same.

Washington constantly felt harassed with suggestions and directions from Congress, and was occasionally downright embittered by its ability to interfere with his handling of the war, at the same time as it manifested its inability to give him the wherewithal to fight it. But as the war went on, for better or worse, he became increasingly certain of his position. There were times during the darkest days, when Congress was in flight and the war seemed all but lost, that it looked as if he would be replaced; there were other times, equally difficult, when Congress granted Washington a virtual dictatorship; eventually, there was increasing confidence in his leadership.

His underlings gave him unceasing trouble. When Congress elected Washington as the commander of its army, it also appointed subordinate officers. Four major generals were chosen: Artemas Ward from Massachusetts, Israel Putnam from Connecticut, Philip Schuyler of New York, and Charles Lee from Virginia. Ward was a rather cantankerous Yankee, and he and Washington did not get on too well; he did not possess any real military talent, and after the operations around Boston, he remained in command of the Eastern Department where, fortunately, there was little action. He usually appears as an old fuddy-duddy, though he was only in his early fifties during the war. Putnam was an old war-horse whose position outstripped his abilities, and after the New York campaign he faded badly; he became a bit of a grumbler, but he was never subtle enough, or indeed intelligent enough, to lead a real faction.

Schuyler was a different matter. As a great New York landowner and a major political figure in an important state, he was a power in the land. He was often embroiled in controversy, sometimes with Congress, usually with his own officers. For example, he fought a running feud with Horatio Gates in 1777. Washington found him useful, however, and mostly helpful, but he had to be handled with great care.

And no amount of care was enough to handle Charles Lee; a retired British lieutenant colonel, he had been in the colonies only a few years before the revolution broke out, and he had married money and set himself up as a potential leader of the Patriot cause. He had great military experience, as well as a great opinion of his own talents. Talent he actually did possess, but not enough to support his aspirations. He was wildly eccentric in his personal habits, dirty and profane, and he kept a pack of dogs which he fed from plates on his dining table. Washington and everyone else initially deferred to his experience, but he was happiest with flights of fancy and plots and schemes to supplant his commander. Opinion is still mixed as to whether he was a hero, a villain, or a fool.

Congress further appointed eight brigadier generals, always paying due attention to political and geographical considerations. Of them John Sullivan of New Hampshire did some reasonably useful work, though he may have been involved in one of the schemes to replace Washington; Richard Montgomery died at Quebec, and young Nathanael Greene from Rhode Island turned out to be a minor military genius. The rest faded into the general tapestry of the period.

Finally, Horatio Gates of Virginia was appointed adjutant general; the son of a servant in England, Gates had difficulty living down his origins, and after military service in the colonies, became attached to the Patriot cause. He had some military talent, and surprisingly, was popular with New England soldiers; his nickname "Granny" Gates derived from his care for his troops, rather than the fussbudget, old-maidish nature it implies. Unfortunately, he was a fussbudget, too, and a conniver as well. His successes in the Lake Champlain area, won perhaps more by other men than by himself, led to ambitions to replace Washington, and he had substantial support in Congress to do it. All he lacked was stature and real ability.

Other men rose and fell through the course of the struggle. Some were remarkably brave, able, and self-sacrificing; some were cowardly, stupid, and venal. A few were both.

The British were much the same. The divided counsels in the cabinet did nothing to make the task of the soldiers easier, and the soldiers constantly vied both with each other, and with their political superiors. At the juncture where high command met political direction, there was a morass of alliance, friendship, ambition, and dislike. At the center of the morass were the generals who had come over to help Gage at Boston. These three, Sir William Howe, John Burgoyne, and Sir Henry Clinton, with the then governor of Quebec, Sir Guy Carleton, dominated the British command for most of the war. All possessed talents, some in greater measure than others, and all had shortcomings that prevented them from succeeding in their aims.

Carleton was perhaps the most enigmatic of the four. He was a popular and effective soldier, and some authorities believe that he might have won the war for Britain; his military maneuvers were well-handled, but on closer examination, they were subject to almost inexplicable periods of inactivity. In actuality, the threats he faced never seem to have been as overwhelming as he conceived them to be. His chief disability, however, was the fact that Lord George Germain thoroughly disliked him, and that was enough to cripple him.

Sir William Howe was the most crucial of the lot, for during his period of command he failed to bring the war to an end, and may therefore be said to have lost it. He was the youngest of three brothers; the eldest, George, had been killed at Ticonderoga in 1758, and the second, Richard, commanded the Royal Navy's fleet in American waters during much of the war. The Howes were Whigs in British politics, and had strenuously opposed the repressive measures that led to the war. Howe had said he would not accept the American command, and given his views, he probably should have stuck to his position; instead, he decided his duty was to obey. At the same time as he took up the military command, however, he also accepted instructions to negotiate a peace settlement; he and his brother were therefore in the highly contradictory position of trying to talk peace with the Americans while trying to conquer them. He thus had muddled instructions to compound his own mixed feelings about the war.

John Burgoyne had no such problems. A man on the make, he had married money for love, and done well out of it. He had a reputation as an expert on light forces and irregular operations, and had literary, military, and even political ambitions. His actual talents would support none of these, but he was an engaging character with a marked skill at intrigue and insinuation. He was close to Germain, and he managed to supplant Carleton in 1777; it was his worst mistake in a life that saw many.

Sir Henry Clinton presided over the endgame. He was a reasonably efficient, somewhat stolid, administrator. He did not do well in field command, and he believed that he did not enjoy unreserved support from home; he was right. His chief claim to fame was less in losing the American War than in writing a massive, and still readable, account proving that he did not lose it.

Generally speaking, though, the British higher commanders were a creditable group, well-trained, knowledgeable in their profession, experienced in the field, and supported by the most prosperous and efficient society of its day. Sometimes that is not enough.

CHAPTER FIVE

War in the Grand Manner

Long before Sir William Howe abandoned Boston, the British had developed an overall strategic plan for 1776. New England they conceived as the heart of the rebellion, and as lost to them for practical purposes. They therefore proposed to isolate the Yankees from the rest of the rebels, and subdue the remainder. To this end, their main effort was to be directed at New York. A two-pronged attack was set up: Sir Guy Carleton would advance south from Quebec, along the Lake Champlain route; meanwhile, the chief British armament would proceed by sea, to take New York City itself. The effectual occupation of the Champlain–Hudson line, and America's principal city, by this logic, would bank the fires of rebellion in the north, and allow the Loyalist subjects of the Crown to reassert their control.

Meanwhile, operations in the south would be aimed at regaining control of Virginia and the Carolinas, in response to the assessments and pleas of the royal governors there. On January 20, Sir Henry Clinton left Boston for the southern theater; he stopped in New York Harbor on his way, throwing the citizenry into a panic that was only increased by the arrival of American General Charles Lee and two regiments of Connecticut troops. But Clinton did not land; he soon sailed again, to meet a substantial fleet and convoy coming from Britain, for the rescue of the southern colonies.

Letters intercepted at sea suggested that this major British force might sail as early as mid-December of 1775. But in spite of the rebellion's being eight months old by then, the British government and armed forces were still only slowly shifting into wartime attitudes. All had to be done from the start, and it was February of the new year before the fleet left from the Irish port of Cork. It consisted of nine warships, led by the *Bristol*, a 50-gun ship, under the flag of Admiral Sir Peter Parker, and more than thirty transports, carrying seven regiments of infantry commanded by General Lord Cornwallis. With 2,500 regular soldiers at his back, Cornwallis was confident he could manage the task at hand.

February is not the best time to try a crossing of the North Atlantic, and after five days at sea, the fleet was hit by a succession of westerly gales that scattered it all over the ocean. Some of the ships went back to Cork, others were lucky to find shelter in the south-coast ports of England itself. While these unhappy vessels, with their cargoes of seasick soldiers, were running before the wind, in the opposite direction to that they wished to go, the Carolina Loyalists, having risen prematurely on assurances the fleet was on its way, were being defeated in the little campaign that culminated at Moore's Creek Bridge late in February. The first British ships did not raise Cape Fear, North Carolina, until mid-April, and the whole fleet was not at their rendezvous point until the first week of May. By then they were six weeks too late.

That being the case, they then spent another three weeks arguing about what they ought to do. Clinton had met them, so he, Cornwallis, Parker, and the southern governors all dined and discussed, discussed and dined, and tried each other's patience until they at last reached a decision. The chief port south of Philadelphia was Charleston, in South Carolina, so they determined to go there. Chesapeake Bay and Virginia, and North Carolina, could be gathered in later. On May 31 the fleet weighed anchor, and arrived off Charleston the next day.

The city lay about six miles inland on an opening in the kind of shore that sailors hate. The whole coast consisted of low-lying, sandy islands and marshes, split by meandering creeks; shallow water and sandbars lay offshore. It took the British a week to find their way over the outer bar and gain an anchorage in Five Fathom Hole, off Morris Island on the southern side of the harbor entrance.

Meanwhile, the citizens of South Carolina were preparing their own defense. Patriot Governor John Rutledge had called up all the state troops he could muster, and had several regiments in hand. At the same time that the British arrived, so did Charles Lee, and he brought with him three Continental regiments, two from North Carolina and one from Virginia. Lee immediately started giving orders to everyone, and the South Carolinians took offense and refused to obey him. The impasse was resolved when Rutledge graciously put his state troops under Lee's command. Eventually the Americans had some 6,500 men available to defend the city, though as it happened, only a small number of them took part in the actual fighting.

The city's defenses consisted of a number of half-finished works, of which the most important was Fort Moultrie, a modest little square fort on Sullivan's Island, the northern and outer island on the harbor approaches. The fort was hardly impressive; it was made of palmetto logs and sand, and only two sides of it were completed, to the seaward and the south, facing the harbor entrance. Hasty breastworks were thrown up along the northern side, but they were far from complete. Sullivan's Island itself was about four miles long, low and sandy; its northern end was separated from Long Island by a low channel called The Breach. Colonel William Moultrie, who commanded on Sullivan's Island, sent some men north to hold The Breach if possible, and he posted other detachments along the middle of the island, with instructions to fall back on the fort as necessary. Lee did not like the position, but then Lee did not seem to like much of anything, and Moultrie was confident he could hold it.

When the British looked about them, they decided that
The Breach was fordable, so Clinton landed most of his troops
on Long Island, with the intention of crossing the little channel
and moving south on Fort Moultrie while Parker's ships bombarded it. Having landed the men, he then found to his dismay
that though rocks and bars in The Breach made it impracticable for boat work, it was still seven feet deep, so it could
not be forded either. The British soldiers were thus reduced
to spectators.

Parker planned to assault the fort on the 23rd, but the
wind turned against him, so it was not until the 28th that the
battle was fought. It turned out to be remarkably uneven.
Moultrie had something more than 400 men in the fort, South
Carolina infantry and artillery. The fleet took up its position
and began firing, first high-flying shells from bomb ketches,
and then a straight naval bombardment. To the Americans'
delight, these did almost no damage at all. The bombs were
well fired, and landed mostly in the center of the fort, but its
parade ground was soft and spongy sand. The shells buried
themselves in it, and burst harmlessly, throwing up great gouts
of sand and little else. The flat-trajectory naval guns battered
all day at the fort, but the palmetto logs were soft too, and
absorbed most of the cannonballs without harm. Parker sent
three ships into the harbor to try to flank the fort, but they
all ran aground; two spent the day hauling themselves off,
and the third had to be abandoned and burned.

By contrast, American return fire was highly effective;
Nelson once remarked that it was foolish to attack stone forts
with wooden ships, and in this case, it was foolish to attack
sand castles with them as well. The Carolinians concentrated
their fire on the bigger British vessels, especially the flagship,
and at several points they swept the quarterdeck clear, including blowing the admiral's breeches off. Not until dark did
the British sullenly give up and haul away, but by the end of
the battle, the Americans had killed or wounded about 225
British, and disabled several of their ships, for a loss of a dozen
killed and two dozen wounded of their own. It was a stunning,
heartening victory for the American cause in the south, and
a defeat of enormous consequences for the British. Clinton
took his useless troops north to rejoin Sir William Howe, and

the fleet, after repairing what it could, eventually sailed away; with it faded any Loyalist hopes for the immediate future.

War is a great destroyer of the comfortable sophistries by which human beings conduct their normal affairs. By early 1776, it was no longer possible to pretend that the American revolutionaries were anything but that; the pretense that this was a loyal protest to His Majesty King George III, that he was a kind and generous paterfamilias who had been led astray by bad advice and greedy ministers, simply collapsed under the weight of events. The conflict in the colonies themselves, the American attempt to suborn Canada, the hiring of German troops and Indians to subdue the rebellion, all these had hardened opinion. Willingly or otherwise, the Americans gradually accepted the logic of the situation, and moved toward actual independence.

Throughout the last year, their various possible positions had been hotly debated. Nothing would be farther from the truth than to see them unanimously clamoring for independence right from the start of hostilities. All but the most extreme of them revered the British connection, or said they did. In their arguments thus far, they saw themselves not as rejecting the Anglo-Saxon political tradition, but as restoring it to its former purity. Even in this, they were well within British norms, for all the great upheavals of the seventeenth century had been made in the name of restoring an older, lost equilibrium, rather than creating a new one.

In July 1775, conscious of the need to justify its actions, Congress had issued a "Declaration of the Causes and Necessities of Taking up Arms." This was primarily the work of John Dickinson, one of the ablest political thinkers of the colonies, and one of the most interesting. Dickinson had been active in both Maryland and Pennsylvania throughout the ten years before the Revolution began; he had consistently written against the British government's policies, and yet had equally consistently been a voice for moderation and against force. A member of the First and Second Continental Congresses, he had authored several of the petitions and addresses to the King. Yet now, in 1775, he wrote that to resist by force was better than "unconditional submission to the tyranny of irritated ministers," and that Americans were, if necessary, "resolved to die freemen rather than to live [as] slaves."

The months since then had shown that the Americans were up against more than just irritated ministers, and it was Thomas Paine, in January of 1776, who stripped away the veils. Paine was an English radical, in his late thirties, who had failed at virtually every job he ever tried; but in the process he had educated himself by intensive reading in politics and philosophy. In the early 1770's he met Benjamin Franklin, then in London as an agent for the colonies, and the latter sent him off to America with letters of introduction. Paine was a natural for the revolutionary cause. In Philadelphia he met Dr. Benjamin Rush, one of the leading and less temperate rebels, and it was Rush who eventually suggested to Paine a pamphlet urging independence.

Common Sense was written for the common man; that was its great defect as political philosophy and, far more important, its great virtue as propaganda. Here were none of Thomas Jefferson's subtleties or John Dickinson's hesitations. Good government is bad enough, said Paine, but bad government is intolerable; the only reason men have governments is to protect themselves from war and invasion, but in the present case, government means just that. Therefore Americans would be better off to get rid of their old, *British* government, and to set up their own. Even more forthrightly, he pointed out that it was not just some ill-defined "government" that was the cause of trouble: it was kings in general, and one King in particular. Painc had made the transition rapidly; he had been in America only a year, yet he hit the heart of the matter, and the whole thrust of his argument was "We are not Englishmen; we are Americans!"

The little pamphlet sold half a million copies; practically every person in America who could read must have bought it. It was an astonishingly successful piece of propaganda, not less so because it convinced those who were already half-convinced anyway.

Gradually over the winter minds moved toward that fatal step. In April North Carolina told its delegates to Congress to join with any others who might be advocating independence; Virginia followed suit in May, and in June Richard Henry Lee moved a resolution for independence. The moderates and certainly the conservatives still hung back, arguing that things were proceeding too rapidly, but on June 11 Congress established a committee to draw up a declaration for possible adoption. Most of the writing was done by Thomas Jefferson, who drew heavily upon former statements of grievances and assorted addresses, as well as his own political philosophy, which went back in a direct line to John Locke and the theory of the social contract. John Adams took charge of steering the document through the Congress. There, the argument was actually over Richard Henry Lee's earlier resolution; that passed on July 2; it was then largely a matter of form to adjust the declaration as a means of presenting to the world the decision for independence. On July 4 the committee's amended draft was adopted, and overnight it was printed up and sent out for distribution, especially among the army.

The Declaration of Independence is one of the great documents of human history, couched very much in the language and political tradition of the eighteenth century. As such, it sums up not only the Americans' grievances, real and supposed, against their King, but it also sets forth the general assumptions and universal aspirations of society at the time. Jefferson quickly reviewed the former, explained how the King stood in the way of achieving the latter, and then, so that Americans might fulfill their destiny, both as individuals and as a society, declared that "these united colonies are and of right ought to be free and independent states," and finally, to do all that was necessary to realize that aim, the representatives pledged "our lives, our fortunes, and our sacred honor." The signing of the document by the various members of Congress actually took place over the next several months, but every man who put his name on it, even John Hancock who wrote large enough so the King "might read it without his spectacles," knew that that pledge was not an idle one. It was one thing to declare independence; it still remained to be conquered on the battlefield.

It might well be argued that all that went before the summer of 1776 was mere preliminary, a drawing of both the political and geographical parameters of the struggle. By mid-summer, the Americans had both declared their independence, and, with one small exception, decided what territories the United States was actually going to encompass. The position was clearly stated; now it had to be made good.

Both sides moved on New York. The day after Sir William Howe left Boston, Washington sent the first of his troops hastily marching southwest through Massachusetts and Connecticut. He thought it quite possible that Howe would go directly to New York, and was later greatly relieved to find that the British had sailed to Halifax instead. Within a month most of the army had gone south, and the commander in chief followed them. As well, new formations were recruited in the middle colonies, and the militia was called out in Connecticut, New York, and New Jersey. How much time the Americans had they did not know, but they must make the best of it.

Charles Lee was already in the city, before going south to Charleston, and he and Washington conferred over its defenses. The bitter truth was plain to see: New York was in fact indefensible against a power that controlled the sea. Just as Boston could be ringed and encircled from the land, so New York, with its series of islands, rivers, and bays, must fall to anyone supreme on the water. Everyone knew that where there was water for ships to float, the long arm of Britain was inescapable.

Nonetheless, the city must be defended; to surrender the greatest center in America without a fight would do immense and perhaps permanent harm to the Patriot cause. Holding New York might not be possible militarily, but politically it had to be attempted. Lee and Washington agreed that at least the British could be made to pay a heavy price for the city, and who knew but perhaps it would prove so heavy they would let it alone. Lee went south, and Washington settled down to make the best of a bad situation.

American numbers fluctuated wildly during the spring months, but by the time the campaign actually opened, there were about 19,000 troops on hand, almost all of them infantry, supported by a little artillery. Something less than half of them were militia, poorly armed, equipped, trained, and in some

THE AREA AROUND NEW YORK

cases led. The regulars, Continentals, were better in all cate-
gories, but still basically untried. It was as yet an amateur
army.

They could still dig, but where to do it was a problem.
The city occupied the bottom tip of Manhattan Island, and
that was dominated by Brooklyn Heights, on Long Island
across the East River. There was no possibility of holding such
extensive territory as all of western Long Island, or Staten
Island, the big flat piece of land south of New York Bay against
the New Jersey shore. The British might come up the East
River and cut off Brooklyn; they might come up the Hudson
and bombard Manhattan from the west, they might make an
amphibious landing at any one of a dozen, or a hundred, spots.
Washington decided he would fortify what he could of Manhattan, which meant digging trenches and putting up earthworks at likely landing sites around the city. He started a
couple of small forts, Fort Washington at the north end of
Manhattan on the Hudson side, and Fort Lee across the river
on the New Jersey side. He put some troops at Kings Bridge
on the mainland above Manhattan. But he put most of his
effort on Brooklyn Heights, where he stationed Nathanael
Greene with 4,000 troops.

While Washington grappled with the tyranny of geography, Howe succumbed to the tyranny of time. Over the
preceding winter, while he was shut up in Boston, the British
government, recognizing its underestimation of the task lying
before it, had embarked on all the measures to put the country
on a war footing. But recruiting had been slow, and putting
ships back in commission had taken longer than it was intended. From Halifax, troops had to be sent to Quebec, other
reinforcements had to come from Britain, orders were issued
and countermanded, commissions granted and revoked, and
while regimental commanders tried to outbid each other for
recruits, ship's captains argued over cordage and spars. Week
succeeded weary week, and still troops did not march, and
transports did not sail.

Finally, however, the British war machine lurched into
motion. On June 25 Sir William himself arrived off New York
with three ships; on the 29th forty-five more appeared, and
the day after that eighty-two more. At last the British had

come. Howe had brought with him 9,300 men from Halifax. They landed on Staten Island and set up camp. But this was just the beginning. In the second week of July Sir William's brother, Sir Richard, appeared from England, with another 150 vessels and more troops. Next came Sir Peter Parker with Clinton's expedition to Charleston, fresh from failure and burning to expunge it. A month later Commodore William Hotham arrived, with thirty-four more ships, 2,600 elite troops from the Guards brigade, and 8,000 Germans. By the time they were all ready, the British forces mustered 32,000 men under arms, horse, foot, and artillery, supported by a fleet of thirty warships with 1,200 guns and 10,000 sailors, plus so many transports and lesser vessels that they whitened the water. It was the biggest, and most expensive, expedition Britain had ever sent overseas. The Americans dug, and drilled, and waited.

Once again the initiative lay with Sir William, and he proceeded deliberately. In mid-July, long before his army was complete, two Royal Navy frigates had sailed leisurely up the Hudson, exchanging shots with the American batteries along the river. The city of New York had been thrown into utter panic by this, but the ships sailed serenely on, all the way to Tappan Zee, where they stayed for six days, and then sailed back again. It may have been a reconnaissance, it may have been Sir William wearing his negotiator's hat and wanting to demonstrate his mastery of the area, it may have been nothing at all. It was another six weeks before the British did anything else.

But when they did move, they did so very professionally; this was clearly an army that knew its business. On the morning of August 22, in six hours Howe landed 15,000 men and forty guns on Long Island, below the American positions at Brooklyn Heights. Three days later German troops made the same move, and Howe was prepared to develop his battle plan.

Unfortunately, at just this time, Nathanael Greene went sick on the American side, and was replaced, first by John Sullivan, and then by Israel Putnam. Sullivan knew less than Greene about the situation, and Putnam knew less than Sullivan. Between them they garrisoned a forward line, along the Heights of Guian, a rather abrupt bluff overlooking Flatbush, where the British were camped. The Heights were broken by several roads and passes; the Americans guarded the three western ones, but left the eastern one, Jamaica Pass, watched by only a small picket.

Howe decided to mousetrap the whole position, and he did so flawlessly. Early on the morning of the 27th, the British and Hessians mounted noisy demonstrations against the western end of the Heights, near Gowanus Bay, and the two center passes. Meanwhile Sir Henry Clinton, Lord Cornwallis, and Sir Hugh Percy, with 10,000 men under Howe's personal command, quietly marched to, and through Jamaica Pass, picking up five sleepy Americans as they did so. By 8:30 they were in the village of Bedford, directly behind the left center of the Americans. At nine Howe fired some signal guns, the Hessians came on in the center and General James Grant led his 5,000 troops on the British left. The trap was sprung.

The next two hours were bad and bloody for the Americans, as the troops fought far better than their dispositions deserved. While Howe rolled up their left flank and rear, Colonel Carl von Donop's Hessians pushed through their center. The units here, caught front, flank, and rear, tried desperately to face about, but ultimately were broken up and driven. Some got away to Brooklyn Heights, many were gathered in by the British, and a considerable number were actually massacred by the Hessians, who refused to give quarter, and often bayoneted men who were trying to surrender.

On the American right were Maryland and Delaware Continentals, among the best-furnished troops in the army. They were now hit by a heavy attack from General Grant, with the Germans coming in on their left flank, and they had Cornwallis and more British in their rear. These troops gave Grant a considerable drubbing before they were pushed into the marshes and creeks along the shore of Gowanus Bay. General William Alexander, who called himself Lord Stirling, led a series of attacks against the British, trying to break the blocking position, but after six tries, could not get through. Again the fighting along the shores was vicious, with the Germans refusing offers of surrender, but most of the American troops seem to have filtered through.

By early afternoon the battle was all over. Generals Sullivan and Alexander were British prisoners, and so were about a thousand other Americans. Something more than three hundred were killed. British and German losses were less than four hundred. To this point it was a very respectable action, both well-conceived and fought by the British, and poorly disposed but well-fought by the Americans. But it was still only half over. The British were now in front of the American fortifications on Brooklyn Heights; the Americans, though bringing reinforcements across from Manhattan, and with substantial troops on hand, were nevertheless in disarray. Many authorities, including some of the British officers there that day, thought that Howe should have kept right on, and that had he done so, he would have carried the works and destroyed much of the American army in the process. Instead he drew off, encamped again, and began preparations for a siege.

Opinions differ as to why Howe made this decision. Some would have it that the long memory of Bunker Hill still followed him, and he would not again attack entrenched Americans frontally. But there may be less dramatic reasons. His ships controlled the river, after all, or would as soon as they bestirred themselves, so he could consider the Americans trapped, to be gathered in at leisure and possibly without much bloodshed. Besides which, the British troops had been up and marching all night, and fighting a battle that had already lasted for several hours. To march for six or seven hours under a sixty-pound pack, then fight a battle for another six hours, running up and down hills, with all the excitement, fear, and emotional exhaustion that entails, does not leave one with a great deal of energy. And in addition to all these immediate considerations, there was still the fact that Howe was a peace commissioner, and would, if possible, prefer maneuvers that would lead to a negotiated settlement rather than a bloodbath that might only increase long-term opposition. Under the circumstances as he saw them, Howe made the appropriate decision. Of course, he had done that at Bunker Hill, too.

                              *   *   *

So the British sat down to rest, and the shattered and scared Americans began pulling themselves back together. But even while he was sending more men across the East River to Brooklyn, Washington was convinced it was now a trap, and that the position must be evacuated, if only the Royal Navy would give him time to do it.

The Americans were lucky; the wind was from the north, and the British ships could not get into the East River; while Sir William Howe opened his first siege positions, the route to Manhattan remained open. Washington continued to move men across to Brooklyn, but that was a ruse. On the afternoon of the 28th it began to rain, heavily and cold, obscuring vision. The next day Washington held a council of war, and the decision was made. That night the troops filed slowly out of their entrenchments, each unit told only that they themselves were being relieved. The rain had stopped, but now a heavy, dank fog lay over the area. There was some confusion as a few units got mixed up in the sequence of evacuation, but the British remained sleepy and unaware of the drama going on before them. By daybreak, as the first curious British patrols entered the empty American works, the last of Washington's soldiers, and he himself, were entering their boats and crossing the East River. Thanks to good staff work and the boating skills of a couple of regiments of Massachusetts fishermen, the American army lived to fight again.

Nothing happened for the next three weeks. Howe went back to Staten Island, where he opened some negotiations with the captured General Sullivan. These actually led to a visit by emissaries from Congress, who had a pleasant discussion with Admiral Sir Richard; Sir William himself, pleading his active military role at the moment, did not take part in the conference, which led nowhere. The general was already planning his next move, while across the water, Washington was trying not very successfully to come to terms with the problem of Manhattan.

He thought Congress wanted him to defend it, though they insisted that he should do whatever was necessary to preserve his army; New York was less important than that. Several of his generals insisted the city could not be held, and should therefore be burned. Knowing the city was untenable, Washington still could not bring himself to give it up, and he therefore committed himself to the worst of several possibilities: some of his army he left in the city at one end of Manhattan, some of it he posted up in Harlem at the other end, and the weak part in the middle he held with militia detachments, using his poorest troops in the most crucial place. The result was disgrace and near-disaster.

On the night of September 14–15 five British frigates crept up the East River and anchored off Kip's Bay. The shore was held by several regiments of Connecticut militia, who had scratched out but a shallow ditch along the water's edge. Before noon on the next morning, Sunday, the ships opened a heavy bombardment of the shoreline. The gunsmoke drifted down on the Americans; after an hour, out from behind the frigates came barges carrying 4,000 British and Hessian troops; these formed up in neat lines and made straight for the shore. The poor militia, battered and totally dazed, took off without firing a shot. Their panic infected support troops behind them, and suddenly, to the echoes of the navy's guns and the yells of the advancing redcoats, the entire center of the American army disintegrated. Men threw down their guns and ran blindly, bumping into each other, tripping over their officers, who in most cases ran with them.

Washington was appalled, and tradition has him cursing, striking at his own soldiers with the flat of his sword, or slashing at them with a riding crop. Whether he did any of that or not, and he probably did, he also had sufficient presence to send orders for the troops in New York City to get out—fast. General Putnam headed south and gathered up units which he began to lead north. The British were already cutting them off, and Putnam's aide, a young New Yorker named Aaron Burr, led them off to the west, so that they got around the British advance. The foremost British troops got as far as Murray Hill, the commanding height in the center of the island, where they stopped. Another legend has it that the British stalled because a Quaker lady, Mrs. Robert Murray, beguiled the officers with wine and cakes, but the truth was that the first troops had orders to take Murray Hill and then consolidate and wait for their supports, and this is what they did. It seemed sensible at the time; some Americans had panicked, but that did not mean the British maneuver would be totally unchecked. Once again a golden opportunity was lost by men who chose the conventional patterns of their day. The American army, out of breath and, when it came to, thoroughly ashamed of itself, paused to regroup on Harlem Heights. Washington was momentarily in utter despair; his men still had to learn to be soldiers. And he still had to learn to be a general.

But the next morning brought a revival of spirits, in the little affair known as the Battle of Harlem Heights. At the end of their exhilarating day, the British had taken up positions roughly at the north end of what is now Central Park. On the 16th they sent parties of light infantry scouting forward. The Americans, meanwhile, were digging in along the heights in the northwest corner of Manhattan Island. Washington ordered a reconnaissance forward from this position, across a sharp dip known as the Hollow Way and into the woods to his front. Lieutenant Colonel Thomas Knowlton led out 150 Connecticut Rangers.

These soon met the British light troops and a detachment of the 42nd, the Black Watch. Knowlton was an outstanding leader, and his men had already been blooded, over on Long Island. Now they stood and exchanged volleys with the British, before Knowlton began to fall back, leading the redcoats on. Hearing the firing and going forward, Washington sent along some supports, including the Connecticut militia that had done so badly the day before. The Americans began to lap around the British flanks, and soon were treated to the inspiring sight of British backs, and the light infantry and Highlanders fell back, in turn, on their supports. The Americans pushed almost down to the main British position, and by midday, both sides had a good 5,000 men engaged. Knowlton was mortally wounded in an exchange of volleys, but his troops stood well to their work, as did all the others involved. By early afternoon, with neither side wishing to get sucked into a full battle, the firing died down, and the Americans went back to Harlem Heights. In the jargon of the time, this all went down as "an affair of light posts," but it was enormously uplifting to American spirits, and Howe spent the next four weeks entrenching his positions.

He was now in possession of New York City, but it did him little good. On the night of September 20–21, much of the city, about five hundred houses, was burned in a fire that started no one knows how. Each side blamed the other, but it was probably a mere accident. Whatever the cause, it deprived the British of substantial billeting resources, and the charred ruins stayed that way for most of the war.

For a month the two armies and their commanders eyed each other warily, but neither did a great deal. Washington was still torn, now by his desire to hold the northern part of Manhattan, especially Fort Washington, and to deny the Hudson to the British, and his suppressed recognition that this was practically impossible. Howe was his usual leisurely self. He may also have been busy with the wife of his commissary general; satiric American songs of the period recounted all sorts of bizarre things going on, each verse ending with, "While Sir William he lay snoring/Snug in bed with Mrs. Loring . . ."

Whatever the source of his delays, eventually Howe moved again. He decided on another envelopment of the Americans, and in mid-October, the British went by boat and ship northeast to Throg's Point. This was along the mainland, east of Manhattan Island, and an eight-mile march to the northwest would bring the British to Kings Bridge, where they would completely cut off Washington's army from any escape routes. They moved unobserved through fog and landed unopposed on October 12. Unfortunately for them, when the fog lifted they found they were not exactly on the mainland, but rather on a sort of peninsula-cum-marsh. To get to solid ground they had to cross either a narrow ford, or an even narrower causeway and bridge. The latter was held by a mere thirty men, but they happened to be from the 1st Pennsylvania Rifle Regiment, and when enough bodies had piled up along the causeway, the British gave up trying to cross. American reinforcements arrived, and both causeway and ford were soon guarded in sufficient strength to hold them indefinitely.

It took Howe another six days to think all this over, and

then he moved again, three miles northeast once more, to Pell's Point. This was not quite as favorable a position for the defenders as Throg's Neck, but it was held by a small brigade, four Massachusetts regiments under John Glover, the Marblehead soldier whose boatmen had rescued the army from Brooklyn Heights. Glover disposed his troops in successive positions one behind the other, and also behind available stone walls. It was practically another Bunker Hill; the Yankees let the advance, led mostly by Hessians, get within a hundred feet before rising from their wall and pouring in volleys. The first Massachusetts regiment delivered seven volleys before falling back on command; the second one held for seventeen. When Glover fell back to a third line, the British called it quits for the day.

Back on Manhattan, Washington knew that he must go as soon as news arrived of the landing at Throg's Point, but the riflemen bought him six days, and Glover gained a couple more. By the time Howe's army reached New Rochelle, on October 21st, the Americans were digging in at White Plains. It took Howe until the 27th to reach this position, but when he did, he prepared for a full-scale attack, including deploying his whole army in the open before admiring and apprehensive American eyes. The next morning, in a confused fight, British and German troops drove the Americans off Chatterton's Hill, the right-flank anchor of their position. Again some militiamen panicked, but some of the regulars held well, while others retreated prematurely. The British did not do much better. General Alexander Leslie pushed his men ahead rashly—he was another, like Grant, contemptuous of American capabilities—and suffered far heavier losses than were necessary. It was late in the day before the hill was finally taken securely, and Howe decided to wait until morning before finishing the job. In the morning it was raining heavily, and by the time it stopped, the rebels were gone again, to another, better position three miles back.

At this Howe gave up in disgust, and returned to Manhattan. He was not quite finished yet, however. Washington had foolishly left some 2,800 men on Manhattan Island, in and around Fort Washington, in the hope that this work, with Fort Lee on the opposite shore, could hold the Hudson. When the commander in chief did want to abandon it, both the immediate commanding officer, Colonel Robert Magaw of Pennsylvania, and the area commander, Nathanael Greene, insisted it could be held for some time, and then if necessary successfully evacuated.

They were wrong; the position was potentially strong, but it had not been well developed, and it was in fact more of a trap than anything else. On November 15 the British summoned Magaw to surrender, in accord with the prescribed military courtesies of the day. He refused. The next morning they launched a coordinated attack that drove in all of his outposts, from north, east, and south. It happened that Washington himself was at the fort that day; he had crossed over to New Jersey, and come over from Fort Lee to consult with Magaw. He, Putnam, Greene, and General Hugh Mercer from Virginia, after seeing Magaw was busy and after receiving his assurances, left the fort and returned to their boat.

During the morning the British and Hessians, after some heavy fighting, gradually overcame the several American positions outside the fort. As they did so, the defenders fell back, often wounded, usually out of ammunition, until by early afternoon the fort was packed with close to 2,500 men, in a space that would hardly accommodate a third of that number. Hessian Colonel Johann Rall was the first to reach the fort, and he demanded its surrender. Magaw had little choice, to his despair, and by midafternoon nearly 3,000 well-trained and experienced American troops were filing out to captivity. Rall, who had fought in both the Prussian and Austrian armies, considered them a rabble beneath his notice. Washington and his officers were still in their boat, halfway across the Hudson; with sinking hearts and tears in their eyes they watched the colors come fluttering down from their little fort.

The tale of disaster was still not told. For once Howe did not rest on his arms, and a mere couple of days later, the British crossed to Fort Lee and descended rapidly on it. Barely warned, Washington, who was still there, led his 2,000 troops out in a hurry. They managed to save the priceless gunpowder, but they lost guns, baggage, tents, and all sorts of military stores, and they just barely escaped across the Hackensack River.

The commander in chief was now effectively cut off from the larger part of his army. By late November there were only about 16,500 Americans left in the army around New York. But 4,000 of these were up the river at Peekskill, more or less uselessly guarding the Hudson Highlands; and the major element was back at White Plains, 7,000 under Charles Lee. The remaining 5,500 were all that Washington had directly under command, and even of these, another thousand were off on detachments. Washington was still too impressed with Lee to send him direct orders, but he repeatedly urged him to come west and south, to bring the army back together; Lee refused to budge. He was quite content where he was.

So, apparently, was Howe. Instead of delivering the coup de grâce to the dying American cause, he sent Henry Clinton off with 6,000 men to capture Newport up in Rhode Island, which the navy wanted for a base. Settling down in New York City himself, he offered an amnesty to any Americans who would come in and make peace with the Crown. Hundreds did; Loyalists appeared from all over the area, and substantial numbers of American deserters and stragglers gave up the struggle. The New Jersey militia refused to come out for the Patriot cause, and it was almost as an afterthought that Howe ordered General Cornwallis to chase Washington out of the state. The British commander was preparing to don his peacemaker hat once again.

The pursuit across New Jersey was a terrible ordeal. Winter was coming on, and the little American army plodded doggedly southwest, with British and Hessians nipping at their heels. The trail was easy to follow, littered with castaway bits of broken equipment, broken-down soldiers, and stragglers willing to surrender and glad it was all over. On December 3 Washington reached Trenton, and four days later he crossed the Delaware River into Pennsylvania. Putting his troops into positions they lacked the numbers to hold, he gathered up all the boats for seventy-five miles along the river, and the army collapsed with a sigh. Cornwallis, closing up to the Delaware, reported to Howe that the birds had flown. It seemed to matter little. Everywhere there were signs of collapse. Lee had finally begun to move, but on the morning of December 13, while his troops were on the move around Morristown, he himself was captured at Basking Ridge, New Jersey, and this was thought to be yet another nail in the Patriot casket. Howe decided that day to go into winter quarters, and Cornwallis, leaving his Hessians to hold outposts along the Delaware, thankfully turned back toward New York. There was not much glory in chasing a rabble of fugitives from one hole to another.

CHAPTER SIX

The Northern Campaign of 1776

Amidst the disaster around New York in the fall of the year, some small mercies and some even smaller losses in the north went almost unremarked. The Americans missed their little chance of extending the Revolution to Nova Scotia, but they bought sufficient time around Lake Champlain to prolong the life of the struggle for another year. At the moment, this did not appear to be of much import, but had the British won here as convincingly as they did around New York City, the Revolution might well have ground to an end. As it was, a few hundred New Englanders and New Yorkers proved once again that in war, time is a dimension every bit as important as space.

After the debacle at Quebec City, the American forces were reduced to utter misery. The wounded Benedict Arnold was now in sole command; Richard Montgomery was dead, Daniel Morgan a prisoner. Arnold commanded a mere skeleton of about five hundred men; he was nonetheless determined to hold on, and asked for whatever reinforcements could be sent to him. There were none. A regiment of American troops back around the foot of Lake Champlain and Montreal was threatened by enemy action from the west, including Indians loyal to Britain. General Schuyler was in Albany, but he in turn was harassed by Loyalists operating in the Mohawk Valley, west from Albany, where many of the great families and their supporters were against the Revolution. Arnold's few men were further reduced by smallpox and disease generally, and by the expiration of enlistments.

Neither Congress nor Washington were insensitive to Arnold's needs, but there simply was not much that could be done during the first months of the new year. Eventually Washington suggested that some of the militia regiments that were being formed for his own use be directed north instead. There was a gradual increase in troop strength in the theater during April, and by the time the campaign opened in May, something in the neighborhood of seven thousand Americans were either in Canada or on the way there. But they were in penny packets; Arnold, now a brigadier general moved to Montreal, had several hundred with him. Major General John Thomas, a capable and experienced officer from Massachusetts, had replaced him in the command at Quebec City. Other troops were strung out back along the route to Chambly, St. Johns, south along Lake Champlain, and then from there all the way to Albany.

All of these dispositions were just too little and too late. Carleton's first reinforcements reached him early in May, the vanguard of an eventual 13,000. Secure in the knowledge of more help on the way, he at last stirred himself; he brought his troops out from behind the walls of Quebec, and easily drove off the Americans whom he had outnumbered three or four to one all along. Several hundred sick were taken prisoner, and the Americans also lost what they could afford even less, substantial amounts of military stores.

By the time the main portion of the American army gathered at Sorel, where the Richelieu River enters the St. Lawrence, they were a disorganized mob wracked by smallpox and dysentery. Thomas himself died of the former, at the beginning of June, and was hastily replaced by John Sullivan. He, thinking to regain some of the initiative, sent troops forward down the St. Lawrence to Trois Rivières; he believed that there were perhaps eight hundred British here, and with a little luck, he might scoop them up. Instead, his force ran into Carleton's vanguard, 6,000 under John Burgoyne. Unaware of what they were up against, the Americans made several attacks before being beaten off; they then broke up and were harried through woods and swamps, losing a fair number of men to the Indian allies of the British. Of some 2,000 involved, only about 1,100 got back to Sorel.

By the end of the second week of June, the last toeholds in Canada were gone. Arnold had abandoned Montreal, just barely getting away; Sullivan had come back from Sorel; and the miserable remnants of the American army were gathered on Île aux Noix, a swampy, fever-ridden pesthole at the northern end of Lake Champlain. They, too, were plagued by the various eighteenth-century diseases that went under the generic name of "camp fever." A Congressional committee that had visited Montreal during Arnold's stay there was convinced that there was no further chance of gaining the territory, and that the whole enterprise had been both ill-judged and poorly managed from the start. Though they were probably right, the simpler truth was that the Americans just did not have the strength to export their revolution into what was basically a foreign territory. In fact, by the beginning of July, as Congress was debating and passing its resolution for independence, it was less a matter of taking new areas than it was of retaining American ones.

Sir Guy Carleton had known from the outbreak of hostilities that the Lake Champlain connection between New York and Canada was crucial, but so far he had managed to do little about it. For a year he had been preoccupied, perhaps overly so, with the defense of his own colony. Canada was now secure, and he was at last ready to assume the offensive, or so he thought. Instead, three precious months were frittered away while both sides postured, and then indulged in a boat-building race. It was a game the Americans were happy to play.

July went in an American retreat back along the lake, first to Crown Point, and then finally to Ticonderoga, so they ended up essentially where they had begun, a year and several thousand lives earlier. There was also a command shuffle. Philip Schuyler was still officially commander of the Northern Department, with his headquarters at Albany; John Sullivan was in command in the field, now at Ticonderoga. Late in June, Congress ordered General Horatio Gates north to take command, but they did not specify which command he was to take. Eventually they decided he was to serve as second to Schuyler, whereupon Sullivan, with some justification, threatened to resign and went off in a huff. This was how he came to be employed around New York, and to be captured on Long Island.

Throughout the Revolution, there was a great deal of what appeared to be unseemly squabbling over who commanded, or was subordinate to, whom. All of these men were indeed Patriots—they would not have been serving otherwise—but they were also men with ambitions, and with careers to make, and as none of them had ever commanded major forces before, any one officer might well consider himself the equal of any other. Even success or failure on the battlefield might not be enough to fix a man firmly in the chain of command, for the separate politics of the states, and of Congress too, had to be considered. But of course it was not simply a matter of pride; it was also a matter of competence, and ultimately, of life and death, for individuals, armies, and possibly for the Revolution itself. No one today can think the Revolutionary War would have been won by the Americans, had Charles Lee replaced Washington, or even had Granny Gates replaced him, but both were quite sure they were more than fit to do so, and both had people who agreed with them. Some men swallowed their pride and served where circumstance dictated; some became embittered by what they perceived as insufficient recognition; some turned traitor. As in all human affairs, most people did the best they could under conditions as they understood them.

It remained easier to appoint commanders than to recreate armies for them to command, and Gates and Schuyler had desperate work to do, trying to put some sort of fighting force back together. A couple of Continental regiments were sent up to Ticonderoga, and the militia of New York and New

England were mustered and sent forward, and slowly, through the summer months, a new army arose from the corpse of the old. But everything depended upon how rapidly the British struck.

Fortunately, they did not move very quickly. Most of the actual summer was spent, unnecessarily it would seem, in securing the line of the Richelieu River, and garrisoning and restoring Sorel, Chambly, and St. Johns. It was well into August before Carleton took Île aux Noix, which he further fortified as an advanced base. And it was the second week in September before he sent his first troops south on the lake, Indians and Canadians traveling in canoes. But he needed rather more than that to command the waters of Lake Champlain, and that was the key to the whole situation.

The lake is about a hundred miles long, and ten miles wide at its widest spot, so it is a very substantial body of water. And water travel in the eighteenth century was so vastly easier than going overland that whoever controlled the lake automatically controlled the land around it. As the Americans had a small fleet, the British must have one, too, so they began trying to outbuild each other.

At the American end of the lake, Gates entrusted the naval side of his operation to Benedict Arnold; since the latter had made some merchant voyages before the war, he claimed a knowledge of things nautical that none of the other American commanders had. He already possessed a small squadron of three little schooners and a sloop, all gathered in or built the year before when the Americans suddenly took Ticonderoga and with it control of the lake. Now he set to work building several smaller vessels, row galleys rigged with lateen sails, and gunboats or gundalows carrying three field pieces on naval carriages.

This all turned out to be an enormous task; most of the men in the country who could build a ship or boat were busy doing so along the seacoast, and such men did not show up in the militia in the middle of the wilderness. Eventually a few companies of shipbuilders were enrolled, at exorbitant rates of pay, and sent to help out on the lake. Additionally, there was hardly a man among the Americans who could not build a barn if he had to. Manpower was actually less of a problem than tools. Connecticut sent a thousand axes, local sawmills were put back into operation, smiths were set to making nails and ironwork. The boats soon took shape—too slowly for Arnold's impatient nature, but far more rapidly than anyone had a right to expect, certainly with amazing speed as far as the British were concerned.

At the other end of the lake, Carleton was wrestling with similar but slightly different difficulties; he had plenty of skilled workers, in sailors drafted from the Royal Navy ships in the St. Lawrence, and he had no shortage of men or materials. On the big river itself he had three vessels, a full-rigged ship named *Inflexible*, and two small schooners. But the Richelieu had ten miles of rapids between these and Lake Champlain. The British tried to move their vessels on rollers over the ground, but it was too soft; eventually they took the three apart, carted them to St. Johns, and put them back together. They would have more than matched Arnold's original three vessels, but as the ambitious Yankees were building more boats, so the British had to do the same. They assembled several gunboats that had been brought in pieces all the way from England, then they built several more local gunboats, then a monster floating battery called a *radeau*, which was a fancy name for a barge, which would carry three hundred men and fourteen heavy guns, and, finally, four hundred bateaux to carry the troops along the lake.

Arnold moved first, and was cruising the lake with part of his little fleet in the last week of August. Every day that went by was valuable, for it brought not only additional vessels, but even more important, it brought the end of the campaigning season that much closer. After scouting the northern end of the lake and doing what little he could to annoy the British, Arnold chose his ground—or water—for a fight. A third of the way from the northern outlet of the lake, a half mile off the western shore, lay Valcour Island. Here, across the little channel, Arnold drew up his fleet in a battle line and anchored, to await the coming of the British.

He was lucky; not until October 11 did they arrive, and when they did, they sailed past him before he was spotted.

They then had to turn about and beat up against the wind to attack. It was noon before the first of their vessels was in range, but gradually several of their gunboats came up. A strange battle then developed, with both sides anchored at about 300 yards' range, firing broadsides at each other, while the noise echoed off the mountains and the Indians on the shore sniped at the Americans. Arnold's schooner *Royal Savage* ran aground early in the action, and was boarded by the British, who turned her guns on the Americans; then they were driven off, and the boat finally burned and exploded. It was almost dusk before the British ship *Inflexible* got into range, but her fire was enough to silence the American line and effectively end the battle; as night came on, the British drew off, satisfied that their enemies were trapped and could be easily gathered in come morning.

Once again their fatal tendency to think they had done enough for one day cost them a clear-cut victory. For during the night Arnold, still full of fight, got away. In the fog, he put his remaining vessels in line—he had lost only the schooner and one gundalow, the *Philadelphia*, sunk in shallow water—and sailed quietly past the whole British fleet. Unfortunately, with dawn the wind turned, and the awakening British saw their quarry only a few miles ahead of them.

The day of the 12th was spent in a terrible pursuit; the wind was from the south, blowing against the sailors, and both sides passed hours pulling at sweeps, long oars designed to move the heavy and unwieldy vessels. The Americans tried to make repairs as they went, and barely managed to stay ahead. By the next day they were exhausted, and then, when the wind at last shifted about midday, it reached the British first. As their sails filled, they began to overtake the desperate Americans, and one by one the slower boats were caught, run ashore, burned, or surrendered by their crews. Four or five of the handier, less damaged little boats got away, but Arnold was finally driven ashore ten miles north of Crown Point, where he beached and burned his boats before escaping into the woods with their crews. Reaching Crown Point, he burned that too, what was left of it, and took his men south to Ticonderoga.

Soon after the survivors of Arnold's force reached the fort, British boats showed up, but not to fight. They were flying flags of truce, and they landed all the prisoners Carleton had taken in the fight and subsequent pursuit, something more than a hundred men. The British general had been so impressed with their stand that he decided to parole them. In fact, he had treated them so well that the American command immediately sent them home, to get them out of camp, so their stories would not depress morale.

This turned out to be unnecessary, for Carleton had had enough. He decided he could not carry Ticonderoga by storm, and that it was too late in the season to besiege it. He would leave it until next year, and that in turn, he decided, also meant he must leave Lake Champlain in American hands. He took his fleet, and his transport boats, all the way back to St. Johns, and closed down operations for the year. Everything was put into storage and snugged down; it was, after all, getting cold. In the light of subsequent events, this decision was undoubtedly wrong; it may, in fact, have cost the British the war.

In a much smaller episode than those others occurring in 1776, the Americans lost, or more accurately failed to gain, Nova Scotia. The area had for a century been a focus of imperial rivalries, settled by the French, taken by the British, restored, and taken again. Most of the French Acadian inhabitants had been expelled from the Annapolis Valley and Minas Basin area during the Seven Years' War, and replaced by settlers from New England. On the Atlantic coast, Halifax had been founded by the British in 1755, the only overseas settlement in America that was a direct result of government action. Since then numbers of Germans had moved into little coves and bays along the shore, as well as more British and Americans, and there was a settlement of Yorkshire English on the isthmus that connected the peninsula with the mainland, as well as a large group of Scots toward the eastern part of the area. There was therefore quite a mix of nationalities and loyalties in Nova Scotia, but at the time, and for many years thereafter, it drew its dominant impulses from New England.

By the standards prevailing at the time of the Revolution, however, Nova Scotia was just too far away for the projection of American power. The Gulf of Maine was a sort of no-man's-land, with British cruisers from Halifax and Americans from Machias and other little towns raiding back and forth, but the key to the area was the Royal Navy's general control of the sea.

Early in 1776, two Nova Scotians, John Allen and Jonathan Eddy, appeared in Massachusetts to appeal for help. There was little to be spared, but the Massachusetts Assembly promised to send supplies to whatever force they might raise in the Maine district. Eventually they recruited a little more than a hundred men, and proceeded up the coast in small boats. The key to an attack on the colony from this side was the position at the Isthmus of Chignecto, a small fort originally built as Fort Beauséjour by the French, and now named Fort Cumberland. It had a small garrison of about 200 troops, a local unit known as the Royal Fencible Americans.

The American troops arrived early in November, and besieged the little fort. Knowing that help for the garrison would soon arrive from Halifax, they tried to storm it on November 13, and again on November 22. Both attacks broke down in confusion, and when relief did appear coming up the Cumberland Basin, the rebels drew off. With bad weather now breaking, the garrison was content to let them go. The British commander then proclaimed an amnesty, which brought in a hundred dubious locals, and broke the back of Eddy's force without fighting. Later the British advanced outposts down the shore of what became the province of New Brunswick.

On the Atlantic coast of Nova Scotia, loyalties were determined largely by the actions of privateering vessels. The Americans were never strong enough to threaten Halifax itself; they did first shelter in, and then raid, some of the settlements along the shore south and west of the port, and gradually they drove the inhabitants there more and more into the arms of the British. At the end of the war the area was so secure in the imperial connection that it served as the initial refuge for many of the American Loyalists.

By the end of a year and a half of fighting, then, the outlines of the future United States were taking shape. Independence had been declared, though whether it could actually be won was still extremely doubtful. But the colonies, or states, from the Atlantic seaboard to the mountains, from the Maine district down to Georgia, were firmly committed to the rebellion. North of there the area was equally firmly held by the British, and whether the inhabitants liked it or not, or indeed cared one way or another, it was going to stay that way. Both Nova Scotia and Canada were dependent upon access to the sea, and controllable by sea power and its ability to dominate adjacent land masses.

The British also, now, controlled the major city and seaport of the infant United States, and they would do so for the rest of the war. Ironically, and somewhat to the discomfiture of the British, this did not do them much good. The military theory of the period held that if you took the enemy's capital, or his major cities, he would have sense enough to make peace. But the Americans were not involved in a conventional eighteenth-century war; they were truly involved in a revolution, and they were not interested in negotiations and a slight readjustment of relations; the time for that was past. They were interested in complete, total, absolute independence, and nothing less. In December of 1776, it looked very much as if their vision exceeded their grasp, but that issue still remained to be decided. For all the losses and failures of the year, there were a few glimmers of hope. The Patriot cause might be burning low, but it was still alight. Something might, indeed must, yet be done.

CHAPTER SEVEN

Small Mercies

WITH THE always accurate vision provided by hindsight, it looks as if the British commanders at the end of 1776 were incredibly supine. A little more concentration by Sir William Howe, a little more effort by Lord Cornwallis, and Washington and his puny remnant of an army might have been destroyed. And a bit more aggressive behavior by Sir Guy Carleton would probably have secured Ticonderoga and all of Lake Champlain; the colonies would have been all but cut in half and their armies dispersed, and the Revolution might well have been suppressed for good.

But as always, there appeared sound reasons at the moment for doing what was done. Sir William was conscious that the Navy wanted a station at Newport, and it would be a useful base. In the field, both Cornwallis and Carleton were sure it was time to quit. Eighteenth-century armies rarely campaigned in the winter, and then only with great difficulty. Indeed, it did not take full winter to shut them down; the advent of poorer weather in the fall, rains that turned roads and tracks into sloughs of mud, the loss of useful forage with the fall season, the wetter, colder nights that lengthened the sick lists, all of these were inducements to stop chasing around the country and look for warm billets. Armies were expensive, fragile organisms, and could much more readily be broken by adverse weather than by an enemy. If the war were ninety percent won, why take unnecessary risks to finish off the remaining ten percent? If American resistance did not collapse of its own weight, it would easily be broken in the spring anyway. In the past year the Americans had demonstrated their inability to mount and sustain major operations, or to field and effectively employ a regular army. There was little reason to fear they would improve their performance in the next few months, and indeed, quite the opposite was expected.

The existing American army was, as usual, in a state of near dissolution. Enlistment in the Continental forces was still for one year only, and the terms of service of most of the current soldiers would expire at the end of the calendar year. Congress had authorized a larger army for 1777, but a variety of circumstances conspired against it. For example, only the states could appoint officers, who would then do the recruiting for their regiments or battalions. But Congress had invited the separate states to send committees to the army, to review their officers' conduct before granting them renewed commissions. By late in November, none of the states had yet sent their committees, none of the officers had had their commissions renewed, and therefore there could be no recruiting. All of this was taking place—or failing to take place—while Washington was retreating across New Jersey, with his army disintegrating anyway.

What the Americans did have, as winter came on, was a series of penny-packet forces scattered about the country. The militia had either gone home, as from the northern front, or failed to come out when called, as through New Jersey. A few regular battalions remained on duty in the Ticonderoga area. There were some units in northern New Jersey, west of New York City; these were the residue of those forces that Charles Lee had commanded, and with which he was belatedly moving west and south when he himself was captured. The small Continental forces in the south were effectively off the board, so that left General Washington and what might laughably be considered the main American striking force, on the western bank of the Delaware River in Pennsylvania. Here the commander in chief, with only about 3,400 men, took up his position. To secure the river, he strung his forces out in detachments, from Burlington up past the large bend at Bordentown, and then northwest past Trenton. More help than his men was the fact that he had gathered up all the boats for seventy-five miles, so the British would have been hard-pressed to get at him even if they had chosen to do so.

In a situation that looked almost irredeemably dark, the most important single fact was that Washington did not know he was beaten, a classic example of the old aphorism that in war, the moral is to the physical as ten to one. The approach of enemy forces had compelled Congress to flee Philadelphia for Baltimore in December, and they then passed a resolution that, in effect, made the general a dictator and free to do as he saw best. And he, in spite of all the difficulties that threatened to overwhelm the American cause in general and his army in particular, was planning to strike back at the British.

There were a few glimmers of hope. Even as his own units melted away, Washington sent the army's quartermaster general, Thomas Mifflin, to Philadelphia to recruit militia, with some success. Sullivan showed up in the third week of December with 2,000 of the troops commanded formerly by Lee, and Granny Gates appeared with 500 more from away up north. Another thousand volunteers, the Philadelphia Associators, came out, and as Christmas approached, Washington could count about 6,000 troops, ready if scarcely fit for duty. They got another boost, moral rather than physical, from Tom Paine, who on December 19 published the first version of *The Crisis*:

> These are the times that try men's souls. The summer soldier and the sunshine patriot will, in this crisis, shrink from the service of their country; but he that stands it *now*, deserves the love and thanks of man and woman. Tyranny, like hell, is not easily conquered. . . . Heaven knows how to put a proper price on its goods; and it would be strange indeed if so celestial an article as FREEDOM should not be highly

rated. . . . The heart that feels not now, is dead; the
blood of his children will curse his cowardice, who
shrinks back at a time when a little might have saved
the whole . . . he whose heart is firm, and whose con-
science approves his conduct, will pursue his principles unto death.

As men's minds had slowly grappled with and then accepted the idea of independence, so too in the middle states
did they lean toward more active support for the cause. Paine's
work was read approvingly in the billets of the hungry army;
he had put his principles in practice, and enlisted and fought
through the retreat in New Jersey; now he had summed up
what many deeply felt but few could enunciate. Outside the
army, too, Pennsylvanians and Marylanders reluctantly accepted that something must be done, and that they themselves
must do it. But it was up to Washington to keep the army,
and the Revolution, alive until spring. Somehow, the few must
buy time for the many. While his redcoated enemies and their
German allies enjoyed good billets in New Jersey and back in
New York City, Washington began pulling all the threads together once again.

The chase across sodden and sullen New Jersey had
convinced the British that the war was all but over. By mid-
December Sir William Howe was ready to go into winter quarters in New York City. He consulted with Lord Cornwallis,
who had handled the actual pursuit, as to the best dispositions
to make. Howe suggested pulling back around Newark, with
advanced posts as far south as Perth Amboy and New Brunswick, roughly the line of the Raritan River. Cornwallis de-
murred; he thought it would be unwise to give up the central
part of the state, where many Loyalists had come out for the
King, and equally many erstwhile Patriots had accepted the
amnesty and taken the oath. Normally it would be a provo-
cation to leave one's advance posts so near to the enemy, but
in this case, the enemy was powerless, so Cornwallis saw a
substantial political gain for a minimal military risk. Since
Howe was still operating under instructions to conquer the

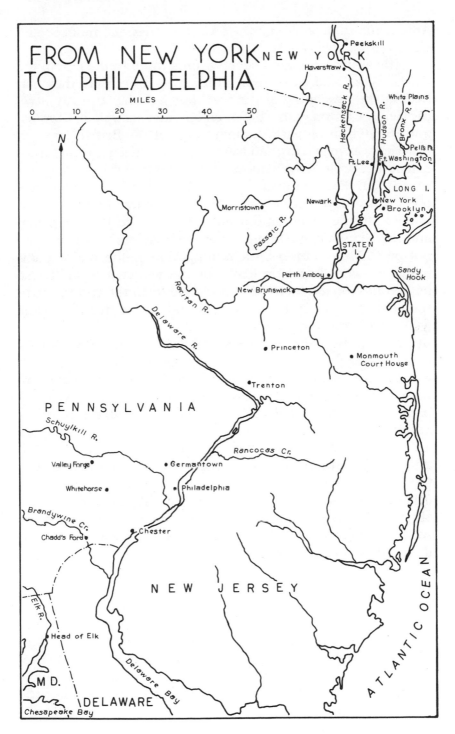

FROM NEW YORK
TO PHILADELPHIA

MILES

0   10   20   30   40   50

N

NEW YORK

Peekskill

Haverstraw

White Plains

Hackensack R.

Hudson R.

Bronx R.

Pells Pt.

Ft. Lee

Ft. Washington

Morristown

Newark

LONG I.

New York

Brooklyn

Passaic R.

STATEN I.

Raritan R.

Perth Amboy

Sandy Hook

New Brunswick

Delaware R.

Princeton

Monmouth Court House

Trenton

PENNSYLVANIA

Schuylkill R.

Rancocas Cr.

Valley Forge

Germantown

Whitehorse

Philadelphia

Brandywine Cr.

Chadd's Ford

Chester

NEW JERSEY

Elk R.

Head of Elk

Delaware Bay

ATLANTIC OCEAN

M D.

DELAWARE

Chesapeake Bay

Americans in as conciliatory a way as possible, he accepted
Cornwallis's suggestion.

The situation looked peculiar on a map. In the north, the
British were back in Canada, holding no more than they had
held at the beginning of the war, but holding it firmly now.
Sir Henry Clinton with 6,000 men had just occupied Newport,
and Howe himself with the main part of the British army in
America was in and around New York City. Then he had forces
extending, progressively more thinly, down through New Jersey to the Delaware. Given the extent of the American colonies,
there was thus a relatively small amount of territory in British
hands. Yet the rebellion did indeed appear to be collapsing,
and the British could congratulate themselves that it was all
but over. Many officers, including some of the major commanders, went home on leave for the winter season. Those
left behind looked forward to a respite from the campaign in
the field. It was nearly Christmas, and it was time for some
well-earned relaxation.

British dispositions in New Jersey were actually such as
to invite attack. The main base was at New Brunswick, which
was about halfway between New York City and the Delaware
River. Then the advanced posts were left along the New Jersey
bank of the Delaware River itself, manned by German troops
at Bordentown and Trenton. The whole of the British forward
area was commanded by the General James Grant who had
attacked the American right at the battle of Long Island, and
the Hessians were commanded by the Colonel Rall who had
accepted the American surrender at Fort Washington. In the
entire British Army there were probably not two men more
contemptuous of the Americans than these; they were the kind
it would be a delight to slap in the face.

Christmas of 1776 was cold and rainy, a thoroughly miserable day. The 1,200 Hessians in Trenton celebrated it in
traditional German style, with feasting, drinking, and song.
The garrison was somewhat isolated, but its commander had
neither strengthened the position nor sent out patrols. As evening came on, he was carried to bed drunk. While the Hessians
celebrated, across the river Washington mustered his little

army and moved. He had planned three separate crossings of the river, but only the one he led himself came into effective action. He left his camp about midafternoon, and marched a few miles upstream to what is now known as Washington's Crossing, and was then McConkey's Ferry. Here before midnight, as the rain changed to hail and then snow, the ragged army crossed the river, fending off ice floes and poling the boats through the shallows. The weather worsened as the first contingent got across, and the whole operation was not completed until about four in the morning, which put them four hours late. The men were miserably cold and tired, some barefoot in the snow and mud. The officers were worried over the time and trying desperately to hurry things along, all too conscious that an attack scheduled for dawn would now have to be made in full daylight, against an enemy who would be up and might well be warned and ready.

The Hessians had indeed been told to be on their guard, but most of the cautions had been disregarded. The pickets they did have out expected no more than perhaps a small raid or some probing, possibly by mounted troops.

Short of the town, Washington detached two smaller columns, one led by Nathanael Greene to go inland from the river and come down from the north, while the second, led by John Sullivan, who had been exchanged soon after his capture on Long Island, attacked along the river road itself. At about eight Greene's advance met the first Germans north of town, and after a short exchange of fire drove them back on their supports. A few minutes later Sullivan's troops also came into contact, and the action soon developed into a full-scale battle. The Hessians hustled out of their billets and formed up in the streets in the center of town, but the Americans had field guns with them, brought forward with enormous difficulty, and as the Germans tried to attack Greene to the north, they were hit in flank by Sullivan's guns. German guns that tried to support their own troops were overrun, and under the pressure the Hessians began to fray out to the south of town. The rain continued falling, and many muskets were useless, but the Hessians could not get close enough to use the bayonet. Several regiments broke up in confusion, Rall was shot off his horse, fatally wounded, and the Hessians began to throw down their arms and ground their colors. In about an hour the battle was over.

Tactically, Trenton was a neat little action that netted the Americans several hundred prisoners for almost no losses of their own. On a strategic level, it was spoiled somewhat by the failure of the two secondary columns to get into action, and to close off enemy avenues of retreat or rescue. Washington had originally hoped to remain on the New Jersey side of the river for at least a while, and perhaps gather in other posts as well, but now he had to go back across to Pennsylvania, an effort that turned out to be even more difficult than the original crossing, and in which some soldiers actually froze to death. But on the overall level, of moral effect, Trenton was little short of spectacular. It did nothing less than keep the American cause alive, and it brought in new recruits, and gave new support and new vigor to a cause many people had seen as all but moribund. In spite of all the failures of the year now ending, here was evidence that the British and their already hated Hessian friends were not unbeatable, and that that blood-tinged trail in the snow and mud might someday lead on to ultimate victory after all.

It was no time to rest on well-deserved laurels. There was some thought of attacking the garrison at Bordentown next, but the exhausted little army could not do it. Nonetheless, on the 30th of December—with less than forty-eight hours to run for some enlistments—Washington crossed the river into New Jersey again. On his own recognizance, he offered a bounty of ten dollars to every man who would extend his service for six weeks, and this and personal appeals to some of the troops kept enough of an army together for some maneuvering to be possible. The British, under Cornwallis himself, who had delayed his departure for London on the news of Trenton, and was now ready to destroy these upstarts for their presumption, advanced south from New Brunswick and Princeton to trap the Americans around Trenton, but after a very creditable delaying action, the little army slipped away again. The noble earl was highly mortified at being made to look incompetent.

Washington then made what would have been a foolhardy

decision had it failed, but turned out to be a stroke of genius because it succeeded. Instead of retreating back into Pennsylvania, he turned the army toward Princeton, about ten miles from Trenton. This had served as a base for the occupation, and held considerable stores. When Cornwallis advanced, he had left about 700 troops from the 17th, 40th, and 55th Foot there as a garrison.

These were split on the morning of January 3, 1777, when the Americans arrived. Colonel Charles Mawhood was marching with the 17th and the 55th to support Cornwallis, having left the 40th in town to guard the stores. There was a short but bloody encounter when the American left, led by General Hugh Mercer of Virginia, met the 17th. The British formed line and broke the American attack, mortally wounding Mercer in the process, then came on, and were broken in their turn by a New England brigade of Continentals. This was little more than a skirmish, though significant for the fact that, almost for the first time in the war, American regulars stood up in the open field and traded volleys with their British counterparts. Even though the 17th was badly outnumbered, it was still clear that some American troops were learning their business.

The Americans then went on to take Princeton itself, hustling the British out of town. Cornwallis returned from Trenton before they could destroy or carry off all the stores, but they did make a pretty good haul; Washington would have liked to move on to the even greater pickings at New Brunswick, but the army was completely exhausted by now, and after getting away from Princeton, they collapsed for the night at Somerset Court House. Two days later, having shaken off Cornwallis and still moving north, they went into winter quarters at Morristown, forty-some miles north of Trenton and about twenty-five miles west of New York City.

The frustrated British, unwilling to pursue winter operations further, were compelled by this move to give up most of central New Jersey. Howe pulled his forces back all the way to the Hudson, holding only Perth Amboy at the mouth of the Raritan, and New Brunswick a few miles up it, as outposts. These served little practical purpose, and New Jersey was essentially returned to the Patriot cause by the first week of the new year. It was a startling reversal of fortune, changing the whole strategic, and even more importantly, the psychological, picture from what it had been a mere fortnight before.

The improvement in the American military position was unfortunately not matched by the general situation. Throughout the period of winter inactivity, Washington continued to plead for more men, supplies, and support in general. Congress, which remained in refuge in Baltimore, responded ineffectually. This was a peculiar hiatus in American governmental development. After declaring independence in July of 1776, the Continental Congress had begun debating a constitution, the Articles of Confederation. These were not ratified, however, until November 1777, and in the interim, Congress continued to function in the old, haphazard way, through committees trying to exercise whatever authority they could manage to assert on the basis of powers delegated by the separate states to the central body.

More important than the constitutional provisions, however, was the actual physical situation of the Congress. Forced to flee from Philadelphia to Baltimore, they left behind a watchdog committee to concert measures with Washington, to whom on December 27 they had granted almost dictatorial powers, and the government continued in this vein for six months. The Congress returned to Philadelphia in March of 1777, after the immediate danger seemed past. During the Baltimore sojourn they resolved to increase their efforts to obtain foreign aid, by sending delegations to other countries in addition to those they were already soliciting, and when they came back to Philadelphia they pursued this even farther.

The main business, however, was support of the army, or, as most of the soldiers saw it, interference with the army. At the risk of oversimplifying, Congress regarded the army as a necessary evil, and whether the necessity or the evil was uppermost in any given member's mind at any given time is questionable. Most of the members were steeped in British political philosophy of the late seventeenth and early eighteenth century. They were full of Cromwell and "the rule of the major generals," of King James II and his threat to build a standing army and with it to trample on "the rights of free-born Englishmen." They were also classically educated, and they were all too conscious of the rise of military men to dominate Roman history. Even though they had granted Washington large temporary powers, indeed perhaps *because* they had granted them, they were always worried that the army was going to get beyond its station in life, namely, that it was going to challenge the supremacy of Congress. They also managed to display a remarkable ignorance of the springs of honor and emotion that kept the army in being. Though it appears a small matter on the face of it, few things are more illustrative of this issue than the matters of promotions and foreign commissions.

The appointment of general officers in the Continental service rested in Congress's hands, and Congress vigorously preserved this right. In spite of the fact that Washington might have been thought to have more intimate knowledge of his officers' capabilities than Congress did, the members of Congress resented his suggestions and often overthrew them. In early 1777, for example, he asked for the appointment of three lieutenant generals, there being none in the army at that time. Congress refused. It did, however, appoint five more major generals. In doing so, it passed over the man who had unarguably the best military record and claim to promotion in the entire army, Benedict Arnold. Its reasoning was simple, and perfectly sensible from the Congressional point of view: Connecticut, Arnold's home state, already had enough senior officers for the number of troops it had in service; therefore there was no room for Arnold. Both Washington and Arnold asked that the latter be promoted, with seniority to date over the other five. Reluctantly, Congress granted the promotion, but refused the seniority; according to one well-disposed member, its refusal was because Arnold had asked for this, and in doing so, had implicitly questioned Congress's right to do as it chose with the army. A number of officers actually resigned rather than continue under what they perceived as such humiliation.

The humiliation was all the greater because Congress seemed to give promotions to foreigners for the asking. There was a steady stream of volunteers from Europe to fight for the glorious cause. Many of these men became American national heroes, men such as the Marquis de Lafayette, Baron von Steuben, Johann Kalb, Thaddeus Kosciusko, Casimir Pulaski, and Louis Duportail. But many of them were mere adventurers, come to pluck the naive Americans for whatever they could get. At Morristown, Washington spent a great deal of his time interviewing men who, to hear them tell it, were a cross between the great Marshal of France, Turenne, and the Duke of Marlborough. Few of them could prove it. What was worse, many had been given commissions, either by Congress or by its agents abroad, so that they actually had paper claims to preferment.

The classic example was a French officer, Philippe-Charles-Jean-Baptiste Tronson de Coudray. A brigadier with sixteen years' service in the artillery, he had connections at court and a well-publicized record as an administrator and innovator. The American representative in Paris, Silas Deane, gave him a commission as a major general, and a promise that he could be the American chief of artillery, a post then admirably filled by Henry Knox, and, if that were not enough, a further promise to commission in American service any of Coudray's associates he took overseas with him. In May of 1777, Coudray arrived in America with an entourage of nearly thirty fellow fortune hunters, demanding everything in sight. Because of his connections at home, Congress had to do something about him, and it actually did honor the major general's commission, though it limited it to a "staff" position. Coudray then solved the problem: he rode his horse at a gallop onto a ferry in the Schuylkill River, then skidded right off the outboard end, and the importunate, and now unfortunate, Frenchman drowned. Most of the foreigners were not so easily gotten rid of.

Congress continually resented the claims of its army officers, to the point of appearing quite mean-minded about them. It refused requests for uniforms and even minor emoluments, and grumbled about allowances and pretensions. John Adams, usually an estimable member of Congress, was quite vituperative on the subject, and harrumphed about well-paid and excessively coddled soldiery waxing fat on society and doing nothing to earn their keep. He did not visit the billets around Morristown to see what conditions were actually like; had he done so, he might have taken a different view. As it was, he suggested officers should be elected annually, to keep them honest. As always in human affairs, it was far more pleasant to apply a strict standard of accountability to another group of people than it was to apply it to one's own.

If a major preoccupation of the infant American government during this period was finding foreign assistance, it became an even more compelling imperative to secure allies for itself. To gain the recognition and aid of sovereign states, however, proved more difficult than to gain the services of individual foreign volunteers. Hardly anyone in Europe liked the British, and most countries would be happy to see "perfidious Albion" taken down a peg, but no one was yet willing to go to war to do it.

This was in fact a many-sided problem. The European states disliked Britain, and vice versa. But the American states were chary of the other powers, at the same time as they sought aid from them. Their potential sources of aid or alliance were, eventually, France, Spain, and the Netherlands, that is, the maritime states of western Europe. France and Spain were of course both Catholic, and both monarchical. Spain, possessing a large empire in the Western Hemisphere, was unlikely to look too favorably upon a revolutionary movement that might well infect her own colonies. The Netherlands were simply not up to measures that might embroil them in war with their enormously powerful neighbor, though they were more than happy to sell war supplies, to have their West Indian islands used as bases for contraband and for privateers, and to make whatever they could out of the conflict. Basically, then, if anything were to be done for the Americans by a European state, it would have to be France.

This was bound to be an uneasy courtship. The Americans were not willing to give much, for their part, and the French did not know what they wanted, for theirs. On the revolutionary side, there was the longstanding distrust of the ancient enemy, and the fear that the French would, if encouraged, attempt to reestablish their American empire, and perhaps expand it. At first all the Americans were willing to offer was a commercial treaty; later they moved to an alliance, and also agreed that the former French West Indian islands might return to France—if she could conquer them.

The French had their own problems, chief of which was lack of money. France had taken a beating in the Seven Years' War, but since then there had been a series of highly effective military reforms. By the start of the Revolution, for example, the French Navy might well have been assessed superior to the Royal Navy, and the French Army was in better shape than it had been for fifty years. Unfortunately, the French treasury was in worse. The country was well down on the slope that led to eventual bankruptcy and a revolution of its own, and fiscal policy and governmental development had simply not kept up with changing attitudes and demands. Nonetheless, the French were very sympathetic to the American cause, and highly enthusiastic for Liberty. This was the height of the pre-Romantic period in French society; gallants in velvet coats and court ladies in huge gowns and towering headdresses wept over Rousseau's "natural" heroines and advocacy of breast-feeding, and the French nobility saw the Americans as the epitome of Man in the State of Nature, a noble being, unsullied by the corruptions of cities and courts.

The Americans finally played to this audience by sending the perfect representative to France, Benjamin Franklin. Here was the natural philosopher at his best, author, scientist, a plain-spoken and avuncular figure; he even wore his own—thinning—hair, instead of a powdered wig! What could be more natural? Paris loved him, and he loved Paris. It was almost impossible not to help him, and the court ladies vied to be of service, or at least to sit on his lap.

There were several American agents abroad, of course. They spent as much of their time undercutting each other as they did aiding the American cause. Arthur Lee, a furious, suspicious, intriguing but shrewd lawyer, was for a time American agent in London, and then made the round of several European courts. He actually succeeded in getting some assistance from the Spanish, though they wisely would not allow him near Madrid itself. Silas Deane was even more unscrupulous; in France he was deeply involved in obtaining early French aid through front companies, and in spite of the fact

that he was wealthy himself—he had twice married money—
he both skimmed off a great deal of cash and sold information
to the British. He and Lee hated, and eventually ruined, each
other.

Franklin was not above a quick dollar, either, and he too
may have sold material to the British, as has recently been
suggested. But this was a period when the lines between personal and public conduct were not clearly drawn; many a
European diplomat or minister saw nothing wrong in making
his own fortune out of his ministry, or accepting favors from
interested parties; this is, after all, not unknown to a later age.

Whatever their faults and failings, these were the sort of
men charged with gaining foreign assistance for the struggling
Revolution. The French government played coy, but gradually
dipped its toes in the water.

In 1770 one of the few first-class French ministers of the
era, the Duc de Choiseul, had wanted to go to war with Britain
over claims to the Falkland Islands. France could not afford
it at the time. For the next five years the French observed with
delight the growth of the American difficulties. They sent
agents to the colonies through the sixties and early seventies,
who reported that there would be war, but that the issue of
it was doubtful. Once fighting began, French agents were more
active, though vague in their promises. The government simply could not afford to be drawn.

But private Frenchmen were willing to do more, and the
most famous of them, in this context, was Pierre Caron, better
known as Beaumarchais, author, adventurer, man of affairs.
With the connivance of the government, he set up an import-
export firm known as Hortalez and Company, to supply the
Americans. He got a million livres as a loan from the French
government, the same from the Spanish, and raised another
million privately. The company bought or leased stocks from
the French arsenals, such as the muskets that were being
replaced in the army, and sent them to America. The original
intent was that the Americans should pay for these, either in
money or in trade goods; in fact, though some forty million
livres' worth of goods went to the rebels, they never paid a
sou. Beaumarchais finally staved off bankruptcy by bringing
back highly profitable West Indian goods. Eventually the op-

eration was outdated by the open French alliance and entry into the war, but until late 1777 it served its purpose. The British knew all about it, and officially protested, but the French government simply returned an infuriating Gallic shrug. They would not interfere in a private matter; after all, were the English not great believers in trade?

While it lasted, this was a great opportunity, not actually to make money from trade, because the Americans, as mentioned, could do little in return. The profit lay rather in skimming things off, and for creative bookkeeping; the operation was a model future businessmen might well envy. Palms were greased, money was laundered, invoices were falsified and lost. It became so tortuous, in fact, that no one knew finally how much money was involved, by what routes it moved, or in whose pockets it ultimately landed. In short, it was an entrepreneur's delight. But it helped keep the American struggle alive, and for a time provided most of the material aid the Revolution got from abroad.

The French government, openly, was still a long way from committing itself. By early 1777 the Americans had still not shown they were capable of winning, or even sustaining, their fight. They would have to do something far more substantial than snap up a few outposts to prove their staying power. Until they did so, official sympathy, and surreptitious help around the edges, was all they were going to get.

CHAPTER EIGHT
March and Countermarch

W HEN THE news of Trenton and Princeton reached London, Lord North's ministry knew it was in trouble. To this point, the government's policy had seemed successful. The alteration of carrot and stick, of conciliation and coercion, had won New York and appeared to have gained them New Jersey as well. The failure before Charleston early in 1776 could be explained away, and their main military operations for the year, those conducted by Howe and Carleton, had been reasonably fruitful. Yet privately, they had to acknowledge that they were both baffled and frustrated. Frustrated because no matter how many battles they won, it did not seem to do a great deal of good. They beat the Americans at Long Island, and they escaped to Manhattan; they beat them on Manhattan, and they escaped to White Plains. They drove them out of New York altogether, and they postured in New Jersey; they drove them from New Jersey, and they survived in Pennsylvania. They captured so many prisoners they could not accommodate them, and new American soldiers apparently sprang out of the ground. Loyalists and spies told them the

129

Americans were always on the point of collapse, yet there still remained an army in the field.

What baffled them was the fact that this was outside the range of contemporary military experience. The British were facing a nation in arms, though the term had not yet been invented; that nation might be weak, divided, mostly friendless, but it was still a nation, and the British did not understand it. Nor did they realize that the more they tried to destroy it, the more of a nation it became. During the past year, for example, while their professional forces tried to defeat the American professional forces, the British had also employed Indian allies along the frontiers, Creeks and Cherokees in the south, the Iroquois in the north. This was far worse on the frontier than Hessians along the seacoast, and Loyalist support in the interior dwindled with every new Indian strike. How could you remain loyal to a king who unleashed Germans on you from one side and Indians from the other? So the more the British did, the worse it got.

The American historian Barbara Tuchman has characterized British policy during the Revolution as "the pursuit of folly"; that is, persevering in a course which is seen to be self-defeating even at the time it is being followed. But the government could not figure out what it was up against. Contemporary social and military theory simply did not contemplate the kind of situation the British faced. The great French soldier, Marshal Saxe, had written a little book in which he had fantasized about armed and trained citizens, rushing to the defense of their country when it was invaded, and harassing and overwhelming the intruder, but even Saxe had not taken the idea seriously; it was too far outside the range of experience for that. European warfare for more than a century had been moving in the opposite direction, toward professionally waged wars that inflicted as little damage and disturbance on the productive civil population as possible. In this kind of war, towns were besieged, battles were fought, pawns were exchanged, negotiations went on, and eventually one side or the other was declared to be the winner, carrying off some prize, an island or a fortress, to display as a trophy. In this kind of war, Indians did not scalp women, riflemen did not aim deliberately at officers, civilians did not come out with muskets in hand to shoot soldiers from behind stone walls. In this kind of war, when you captured the enemy's major city and drove his major army from the field, he had sense enough to admit he was beaten and to make peace. Why could not these stubborn colonials see that they had lost? Why, having lost, did they go on fighting?

The water was threatening to wear away the stone. War was expensive. After Trenton Sir William Howe demanded an additional 20,000 troops to finish things off, in the familiar cry of generals ever since: I am winning the war! Send me more men! The ministry agreed to send 2,500. France and Spain were known to be waiting in the wings, chortling and rubbing their hands; sixteen more ships of the line had to be commissioned because of the increasing activity of American privateers. But the real problem was at home. The national debt was rising; worse, horror of horrors, the land tax had to be raised to four shillings on the pound, a rate as high as during the Seven Years' War. The King had overspent the civil list—officially his expense account to maintain the royal establishment, but actually a vast slush fund to allow the government to play politics without being accountable for it—by £600,000. Even the Speaker of the House of Commons, normally a safe government man, had lectured the King and his cabinet on the need for better financial management. In other words, people—people who counted, people who paid taxes —were becoming impatient with a war the government said did not really exist, and that it insisted it was winning.

Lord North had made his reputation as a good financial manager, and he knew all the signs of trouble: rising taxes, rising insurance rates for shipping, difficulties with foreign governments. He himself was both indolent and pacifistic; but his master insisted the war must be waged, and won. George III was not going to give in because the rebels refused to see reason, or because a pack of backbenchers in Parliament were complaining about taxes. Let them all stand to their task like Englishmen, and all would be well.

Easier said than done. They knew they must win, and win soon, before foreign intervention or domestic opposition forced them into acknowledging defeat. But they had done all they could in 1776; they had sent the greatest expedition overseas that had ever been mounted. What more could be done? What new strategy could they devise? Where was the head of this hydra, and how could they strike it off?

Enter General John Burgoyne, the warrior home from the battlefield, home for the winter season, to conquer the drawing rooms of London, to consult with the ministry on plans for the future, to ensure his own place in great events, to undermine his superiors, to play his part upon the stage of history. Debonair, handsome in the fleshy way of the time, witty and well-connected, Burgoyne saw his hour dawning. At the end of February he submitted to the government his "Thoughts for Conducting the War from the Side of Canada" (Burgoyne habitually spoke or wrote in capital letters). This was really a repetition of the 1776 plan, with variations. It called for a strike south from Canada on the Lake Champlain–Hudson route to Albany. This time, of course, it was to be led by John Burgoyne rather than Sir Guy Carleton, a change that was acceptable to Lord George Germain, whose dislike for Carleton was well-known. Then, when Burgoyne's expedition was under way, Sir William Howe would proceed up the Hudson; the two would meet at Albany, the New England colonies would be cut off, and the Revolution would collapse.

Why the New England colonies would be "cut off" by this move was never examined by men who thought in terms of the distances of the English scene, where there were not miles and miles of untended wilderness, and why the Revolution would collapse if they were was again left unexplored. These two points were always taken simply as an article of faith. Given what eventually happened to Burgoyne's plan, its underlying assumptions never needed to be challenged.

This operation would have reduced Sir William Howe and the forces in New York, the major British contingent in America, to a secondary role. Howe, when apprised of the plan, thought that the effect of his own inactivity for several months while Burgoyne made his move would be disastrous, and he therefore suggested that he might be better employed operating independently out of New York. Lord George Germain on reflection agreed, so the plan was altered: Burgoyne would move south; Howe would move wherever it seemed most opportune for him to go. From one coordinated operation, the British now had two, that might or might not converge.

The spring season did not get off to a good start. Sir William Howe soon decided he would be best employed capturing the rebel capital at Philadelphia. To do that, he could either march across New Jersey, hoping to draw Washington out into a battle, or he could go by sea. Though no one seems sure exactly why, he decided to go by sea. He sent off a series of dispatches to Lord George Germain, through which his plans and thoughts evolved; the significant element in them was that cooperation with Burgoyne's march south from Canada was progressively downgraded. Nobody worried over this as much as he should have, and Germain replied only that he hoped Sir William would complete his maneuvers in time to move on Albany.

But Howe did not hurry; quite the contrary. He spent the month of June traipsing about central New Jersey, sparring unsuccessfully with Washington. Then by the end of the month he abandoned all of New Jersey, pulled his troops back onto Staten Island, and sat there for another three weeks before he loaded his men aboard ship and sailed off into the Atlantic.

Washington was totally nonplussed by this. There was any number of places the British might be headed, and the commander in chief had considered all of them. It was possible, but not too likely, that they were going to Newport, to operate against Providence, or even Boston. They were gathering large numbers of ships, but even so they might be planning to sail up the Hudson to Albany. But then, perhaps they were going to have another try at Charleston down in the Carolinas. Nor did the threat to Philadelphia escape consideration. They could move to that city either by way of the Delaware River, or through Chesapeake Bay. The evidence was contradictory; the size of the forces being gathered, and the type—including cavalry and guns—suggested a move south from New York. Yet the longer Howe waited, the more it seemed he must be planning to go to Albany. Burgoyne captured Ticonderoga on July 5, but two weeks later Howe was still sitting on Staten Island. It only made sense if the two

British generals were intending to support each other. Washington slowly moved his army northward, skirting New York City, and ready for a dash up the Hudson.

Sir William finally made his move on July 23. The fleet weighed anchor and put to sea, standing to the southward, 15,000 soldiers on 260 ships. Albany was out, then. Hastily, Washington began marching his regiments south. He reached the Delaware on July 29, expecting to find his enemy before him. But there was no word of the British; they had not yet even been sighted off the Delaware Capes. Maybe it was all a feint, and they were going to double back for the Hudson after all. The frustrated Americans began to move back into New Jersey. Next, on July 31, an express came in from the Capes; the British had been sighted there the day before. Hastily Washington countermarched once again. But then the British sailed out to sea once more! This time they were gone for nearly three weeks. It must be Charleston after all.

Finally the dilemma was resolved. On the 22nd of August the British armada was sighted sailing up inside Chesapeake Bay; they were committed now, and Philadelphia must be their objective.

Washington at this time had an army of about 12,000 men present and fit for duty, and he marched them through Philadelphia on August 24, a Sunday. The troops were lean and hard after several weeks of field operations, reasonably well equipped though hardly uniformed. They put on a brave show to impress Congress and the citizens of the City of Brotherly Love, and then they moved on and took up positions near Wilmington.

The British had had a difficult passage, with storms and adverse winds. Sea travel may have been more expeditious than land at the time, but only if the winds were fair and the sea calm. Howe and his troops in fact had a miserable time of it, beating back and forth, and the transports were scattered all over the ocean. While Washington awaited them at Wilmington, they disembarked at Head of Elk and sorted themselves out, delighted to be on dry land once more. It took several days to get organized before they began an advance on Philadelphia.

   Washington shifted his forces to meet them, and eventually took up a defensive position along Brandywine Creek, a tributary of the Delaware River, twenty-some miles west of Philadelphia. The situation was not a particularly good one; the creek was a substantial feature, but there were many roads in the vicinity, and there were no less than eight fords within the seven or so miles that had to be covered. The British had ample scope for maneuver.

   The main American force, under Nathanael Greene and Brigadier Anthony Wayne, was concentrated around Chadd's Ford, on the left of the position. Beyond it were covering forces of Pennsylvania militia. The Americans were then strung out to their right, with Sullivan's division guarding all the rest of the fords. Troops under Lord Stirling, or General Alexander, and General Adam Stephen of Virginia, were stationed in backup positions. All they had to do was wait and watch.

   On August 10 the British camped within five miles of the American lines. The morning of the 11th saw them up and on the move early. Howe knew the American dispositions—there were plenty of loyal subjects in the area to tell him anything he wanted to know—and he intended to repeat the Long Island gambit all over again. The Germans under General Baron Wilhelm von Knyphausen, their new commander in chief, would demonstrate noisily but harmlessly in front of Chadd's Ford. While this entertained the Americans, Howe would march with three fifths of his army upstream, cross the creek, and come down on the rebel right and rear.

   The plan worked every bit as well as it had a year ago. All of the Americans around Chadd's Ford, including Washington himself, were completely bemused by the Hessian maneuvers, and they spent the early morning hours waiting for something to happen. Eventually reports came in that a large force had been seen moving up the creek on the other side. For some time Washington considered that the British had foolishly split their forces, and he issued orders to attack both groups, in other words, to split his own command. But then suspicious signs multiplied. First, there was word that the British were across the creek, on the American side; but Washington discounted it. Next, a farmer came in, swearing they were across in strength, but he was received skeptically. Finally there was a hasty message from Sullivan: we are flanked and in trouble! At last the Americans began to move.

Convinced by midafternoon that things were degenerating, Washington ordered Sullivan, Alexander, and Stephen to take up a new line perpendicular to the creek, and facing north. Howe gave them time to do this; his troops, still unsteady after six seasick weeks, had been on the move for hours, marching fifteen miles on a hot September day. It was after four when Howe developed his attack on the new American line, which Washington left under the overall command of Sullivan. But as the British came down from the north, Knyphausen also attacked across the creek at Chadd's Ford, his assault led by the 71st Highlanders and the Queen's Rangers. These slowly pushed back Greene's troops, while the Guards hammered at Sullivan's men. The Americans resisted stubbornly on both fronts, making spirited little counterattacks when possible, and their artillery was especially well served. But the army was now bent into an acute angle, and in serious danger of being trapped and perhaps surrounded. No amount of battlefield tenacity was going to redeem the poor dispositions, the failure of reconnaissance, and the lost hours of the morning.

Finally Sullivan's men broke and began to pull out. Washington's new teenage volunteer, the Marquis de Lafayette, was slightly wounded trying to rally them, but as dusk came on, the American army hastily fled along the Chester road, beaten again with almost casual ease. In the year since Long Island, though they had gotten troops who would fight, and officers who would lead, it looked as if they still had not got generals who could command a battle.

That impression was reinforced in the next two weeks. During that time, Howe played with the Americans as a cat does with a mouse, outflanking, outmarching, and outmaneuvering them. Several times Washington tried to stand, but could not find a place to do so successfully. His troop strength dwindled, from desertion, and from sickness—the rainy season was starting—and from battle. In the early hours of September 21, a British force under General Charles Grey attacked and overran Anthony Wayne's division at Paoli. Grey made his men remove the flints from their muskets and attack solely with the bayonet, earning himself the nickname "No Flint" Grey. Wayne lost 150 men, including seventy prisoners, in what Americans promptly called "the Paoli massacre." On September 26 Howe marched triumphantly into Philadelphia, having totally outgeneraled his opponent.

A half century after the Revolution, the great German theorist, Carl von Clausewitz, wrote that the true aim of war was the mind of one's enemy, that wars were won when the losing side was ready to acknowledge that it had lost, and not before. The British forces in America had once again convincingly demonstrated their superiority over the American, and done so where it counted, on the field of battle. But as long as the Americans were not ready to concede that they were beaten, they were not in fact beaten. Therefore, Howe was up against the same old problem, as the next month clearly demonstrated.

Having moved via the Chesapeake rather than the Delaware, Howe now decided to shift his route to Philadelphia. It was obviously easier to bring shipping right up the river than it was to have to unload at Head of Elk and carry supplies overland from there. The Americans were as aware of all of this as the British were, and had blocked the river some miles below the city, about halfway down to Chester. These fortifications had been what dissuaded the Royal Navy from a direct attempt on the capital. Now, a good month later, they were going to attack them anyway. It was October 12 before the British fleet reached Chester, where it anchored while the Navy had a look at what lay ahead of them.

The American works were unimpressive. First they had blocked the river channel with a line of sunken stakes, and covered them with a small battery at Billings Port. A couple of miles farther upstream, where the main channel passed between Red Bank on the New Jersey side and Mud Island, was the main position. Here were more stakes, and Fort Mercer on Red Bank and Fort Mifflin on Port Island. Both forts were merely earthworks, with palisades; the former was too large for its garrison to hold, and the latter was mostly open from the rear, or northern side. Fort Mercer was garrisoned by two Rhode Island Continental regiments, and Fort Mifflin

138   A Short History of the American Revolution

had about 450 men, reinforced during its siege by several further detachments.

Finally, upstream beyond the forts lay several American ships, including a frigate, fire rafts, and assorted gunboats of one type or another. Washington was charged with the defense of the forts, but the navy was supposed to be responsible for the river, a confusion of command that did nothing to help the American situation. The general knew that if Howe could be deprived of easy supplies while in Philadelphia, for however long, life would get difficult for him. But the naval people did not possess the same sense of urgency.

The British opened their operations early in October by easily overrunning the Billings Port work and cutting their way through the stakes. They then moved up to the main position and went to work on it. Fort Mercer was attacked on October 21 by about 2,000 Hessians, whom Howe sent marching downstream from Philadelphia. Colonel Carl von Donop summoned the American commander, Colonel Christopher Greene, to surrender, and said that unless he did so, the Germans would give no quarter. Greene invited him to come on.

Carelessly the Germans did. They attacked the work from the north, and got inside without a shot being fired—only to find their way blocked by a second palisade across the inner part of the fort. From the east they stormed into the ditch and up to the palisade, then discovered they had forgotten to bring along any scaling ladders. At this point, with several hundred Germans milling aimlessly about, the Americans opened a concerted fire. Within minutes the Germans were broken, several officers, including von Donop, killed, and the attack collapsed. The shattered formations were regrouped, and the Germans tried again, from the south, but they were swept away as before, and they gave up the attempt. The Americans suffered 30-odd casualties, and inflicted close to 400, including killed, wounded, and prisoners, the latter of whom Greene need not have taken, in view of von Donop's "no quarter" threat.

In spite of this success, it soon became apparent that Fort Mifflin could not be held. The British worked up the south bank of the river and got behind the Americans, from where they could bombard the open side of the fort without any effective opposition. This they did after several ships had run aground and been burned trying to get past the line of stakes. For a week they bombarded the fort from batteries on the Pennsylvania shore, from floating batteries as close as forty yards, and finally from warships that got so close their Marines could stand in the rigging and shoot down on the defenders. Under this punishment the fort simply melted away, until there was literally nothing left, just a few mounds of earth and splinters of wood. Having sustained 200 casualties, with all their guns dismounted and with nothing left to fight with, the garrison got away in darkness. Fort Mercer was now untenable, and though Washington would have liked to hold it, Colonel Greene wisely evacuated. The American naval vessels, having done nothing at all, were then burned by their crews, and the river was open to Philadelphia by mid-November.

Meanwhile, Washington had fought yet again, to everyone's surprise but his. After Howe had entered Philadelphia in triumph, he camped at Germantown, about five miles north of the city. The Americans, several miles north of that, began again the oft-repeated process of rebuilding. In spite of the recent defeats and the humiliation of being consistently outmaneuvered, recruits came in, militia units rallied, and, like the Phoenix, the American army arose once more from the ashes of defeat. By early October, Washington was ready to try conclusions. He now had about 12,000 men under arms, though most of them were new, while Howe, through detachments and escorts for supplies, had perhaps only 9,000 at Germantown. On October 2, the Americans were at Centre Point, fifteen miles away from the British camp.

The plan they developed was ambitious. Four separate roads led from their camp to the British one, and Washington advanced along all four of them. Maryland and New Jersey militia used the left-hand, northern road, and Pennsylvania troops used the right-flank road. The main attack was by three big divisions under Nathanael Greene on the American left center, and three smaller ones under Sullivan on the right center. The army mustered and started out at dark on the night of October 3, and moving over rough roads in country that was unfamiliar to most, they were soon behind schedule.

Dawn saw Sullivan's men, leading the way, three miles short of where they should be.

Howe knew they were coming, but he refused to take it seriously. The Americans had just been severely handled at the Brandywine; they had lost their capital, and been chased all over the countryside for three weeks. They could hardly be much of a threat; Howe doubled his pickets and relaxed.

Yet there they were. Sunrise brought the Americans, some light horse leading Sullivan's advance straight down the Shippack Road into Germantown. There was no sign of Greene, nor anyone else much. Sullivan threw out Anthony Wayne's regiments to cover his left, some others to watch the right, and swung ahead. There was fog over the battlefield. British Colonel Thomas Musgrave and his 40th Regiment reinforced the British light infantry pickets, and stopped to volley at every fence along the road. But the Americans were lapping all around him, and the redcoats went back and back again. Musgrave threw a few companies into a substantial building in the middle of town, the Chew House, but Sullivan's leading formations went right on by.

Howe was forming his main body south of the town, and starting regiments forward. These began to come into contact with the advance of Greene, delayed by wrong turns and confused by the fog, but finally coming onto the scene. The advance was led by General Peter Muhlenberg of Virginia, a Lutheran pastor who had stood up in his pulpit one day, taken off his clerical robes to reveal his militia uniform, and enlisted his congregation in the army on the spot. They drove deep into the British position, took a hundred prisoners, and then had to turn around to fight their way back out.

Neither side was as yet in serious trouble, but things began to go wrong for the Americans. The fog still hung heavily over the field, mixed now with the smell of the gunsmoke wafting through it. American guns and infantry were banging away at the Chew House, holding out back up the road. Then General Stephen on Greene's right ran into Wayne's men on Sullivan's left. There were British companies floating about in the fog, and shadowy figures loomed up, exchanged volleys, and faded back into the gloom. Some of the troops began to go back. There was more blundering, officers shouting to men to turn around; those facing front turned, those facing back kept going. Panic spread over the American army, Wayne's men fired on Stephen's, or Stephen's men fired on Wayne's; Knox's guns were still banging away at the Chew House while "those behind cried 'Forward!'/And those before cried 'Back!' " Suddenly, the army dissolved almost as it had on Manhattan, and went streaming up the roads away from Germantown, in spite of efforts from Washington on down to make the men stop and form.

The panic was in fact short-lived, and within half an hour the embarrassed troops were collecting around their colors, asking each other what had happened, everyone sure that someone else had panicked, but not himself, and they were ready to go again. But the momentum was lost, and there was nothing to be done but draw off and leave the relieved British to take the honors of the day. American losses were slightly higher than British, something more than 500 on either side.

The result was unexpected. General Stephen was dismissed from the service, but that was an incidental. More important was the fact that, though Americans had run, they had seen British backs before they did so, and they liked it. This time they had not really been outgeneraled—though their plan was far too ambitious to have expected success—and they had not been outfought either. They had in fact beaten themselves. If that was the case, well, that could be overcome. Then, after the Germantown battle, came the events on the Delaware, and again the Americans handled themselves well. Signs might be difficult to discern, in the midst of the loss of Philadelphia and the flight of Congress to Lancaster, but nonetheless, things were changing. A confident little army went into winter quarters at Valley Forge; come spring Mr. Howe might find himself in trouble.

CHAPTER NINE

"Agin Burgoyne"

WHILE HOWE fiddled, Burgoyne burned. At home during the winter of 1776, the flamboyant British general had waged the most successful campaign of his career, the one by which he engineered his supersession of Sir Guy Carleton in command of the British forces operating out of Canada. The latter was left only as governor of the province, while the actual handling of operations was entrusted to Burgoyne, who returned to Quebec in early May, bearing with him the letter that instructed Sir Guy to cooperate in every way. It would have been interesting to have been present at the first interview between the two.

To his credit, Carleton did indeed cooperate, and the shores of the St. Lawrence soon rang with martial music and the sound of hammers, as the British prepared to do again what they had already tried last year. This year there were few delays. All was ready by early June.

The plan Burgoyne had submitted to Lord George Germain and His Majesty was broad in scope. It was in fact for a three-pronged move toward Albany, from the south, north, and west. The confusion over the southern element of this, however—Howe's disinclination to play second fiddle to Burgoyne, his move to Philadelphia, and the progressive downgrading of this part of the plan—left Burgoyne with a double rather than a triple envelopment. The western part of it was a long hook, beginning all the way up the St. Lawrence to Lake Ontario. From there, Colonel Barry St. Leger was to lead some 1,700 men east through the Mohawk Valley. Much of this was Tory country, and it had already produced many of the outstanding figures of the northern Loyalist military effort. It was also, in its western portions, the traditional territory of the Six Nations, the Iroquois Confederacy. Though the Indians had initially decided to stay out of the white man's war, they had long been British allies in the French wars, and they soon joined in on the old side, lured by promises and presents. Given the fear and hatred they inspired among the white settlers, their adherence to Britain was a mixed blessing. St. Leger was to gather up additional Indians, rally the Tories, and distract American resources as he rolled east along the Mohawk.

Finally, Burgoyne himself was to drive straight along Lake Champlain, take Ticonderoga, and proceed on to Albany. As much of the preliminaries to this had been accomplished last year, it was anticipated that the operation should succeed with little difficulty. To effect this, Gentleman Johnny, as he was known both to his troops and to London society, wanted about 9,000 men. He actually got 7,200; the Canadians were not interested in his war, so few French volunteered. Most of the American Loyalists in Canada who were willing to fight were already doing so, and the same was true of the Indians. So Burgoyne had as many British regulars, and German auxiliaries, as he expected, but far fewer irregular troops.

The regulars were good troops toughened by their earlier experience, and leaned down by a winter in Canada. Seven regiments, they provided a backbone of about 3,700 men. The German contingent, commanded by Major General Baron von Riedesel, was five regiments strong, plus some attached artillery, light infantry, and a notable group, a regiment of dismounted dragoons from Brunswick. The British commander expected to mount these troops on horses to be acquired when

the expedition reached more populous country south of Lake
Champlain. Meanwhile they must get along as best they could.
Since they carried heavy dragoon broadswords, wore their
hair in tightly pulled queues under enormous cocked hats,
and worst of all, marched in heavy, stiff jackboots, designed
for mounted action in north Germany, they were going to
have a long, footsore trip to the south. Altogether the Germans
numbered slightly more than 3,000 men. To these auxiliaries
were added the Canadians, Tories, and Indians, as well as
several hundred noncombatants, sutlers, soldiers' wives, and
officers' ladies, the most famous of them being the charming
Baroness von Riedesel, wife of the German commander, and
her three small daughters.

Wives and children notwithstanding, it was a tough little
army that concentrated at St. Johns and moved from there
into Lake Champlain in the middle of June. The soldiers were
well trained, the officers knew their business, and there was
every reason to think that they were on their way to a re-
sounding success. Screened by larger warships, the troops
advanced down the lake in a brilliant show, the bateaux gay
with red British and blue German coats, the sun twinkling on
brass and polished steel, and the bands playing airs that
echoed over the sparkling waters. It was almost a sin to be
paid for such an excursion as this.

The Americans did not have much with which to meet
Burgoyne's and St. Leger's combined nine thousand men.
Philip Schuyler was still commanding the Northern Department, but at the moment, he was more heavily involved with
Congress than with his own army, small as it was, or with his
enemies. In March and April, he, Congress, and Horatio Gates
got into a three-cornered squabble that saw Schuyler victorious only after a personal visit and appeal to Washington.
Obviously American as well as British generals had to fight
with one eye looking backwards, and as the spring opened,
Schuyler's position was insecure both front and rear.

For the actual fighting, Schuyler had some 2,500 troops
at Ticonderoga, Continentals commanded by Major General
Arthur St. Clair, a former British junior officer who had married money and become a power in western Pennsylvania. He

did not arrive to take up his command until June 12. There were also about 900 newly raised militia around the fort. More militia were strung out at the several small posts along the route to Albany, and there were some Continentals ninety miles west of Albany, at Fort Stanwix at the head of the Mohawk Valley. Taken all in all, the Americans were probably outnumbered about two to one at the start of the campaign. Whether the civilian population would rally—and indeed to whom—might turn out to be one of the key points in deciding the whole issue.

Both Schuyler and St. Clair recognized that it would be impossible to hold Ticonderoga with the available force. The Americans needed three or four times as many men as they had even to make a passable defense. On June 20, the two commanders met, and agreed that the fort should be held as long as possible, but that at the last moment St. Clair should abandon it and move his troops across the lake to an earthwork on Mount Independence, where they might be able to stall the British indefinitely. They conveniently neglected the question of getting the garrison across a British-controlled lake, but on the other hand, they showed wisdom in deciding to save their force rather than sacrifice it for a piece of real estate, a wisdom not at all appreciated by those who saw in Ticonderoga "the Gibraltar of America."

While the Americans were making this decision, Burgoyne was succumbing, as usual, to the temptations of pen and ink. He decided to issue a proclamation, which he did as the British started down the lake. It recalled the population to allegiance, and promised death, destruction, and Indian massacre if they refused. It was the general at his pompous worst, and when distributed, it caused an equal mixture of rage and laughter, on both sides of the Atlantic. Americans produced any number of parodies on it, and in Britain, the Opposition had a field day in the House. Horace Walpole, the acidic critic, referred to Burgoyne as "Pomposo," and "Hurlothrumbo." Edmund Burke took him off as well, mimicking him while Lord North rolled on the front benches of the Government side, tears of laughter streaming down his face. To make it all worse, Burgoyne had addressed his Indian allies in the same terms, intending to limit their tendency to commit murder, but in fact unwittingly encouraging it. And at the same time he was appealing to the loyalty of the "suffering thousands" of Americans, he was also threatening them with "the Indian forces under my direction." It did not play in London, and it went down even worse along the northern frontier, where Indian threats had to be taken all too seriously.

None of this might be enough to save the Americans, and the British washed south with ease. They left Cumberland Head, near modern Plattsburgh, on June 17, and reached Crown Point on the 27th. By the first of the month, they were ready to attack Ticonderoga itself.

This position was actually less impressive than it looked, especially given the fact of its being undermanned. In addition to the fort, there was an outerwork on a hill called Mount Hope, to the northwest, and the work across the narrow lake, only a few hundred yards wide at this spot, on Mount Independence. The two sides were connected by a wooden bridge of boats, and it in turn was guarded by a heavy chain-and-log boom. Around to the southwest was a commanding height, steep-sided, known locally as Sugar Loaf. Several American officers had suggested fortifying this as well, but General Gates, during his short tenure of command, had dismissed it as unscalable—in spite of his officers' frequently climbing it for the view—and nothing had been done about it.

The British were soon at work. They went ashore three miles above the fort, British on the west shore and Germans on the east, and rapidly moved to invest the garrison. The Americans on Mount Hope burned their little fort and fled down one side of the hill as the enemy climbed the other. Soon Burgoyne's chief engineer, a Lieutenant Twiss, was standing on top of Sugar Loaf, and he reported to his commander that he could build a road and put guns up there in a mere twenty-four hours. So placed, guns would command not only Ticonderoga, but Independence as well, and perhaps even the escape routes to the south. He immediately set to work. By the morning of July 5, there was a British battery setting up on top of Gates's unscalable hill, and St. Clair knew he was in very serious trouble indeed.

That night the Americans abandoned their position; what

stores and sick could be moved were loaded aboard the hundreds of bateaux behind the chain and bridge of boats, and they started south toward Skenesboro, twenty miles away. The rest of the troops filed across the bridge in the dark, and began a roundabout march for the same place, but by a longer route via Hubbardton. This was all a lengthy and noisy process, but it was covered by a terrific cannonade, which entertained the British without arousing their curiosity. Next morning they approached the works to find them burning, partly blown up, and empty except for four drunken gunners who had stayed behind with a cask of Madeira wine.

So fell "the Gibraltar of America"; in England it was regarded as a great victory, and when news reached the King, he rushed into his wife's sitting room, startling her and all her ladies, shouting, "I have beaten them! I have beaten all the Americans!"

Burgoyne immediately took up the pursuit. The Americans were leisurely boating their way to Skenesboro, confident that the boom at Ticonderoga would delay the British fleet. Their confidence was sadly misplaced; a few cannon shots broke the chain, and the British were off after their prey once again. They very nearly snapped up the Americans around Skenesboro, and if their attack had been slightly better coordinated, they would have got the whole force. As it was, most of the American supplies were abandoned and lost, the town was garrisoned by redcoats, and the retreating St. Clair had to make a long overland detour once more, to avoid being cut off.

His other troops, those going via Hubbardton, were not doing any better. On the 7th, his rear guard, about a thousand men commanded by Seth Warner of Vermont, were surprised there by the British advance under General Simon Fraser and Baron von Riedesel. Attacking at dawn, Fraser began developing the American left. Though surprised, the Americans soon formed a good line, and in the forested country, were doing very well for themselves when von Riedesel arrived to hit them on the right. The pressure was too much, and the line buckled and broke. It was a very hot little fight for the forty minutes it lasted; the British had perhaps 200 casualties, and the Americans twice that many, before scattering in the woods.

St. Clair now continued his retreat, going a long way by little-used trails around Skenesboro, and he finally rallied the remains of his command at Fort Edward, twenty miles south of Skenesboro and on the Hudson River, on July 12.

To this point all had gone surprisingly well for Burgoyne. The Americans, even though some allowance had to be made for their lack of numbers, had still not conducted an effective defense. They had been maneuvered out of Ticonderoga, they had been caught loafing at Skenesboro, and napping at Hubbardton. There was little reason to think their performance would improve in the future. In fact, Burgoyne had now been led, though neither side realized it, about as far out on a limb as he could well go.

He now had two alternative routes before him. He could march almost due south, from Skenesboro, up Wood Creek to Fort Ann, which his advance patrols had already reached, and from there to Fort Edward. Or, he could go back to Ticonderoga, and then move onto Lake George, which ran almost thirty miles slightly west of south. At the end of the lake was a small work called Fort George, built near the scene of the massacre in 1757 that forms the central scene of James Fenimore Cooper's *The Last of the Mohicans*. Though this was an insignificant fort, it was an important position, for Fort George was only ten miles from the Hudson River, and was the normal route taken by travelers passing from one water system to the other.

Burgoyne thought the Lake George route was the better of the two, though he expected the Americans to try to block it with gunboats. But he was already at Skenesboro, at the end of Lake Champlain and ready to move up Wood Creek. This too he thought the Americans would try to block, but there seemed to be relatively little difference between the two possibilities. For years there was a story that Burgoyne was finally influenced in his decision by Philip Skene, his principal Loyalist adviser. The major landowner of the area, claiming about 60,000 of some of the nicest acres in America, Skene was supposed to want a road from Fort Edward to the town —actually no more than a small clearing and settlement—

named after him, and to have tricked Burgoyne into trying to build it. Burgoyne himself never said anything but that he was influenced by his transport problems and the desire not to appear to be retreating. So he chose to send his guns and heavy supplies by the Lake George route, and to march his combat troops up Wood Creek to Fort Ann, and overland to Fort Edward. It was, after all, only twenty-two miles, and, by land, only ten miles longer than the other route anyway. He might, indeed, have sent his light troops ahead immediately; there was little enough in front of them, and only a poor hundred men in a rotten palisade at Fort Edward. A coup de main might have carried the whole enterprise through.

Burgoyne decided instead, in the correct military way, to build the road and do it right. He had wagons and carts and baggage and some guns with him, those that had not been sent by way of Lake George. The country ahead was rough, tumbled and full of little streams running between deep banks. There were in fact some forty or more ravines to be crossed, creeks to be bridged, trees to be cleared, and trails improved.

What followed, therefore, was a battle of the axes. For while the British tried to improve a road, the Americans cleverly decided to ruin a trail, and this was a game the British were not going to win. American farmers might not like to stand up in a straight line and be shot at, which seems a sensible attitude after all, but put axes and shovels in their hands, and they could outchop and outdig the world. This was what General Schuyler clearly perceived, and his men set out to bury Burgoyne's whole army. The call went out for axmen and diggers. Schuyler put a thousand men to work on Wood Creek while Burgoyne was figuring out what to do. They went at it aggressively. They felled huge trees across the creeks and brooks, damming them and flooding the low-lying ground. They rolled boulders into the water to stop boats going through; they cut ditches and changed watercourses. Where the British expected to find dry ground the Americans made a swamp; where there had been wet ground there was now two feet of water; everywhere was tangled trees, mud, and rocks. Had the Belgians had those axmen in 1940, there might never have been a blitzkrieg. The redcoats made a mile a day, and it took three weeks to push through to Fort Edward, which they finally reached on July 29. The same day, their other supply route reached Fort George. At last, Burgoyne thought with a sigh of relief, through the cursed wilderness and into the Hudson Valley.

One of the things that makes military history so fascinating is the mixture of the physical and the spiritual. The projection of power, actual military operations, can be calculated almost mathematically. This kind of calculation was now to contribute to Burgoyne's undoing.

The general knew, though he had hitherto managed to suppress or ignore it, that he was short of transport. His situation was peculiar in that, though he was virtually in the heart of America, he was dependent largely on waterborne supplies. His route ran up the St. Lawrence, up the Richelieu, south through Lake Champlain, and then along either Lake George or Wood Creek, in both instances to within ten or twelve miles of the Hudson. But for those ten or twelve miles, he needed carts, and then on the Hudson itself, he needed more boats. All of this could be computed: so many men required so many rations per day, and these could be carried so far by so many boats or carts. The boat problem had been solved by the ubiquitous bateaux, of which there were now hundreds on the lakes. For land transport Burgoyne had obtained several hundred two-wheeled carts such as were found in Quebec. These, however, were built of green lumber, and they proved totally inadequate to the demands of service as the army struggled ever farther from its supplies, or from its water terminals. American armies in World War II solved this problem with the truck; Union armies in the American Civil War solved it with the railroad, each of these in its day being an innovation that totally confounded enemies who thought they were far superior militarily. Burgoyne's army was incapable of solving it. As he began to flounder, other factors and incidents started to have their effect as well.

To the westward, St. Leger was running into trouble. He left Fort Ontario, on the southern shore of Lake Ontario, on July 26, and marched up the Oswego River, then came east via Oneida Lake, and arrived at Fort Stanwix on August 3. He expected to find a rotten old fort and a few militia. Instead he found nearly six hundred regulars of the 3rd New

York Continental Regiment, under Colonel Peter Gansevoort, who had busily repaired and strengthened the position. St. Leger, lacking sufficient guns to do anything else, sat down to besiege them. Even at that, he had enough men only for a loose blockade.

Meanwhile, the local militia leader, Nicholas Herkimer, bullied and cajoled some eight hundred of his men to attempt a rescue. These marched up the Mohawk Valley to within ten miles of the fort. At Oriskany, on August 6, as they hurried rashly ahead—Herkimer's subordinates having taken his caution for cowardice—St. Leger's Indians and Tories ambushed them. The mile-long American column walked into a well-laid trap on perfect ground. Some units panicked and fled, pursued by the Indians, but after the first shattering volley, most rushed from the road into the undergrowth on either side, and met the enemy on his own terms. There was a terrific fire fight, interrupted at its middle by a heavy rain. At several points the fighting was hand-to-hand, with knife, hatchet, and musket butt. Many of the Tories were local men, and neighbor strangled neighbor under the blood-spattered leaves; Herkimer himself had a brother on the other side. He was wounded in the leg, and died from it some ten days later. The battle lasted for six hours, after which the Indians had had enough. They broke off, forcing the Tories to retreat as well. The Americans lost almost a third of their men, the British probably less, and the relief column turned back.

However, while the battle was being fought, the Fort Stanwix garrison sallied out, and systematically looted and destroyed the British camp, the latter not having enough men to prevent it. The victors of Oriskany therefore returned to cold comfort.

Nevertheless, the siege went on. When St. Leger summoned the fort to surrender, under threat of the Indians to massacre the garrison and everyone else in the Mohawk Valley, the Americans replied that that was a degrading threat for a British officer to make. St. Leger opened regular siege approaches, and prepared to storm the fort. Meanwhile, Schuyler, back facing Burgoyne, decided to send another relief column, much to the disgust of his New England officers, who accused him of being more concerned for New York than for

New England. Still, Benedict Arnold volunteered to command the expedition, and left with nine hundred men. Just before he got to Fort Stanwix, the British gave up; the already discouraged Indians, further soured by exaggerated news of Arnold's strength, began to desert. Without them St. Leger could not maintain his position, so on August 22 he began his retreat. His disgusted Indian allies scalped British stragglers as they went. Arnold got to Fort Stanwix, shuffled troops about, and headed back in a hurry for the Hudson, where even greater events were afoot.

Burgoyne had hoped that when he reached the Hudson Valley, large numbers of Loyalists would show their true colors, and rally to the Crown. This was a perpetual underlying assumption in the British view of the war. They were always certain that many Americans had been coerced by their more radical neighbors, and that if but given the chance, they would show themselves to be loyal subjects after all. This thinking had been behind their expedition to Charleston in 1776, and would figure again in their later transfer of operations to the southern theater. It was equally prominent in their northern plans. There was indeed some foundation for this, as has already been seen in the divisions of opinion in New York State. Equally, there were those in the Vermont area who were, or who were thought to be, well-disposed to the British. At one point later in the war, some of the Vermont leaders actually negotiated with Canadian authorities over retaining a British connection. But such an assumption was a weak foundation for military operations. To say that many people north of Albany were probably loyal, and that they would probably come out for the King, and that they would probably provide supplies and transport to an army that would starve without them, was simply not a sound way to run a war or a campaign, and Burgoyne was about to pay for it.

A peculiar incident now worked against him. There was one Loyalist who was anxious to meet the invading army. She was a young lady named Jane McCrea, and she had gone from Albany to Fort Edward, because her fiancé was a Tory officer with Burgoyne. On July 27, she and a Mrs. McNeil, an elderly cousin of General Simon Fraser, started out with some Indians for Fort Ann, where the British headquarters were then located. Unfortunately, the Indians fell first to drinking, then to quarreling, on the way, and they shot and scalped Jane McCrea, after which they took the other woman, and Miss McCrea's scalp, to Fort Ann, where the trophy was recognized by her fiancé.

Burgoyne could not punish the Indian, for his allies were unhappy enough already, and might well desert him if he took any action. There was an acerbic exchange of letters between him and General Gates, who had just relieved Schuyler, but this was proof of the difficulty of employing auxiliaries who could not be controlled. The most important consequence of the affair was that the Americans seized upon it, and spread news far and wide of the atrocities one could expect from the British. The story was thoroughly embroidered; the unfortunate victim soon lost her Loyalist status, becoming but a blond- or black-haired beauty in the process, whatever she was in fact. Like summer lightning the story spread through New England and the northern districts, and the inhabitants came out, sure enough, but not for the Crown. In the first weeks of August, all over western Massachusetts and Connecticut, and central New York, little groups of men in homespun, muskets over shoulders, trudged along the tracks and dusty roads. Stopping at farmhouses to drink from the wells, they displayed an ignorance of larger issues, but they were going "agin Burgoyne"; no one was going to scalp *their* wives and kids, by God!

Burgoyne soon received a painful illustration of just what a bunch of outraged farmers could do when they took things personally. There was an idea among the British that they could obtain forage, draft and cavalry horses, and local recruits for their cause by a move eastward into the Connecticut River valley. It was suggested to Burgoyne by General von Riedesel, and the commander in chief then picked it up and expanded upon it. He finally sent about 800 men off; almost half were Germans, mainly the Brunswick dragoons; there was but one company of British regulars, and the remainder were Tories, Canadians, or Indians. The commander was Lieutenant Colonel Friedrich Baum of the dragoon regiment, a man who proved to be a rather poor choice for such a mission.

For one thing, he could not speak a word of English, which would have made it difficult for him to gather up Loyalist supporters. To speak English for him, Burgoyne sent along Philip Skene, but since he had long been involved in border disputes with the Vermonters, he was an almost equally poor choice. Baum's orders were to march to Manchester, Vermont, from there to the Connecticut River, to follow it down to Brattleboro, and then to move back west to Albany, a trip that should otherwise take about two weeks. Baum started on August 11, but made only four miles the first day, presumably because his dragoons were so clumsy, and because he stopped every few hundred yards to dress ranks and neaten up the formation. On the 12th he did not move at all, but on the 13th he made twelve miles. Meanwhile Tory intelligence came in of a Patriot supply depot at Bennington, so Burgoyne amended Baum's orders, and off they all went toward the new objective.

The Americans were reacting to this threat to New England; Vermont was too thin to do much, but New Hampshire voted to raise troops, and the state gave command of them to John Stark, who had recently returned home after resigning from the Continental service from having been passed over by Congress in a round of promotions. Congress compounded the insult by sending up General Benjamin Lincoln, one of the officers jumped over Stark's head. Stark insisted he would serve only as an independent commander, and Lincoln had enough sense and good grace to let him do it. They agreed that Stark's New Hampshiremen would fall in on Burgoyne's left rear and harass him. Stark headed for Bennington, where there were already some Vermonters, the residue of Seth Warner's men from Hubbardton, gathering to fight again.

As Baum advanced toward the little town, his Indians destroyed everything they could not carry off, so no supplies were gained. Baum sent back word that the militia were reported to be congregating, and Burgoyne responded by sending out reinforcements under another German, Lieutenant Colonel Francis Breymann; he started almost immediately, but his troops were grenadiers, heavy, slow-moving infantry, and in the rain they made only five of the twenty-five miles to Bennington, before stopping for the night.

The scene was thus set for what became one of the most typical American victories of the entire war, the kind of amateur-over-professional story that has infused American military tradition ever since. Baum had advanced to contact on the 14th, then took up a rather scattered position on both sides of the Walloomsac River, where his troops threw up several little redoubts, most of them beyond mutual supporting range. It rained on the 15th, and he did nothing, while the Americans felt out the position. On the 16th he sat and waited for his reinforcements, and late in the afternoon, Stark and Warner attacked him. First little parties of Americans filtered over the hills, then there was a general rush, and most of the British positions collapsed; a redoubt manned by the Tories gave way, the Indians discovered things to do elsewhere, many fugitives fled to the redoubt held by the Brunswick dragoons, and in a half hour or so, the Germans were penned in. They held on grimly until they ran out of ammunition; then they drew their heavy cavalry swords, formed a square, and began to cut their way out. They were actually making pretty good progress—the Americans had no bayonets for close action—when Baum went down with a bullet in the stomach, and then resistance collapsed. The Americans practically collapsed with it, stopping to loot, herd prisoners, or simply catch their breath.

At that point Breymann arrived with the German reinforcements on the one side, and Warner brought up fresh militiamen on the other. Both sides collided, there was a very nasty fire fight for three quarters of an hour, and the Germans, running low on ammunition, began to retreat. Breymann finally tried to surrender, but when his drummers beat for a parley, none of the Americans knew what they were doing, and kept on fighting. This force too began to disintegrate, but since he could not surrender, Breymann, wounded, eventually fought his way clear with something more than half his men as darkness fell. When the victory was tallied up, the Americans had suffered about fifty casualties, of some 2,000 participants, while the Germans had lost nearly a thousand, of perhaps 1,600. The Brunswick dragoons were virtually wiped out; 9, out of 374, got back to Burgoyne. It was an absolutely stunning victory, in which all the German mistakes worked against them, and all the American mistakes worked for them.

Gentleman Johnny was now well and truly stuck. His western support, St. Leger, had failed; his eastern raid had failed. Howe was off God knew where—actually afloat off the New Jersey coast—and Burgoyne, two hundred miles from Canada, was in the middle of the wilderness: no supplies coming in, no transport to develop, no "suffering masses" hastening to his colors.

Nonetheless he decided to press on; something might happen to turn his luck for the better, which is what losers always think before they totally ruin themselves. He chose to cross the Hudson—better here than later—abandon his route behind him, and fight his way through to Albany. It took a month to gather enough supplies even to do this, but on September 13, his army a reduced but compact 6,000, he crossed the river and started south.

The American side, of course, was not idle through this period. Led by Gates, the militia, enraged by Jane McCrea's death and heartened by Fort Stanwix and Bennington, began to gather. As Burgoyne moved south from Saratoga, they moved north from Stillwater and dug in along Bemis Heights. Benedict Arnold and a Polish officer, Thaddeus Kosciusko, worked out the position.

The first battle of Saratoga, or Freeman's Farm, was fought on September 19. There was a higher hill on the American left flank, unfortified, and Burgoyne decided to take it and lever them off their line. He sent out General Simon Fraser to make a wide sweep around to the right, supported by several other separate columns. As the British swung around Freeman's Farm, a clearing above their lines, Burgoyne stopped to allow all his forces to develop the proper alignment. American scouts reported all this to Gates, but he did nothing about it. Finally, after repeated urgings and some intemperate language, he allowed Arnold and Daniel Morgan the rifleman to lead out about 3,000 men.

Morgan's riflemen bumped into Burgoyne's center column in the clearing soon after noon, and a fierce fight broke out, in which the American marksmen took a deadly toll of

British officers. Arnold brought up musketmen in support, and the battle blazed back and forth across the farm. Both sides tried repeatedly to charge across the open ground, but neither could make any headway. Meanwhile von Riedesel, over on the British left, turned his men toward the sound of the firing, and eventually came in to support the engaged column. This left Burgoyne's base and supplies vulnerable to an advance by the so-far unengaged American right, although, again, Gates did nothing. Arnold was with him, pleading for more troops, when von Riedesel came into action. The fiery Connecticut general returned to the scene of the battle, but the Germans' arrival had saved the day for the British; the Americans could not muster enough strength around the farm to win back the initiative, and they finally drew back sullenly, leaving Burgoyne in possession of both the battlefield and an advantageous situation for the next day.

There was little doubt that Burgoyne morally dominated Gates, and had he continued on the morrow, he might well have won through. Instead he stalled. He was able to get letters to and from Clinton in New York, and these led him to expect some diversionary relief action from that quarter. So he sat and waited for two and a half weeks. To give the Englishman his due, so did Gates, with even less reason, and thus neither army moved at all. But time was on the Americans' side; during this interval, Burgoyne's force settled out at about 5,000 combatants, what with poor rations, sickness, and desertions, while Gates's numbers increased to nearly 11,000, with more militia arriving to swell his ranks every day. Burgoyne had to act. Unable to decide on how, he attempted a reconnaissance in force, which is a contradiction in terms that soldiers often resort to when they are totally bereft of ideas, but think it must be time to do something.

Meanwhile, unknown to Burgoyne, Sir Henry Clinton had also decided to do something about the situation. Knowing there was nothing to be hoped for from Howe, just then entering Philadelphia, Clinton mustered 4,000 men for a move up the Hudson toward Albany. What with the uncertainty of communications, this operation could not really be coordinated with Burgoyne, and actually had the effect of encouraging the latter in his idleness, rather than stirring him to decisive action.

Clinton, who was an able general once he finally overcame a tendency to make too much of his difficulties, undertook a very creditable little campaign. The Americans had garrisoned and fortified the Hudson Highlands, a dramatic range of hills thirty-some miles above New York City. There were forts, and a chain and boom, above Peekskill, and the same again at West Point. Clinton moved against these in the first week of October, his four thousand men outnumbering Israel Putnam's Continentals and militiamen by at least two to one. The British took forts Montgomery and Clinton—named after the Patriot governor of New York, not the British general—by storm and after substantial losses. On October 7 Clinton broke through the first chain. He was still almost a hundred miles from Albany, and that was as far as he intended to go. However, just as he did this, he got letters from Burgoyne asking for more assistance, so he sent an advance corps upriver by boat. These got as far as Esopus, the present town of Kingston, which they burned on the 16th. They stayed there a few days, venturing a bit farther north, but Clinton felt threatened by Putnam, who had withdrawn north before him, and still barred the way to Albany, his strength increased by rallying militiamen. When Clinton received a letter from Howe, ordering him to fall back on New York and send reinforcements to Philadelphia—Howe fought Germantown on October 4, as Clinton was moving on the Hudson Highland forts—he was more than happy to comply. By then it was all over with Burgoyne, and Clinton's move had served to do nothing more than to confuse the considerations of both generals in the north.

Burgoyne undertook his reconnaissance in force on October 7. By this time he was thoroughly distressed; the Americans were all around him like packs of wolves in winter. His supplies were raided back along the route to Canada; his allies were deserting; his patrols could barely get outside their own lines; he had almost no idea what exactly was going on; his communications with Clinton depended upon a few brave Tories who would carry messages, in some cases, swallowed

in capsules in their stomachs. He had either to go forward or
go back, and there did not seem much choice which.

About all the British general knew for sure was that the
Americans were still entrenched to his front on Bemis Heights,
and that there were a lot of them. He sent out three columns
of troops, about 1,500 strong, light infantry on his right; von
Riedesel with some Germans, General Simon Fraser and the
24th Foot in the center; and a composite force of grenadiers
on the left or inside column. These advanced toward the American position, then drew up in a line; they had about ten field
guns with them, which showed up the absurdity of the idea
of a reconnaissance in force; it was really a feeling attack: go
forward and see what happens.

What happened was Daniel Morgan and his riflemen. The
British had an open field to their front, but woods on either
flank. Gates gave Morgan permission to work his men around
their outside flank; while they did so, two American brigades,
New Hampshire Continentals and New York and Connecticut
militia, under brigadiers Ebenezer Learned and Enoch Poor,
came forward to dispute the field. The Americans substantially
outnumbered the British. When the grenadiers advanced, they
were rocked by well-delivered volleys, sent reeling back, and
then the Yankees swept forward, up a slope across the field,
and right over them. Meanwhile Morgan hit the outside flank
and shattered it, driving the light infantry before him. Von
Riedesel and the center column were left out in the open all
alone; orders to retreat were lost in the American fire.

At this point Benedict Arnold arrived on the scene. He
had been relieved of command after Freeman's Farm, presumably for overshadowing Granny Gates, and had been
hanging about looking for something to do ever since. Now
he took over the battle, and directed the assault upon von
Riedesel's column, which had settled down to a deadly fire
fight, centered around Simon Fraser and the 24th. Arnold
directed Morgan's attention to Fraser's leadership, and Morgan put rifleman Timothy Murphy to stopping it. Fraser fell
mortally wounded, and the stand collapsed. The British and
Germans began to fall back.

The battle might have ended here. Gates certainly wanted

it to, and his contribution to it all consisted largely of sending orders to Arnold to desist, while arguing the merits of the American cause with a dying British officer who had been brought in. But Arnold had his blood up, and so did the men on the field. He led them on against the flanking redoubts of the original British encampment, and here there was storm and volley, both sides taking heavy losses while Arnold galloped madly about the field, trying to find fresh regiments to throw into the attack. Finally the British and Germans, mostly the latter, could stand it no more, and were worn down and overrun. Arnold was wounded in the leg, Burgoyne's men fell back into their main entrenchments, thoroughly trapped now, and the battle died out from exhaustion.

Virtually every episode about this second battle of Saratoga has been disputed, and both Arnold and Gates have vigorous champions and detractors. The battlefield itself has been preserved and restored, though it is one of the more difficult historic sites to make sense of; an Irish-American society raised a monument to Tim Murphy, and there is probably the strangest monument of the entire war, a monument to Arnold's leg, which refers to him only as the "most brilliant soldier of the Continental Army" without mentioning him by name. But whoever deserved credit for doing what, the result was decisive. On the night of the 8th, Burgoyne started to retreat. He dragged his army back to Saratoga, and there took up a strong position, where he made the now-fatal mistake of digging in again.

While the British dug, the Americans took up a tardy pursuit, and by the 12th Burgoyne was virtually surrounded; from then on, it was just a matter of getting through the formalities. Burgoyne held a council of war, a euphemistic device by which a commander concedes defeat and attempts to spread the blame for it. His officers agreed it was time to ask for terms.

There followed an interlude of several days, while both sides sought to outmaneuver each other, with demands and concessions fluctuating on the basis of news and rumors of Clinton's activities to the south. The upshot was a "convention" rather than a surrender, but the result was the same. On October 17 the British army laid down its arms and passed into captivity. Gentleman Johnny, splendidly attired, played his part to the full, and each general tried to outdo the other in the extravagant compliments of the day. The less effusive New Englanders wanted to tar and feather Burgoyne, and massacre his few remaining Indians, but the surrender ceremonies finally went off without a hitch.

This was Burgoyne's major appearance on the world stage, and it played to mixed reviews. In London there was confusion. Leading opposition politicians openly and shamefully rejoiced at their country's defeat, and gleefully anticipated how they would bring the government down. North, Germain, and above all the King were dismayed, but grimly determined to hang on. But London's reaction turned out to be less important than that of Paris. The news there was received with unrestrained delight. The streets were illuminated, and Franklin and the other Americans were hailed and congratulated wherever they appeared. Early in the new year, on February 6, France and the United States signed an offensive and defensive alliance. Britain responded by declaring war on the ancient enemy. The American Revolution became a world war.

CHAPTER TEN

The War at Sea

W HETHER OR not French intervention might be decisive was a matter of sea power, but indeed, the entire war was that. Great Britain was a thalassocracy, its power dependent not on land force, but on the ability to dominate the oceans of the world, to keep the waters safe for its own trade, and to deny that trade to its enemies. To the British, this was a truism so obvious that it was not even examined in any theoretical sense for another hundred years: they did what they did because they *knew* that they had to do it. France had armies, Britain had navies; that was the way the world worked.

The concept of command of the sea, fully enunciated by British, American, and a few French theorists only at the end of the nineteenth century, was a somewhat elusive one, often appearing as fluid as the medium on which it was exercised. Ideally, at a logical extreme, it would mean that a navy totally dominated all the waters of a given area, so that an enemy could not even get out of his harbors. There were but a few short periods in history when the British approached this: when they blockaded the American coast in the War of 1812;

when they patrolled the coasts of France after Trafalgar in 1805; when they kept the German High Seas Fleet bottled up in its bases in 1915 and 1916. Most of the time, however, control of the sea could not be this near totality. Weather and technology both militated against it. An inferior enemy could usually manage to slip a squadron out to sea, as the French and Americans did repeatedly in their wars with Britain, and as the Germans did occasionally during both world wars. Beyond that, it was almost always possible for the weaker force to get single vessels to sea, to prey on British or allied commerce. This might not be capable of producing a decisive effect: the great American theorist of sea power, Admiral Mahan, argued that it was a waste of time, and that only a battle fleet was able to challenge for and attain command of the sea. German submariners very nearly, but not quite, proved him wrong.

If preying on commerce, *guerre de course*, as the French called it, could not achieve decisive results, it could prove both annoying and embarrassing. The loss of merchant ships to enemy raiders, either national or private armed vessels, the privateers, caused shortages at home and abroad, made prices rise and insurance rates go up, and therefore gave governments heartburn. Throughout its wars the Royal Navy, attempting to concentrate on the enemies' battle fleets, when they had any, was always distracted by the necessity for protecting British commerce, and at some points, when the opposition's main force either was nonexistent or already contained, commerce protection became virtually the primary task of the navy, as in the battle against American raiders in the War of 1812 or against the U-boats in the Battle of the Atlantic.

The infant United States had not the slightest chance of overturning British sea power; there was never even a thought of it. But the Americans could harass the British, they could obtain stores for themselves by capturing them at sea from their enemy, and they could make fortunes in the process. Very quickly they set out to do all three of these.

Shut up in Boston in 1775, the British were resupplied by sea. Reinforcements arrived from Britain and Quebec, forage and food came in from coastal areas whose merchants were still willing to sell to the British, and it was immediately obvious that ships and sailors were a necessity to the Revolution. General Washington, using his powers as commander in chief, commissioned several small coastal schooners, and sent them out after prizes. The first American naval vessel was thus the schooner *Hannah*, though there are people in Machias, Maine, who insist their town was first with a schooner of its own that fought the British off the little port. In any case, *Hannah* and her colleagues were soon bringing in British prizes, snapped up off Boston Harbor, and making a general nuisance of themselves, both to the British, and to Washington, who found his new sailors distressingly indisposed to take orders, and more inclined to play pirate.

Meanwhile, in Philadelphia, Congress was also deciding, somewhat grudgingly, that it needed a national navy. John Adams suggested the idea in October 1775; the New England members tended to like it, while the rest were not too interested. Nonetheless, a Naval or Marine Committee was set up, a proposal was brought forth, and finally a navy, and then a marine corps as well, were enacted. There were several problems with this, the most significant of them being in the areas of competition, administration, personnel, and equipment.

The competition came from two sources, private enterprise and the separate states. It had long been the practice in the imperial wars for governments to issue commissions to private individuals, merchant ship owners and captains. These would then go out raiding enemy commerce, to the annoyance of the enemy and to their own enrichment. Indeed, many early American fortunes were made by privateers in the old French wars. Most ships in those unsettled times carried some amount of armament, and it took little more than a piece of paper to transform a merchant vessel into a quasi ship of war. The chief limitation on the privateers was that they did not like to fight. Their reason for existence was the snapping up of merchant ships weaker than themselves, and there was no profit in lying yardarm to yardarm and fighting to a conclusion with a ship of the Royal Navy. Faced with that prospect, the privateers usually chose the better part of valor. The United States produced hundreds of privateers during the war, some of them very successful. The chief difficulty they presented to the Americans themselves was that they absorbed seamen who might otherwise have gone into the navy. The life of a privateersman was both far more rewarding, and generally far less risky, than serving in the navy itself, so most sailors preferred the former whenever possible.

The individual states also developed their own navies, again in competition with a national service. Connecticut and South Carolina both had good little navies, and Massachusetts and Pennsylvania, even though the latter had no coastline, both had substantial fleets. So here again there was competition for resources, and crossed lines of command between the several services. Nicholas Biddle, for example, one of the first men appointed a captain in the Continental Navy, had earlier commanded a river galley in the Pennsylvania State Navy.

When the national navy was established, Congress was at a loss how to run it. For most of the war, the job was done by a committee, whose name, numbers, and personnel fluctuated as time went on. At one point the Marine Committee had thirteen members, one from each state, an awkward arrangement that encouraged members to be present more to look after their own parochial interests than for any larger purpose. For instance, they squabbled incessantly about which state was going to get which contract for building ships, one of the earlier forms of pork-barreling in American politics. The committee eventually became all but moribund, and by the end of the war, the navy was being administered as a sideline by the de facto financial minister, the great Philadelphian Robert Morris.

Who should get commands was as much a subject of contention as who should build ships. There were in the United States a great many men who had seafaring experience, as masters or owners of their own vessels. So there was a tendency to follow the accepted eighteenth-century precept that if a man could make money, he must be smart enough to be an officer. The first commander in chief of the Continental Navy, therefore, was a successful Rhode Island merchant, Esek Hopkins. It did his candidacy no harm that his brother Stephen was Rhode Island's member on the committee; indeed, Stephen also secured a captaincy for Esek's son

John, adding nepotism to the pork-barreling. But just as in the army, it would take the test of war itself to show who was a good commander and who was not. While Biddle was one of the first captains commissioned, the senior lieutenant of the new navy was a Scottish adventurer named John Paul, who added the surname Jones to cover his tracks.

The ships of the little navy were as mixed a bag as the officers. The first American flagship was the *Alfred,* a converted merchantman formerly named *Black Prince;* the only other full-rigged ship—properly speaking a "ship" has three masts, with square sails on all three—was the *Columbus,* a name presumably more impressive than that of her former life when she was the merchant ship *Sally.* Both of these were transformed into frigates of 24 guns. In addition there were two brigs, two sloops, and two schooners, the little *Wasp* and *Fly,* both with 8 guns.

The Americans did have a substantial shipbuilding industry, one of the few types of manufacture that had flourished under the imperial connection. All along the northern coast, down as far as the Chesapeake Bay area, there were yards capable of turning out well-built vessels. Most of the yards were small, with a capacity for sloops and schooners and other coastal craft, but there were also those that could build vessels of greater size.

During these later years of the age of sail, the arbiter of naval warfare was the ship of the line, that is, a ship big enough, strongly enough built and heavily enough armed, to lie in the line of battle. The largest of such ships went up to 120 guns, but there were few of them in the entire world. The lower end of the scale was about a 60-gunner, and the standard was the 74, with two full gun decks plus extra guns on forecastle and quarterdeck. The Americans knew that they could not challenge the Royal Navy at this level. They did decide to build three ships of the line, but even this proved beyond their limited resources. Only one of them, the *America,* was actually completed. She was laid down at Portsmouth, New Hampshire, in May 1777, and not launched until November 1782. Preserved drafts show a handsome ship, but she did not do well. Immediately upon launching, she was given to the

French, in return for one they had lost, and she was broken
up a few years later.

The ship of choice in the American navy, throughout its
sailing years, was the frigate. Next below the ship of the line,
these were vessels with one full gun deck rather than two, and
ranged from a lower limit of perhaps 24 guns, up to about 50.
The standard frigate of the Revolution carried 32 guns. The
big, famous American frigates such as the *Constitution*, which
was rated as a 44 but actually carried 50 guns, came along in
the 1790's. The American builders turned out some excep-
tionally fine frigates. The government decided initially to build
thirteen of them, five 32's, five 28's, and three 24's, which
would have given the nascent navy three distinct classes of
ships for operations. They were generally much admired by
seamen, and the *Hancock*, built at Newburyport, Massachusetts, enjoyed the universal reputation of being "the finest and
fastest frigate in the world." She served only a few months in
the Continental Navy, for she was captured by the British in
mid-1777. Renamed *Iris*, she made a fortune in prizes for her
British captains, before being captured by the French in 1781.
She then served them for several years, and was finally hulked
at Toulon, where she was blown up during the French Revolution. In their David-against-Goliath contest, the Americans
lacked neither good men nor good ships.

But Goliath had much more of both. The British began
the war with 131 ships of the line, and 139 smaller vessels,
frigates and brigs and suchlike. Most of these were actually
out of commission and in poor condition, the navy having
been struck, as usual in Britain, by a governmental passion
for economy during the years of peace. Ships had been allowed
to rot, dockyard stores had run down, sailors were beached
and officers dismissed. The Admiralty, which administered
the navy, was in a classic muddle, and the whole operation
was coasting on its past reputation and glory. Nonetheless it
was still a formidable force, with substantial elements on the
North American station, ranging from Newfoundland to Halifax and down to the Caribbean.

One authority has suggested that the Royal Navy alone,
with a few landing parties and some marines, ought to have

been able to nip the entire Revolution in the bud. The navy did indeed bombard Falmouth, Maine, and Gloucester and New Bedford in Massachusetts, it quickly scooped up the New England fishing fleets and West India traders, and decimated the whaling industry based on Nantucket. But the navy was not configured to do more than that; indeed, to do more than that never occurred to it. Standing armies have always been perceived as a danger to the civil power, but standing navies have never been perceived as such, and the thought of using sailors and marines ashore as an aid to preserving royal authority hardly crossed anyone's mind. Rather than doing anything positive, the navy stayed offshore and said to the soldiers, "Oh, isn't that your problem? Let us know if you need any help."

So the navy was there to help, to bring British and Germans over from Europe, to evacuate Boston, to carry expeditions to Charleston, and New York, and Quebec, to build boats on Lake Champlain, and to carry Howe from New York to Philadelphia. Most of this it did competently. But it did not exercise a great deal of initiative, on a strategic or a tactical level. Strategically, the best it could think of was that it would like Newport for a base; tactically, it never crossed an admiral's mind that, with hundreds of ships sitting in New York Bay, a few ships' boats could with ease have towed vessels into the East River, and cost George Washington his army after the Battle of Long Island. On sea, Sir Richard Howe proved about as competent, and as uninspired, a commander as his brother was proving ashore.

The Americans were more ambitious. In its first orders to Esek Hopkins, Congress directed him to take his squadron, all eight ships with less than a hundred little popguns, and clear first the Chesapeake, then the Carolina coasts, and then go up and drive the British away from Rhode Island. This was, to be fair, before the great British armada of 1776 had arrived, but it was still a heavy assignment. Hopkins immediately decided to pay no attention to it—commanders always had to have a discretionary clause in their orders in those days of slow communications—and as soon as he got his ships to sea, he sailed south for the Bahamas. There he handily captured the island of New Providence, now Nassau, with its fort and substantial military stores. This little action provided the first battle of the Continental Marines.

Unfortunately for Hopkins, on the way home five of his little ships fell in with a small British frigate, H.M.S. *Glasgow*, 20. For three hours the Britisher beat away at the Americans, several times raking *Alfred*, before he made his escape. The American performance was so poor that Hopkins and a couple of his captains were court-martialed, a procedure which made room for John Paul Jones to get his first command. The New Providence expedition was the first, and practically the last, fleet operation the Americans mounted during the entire war. Everything after that was done either by single ships, or by small squadrons that happened to come together for some ad hoc cooperation.

The effect of this was that the British Goliath was attacked less by an American David than by a swarm of Yankee bees. The American naval vessels were used as independent raiders, and whenever they could get to sea, they went looking for a fight. The privateers quartered the trade routes, snapping up prizes, and between the two of them, they caused the British a great deal of pain.

It worked both ways, of course. During the war the Americans commissioned more than 2,000 privateers, and they took more than 3,000 British vessels. The Admiralty was forced to provide convoy escort service around the British Isles themselves, and even for the packet services across the Irish Sea, something that had never been necessary before. But a good half of the American privateers were in turn taken by the British, and American merchant vessels were practically chased off the seas altogether. Thousands of American sailors languished and died in British prison hulks and in overcrowded jails in Halifax, the West Indies, and Britain.

The infant navy turned in some notable single-ship actions. In 1777 Captain Nicholas Biddle was given command of the new frigate *Randolph*, 32, and made a successful cruise in the West Indies, taking a Royal Navy ship and her convoy of three merchantmen. In early 1778 he broke out of blockade at Charleston, South Carolina, and got to sea again. On March 7 he sighted a sail and made for it. Unfortunately for him, it turned out to be a ship of the line, H.M.S. *Yarmouth*, 64. The Britisher not only had twice as many guns, but they were of course heavier as well. Instead of fleeing, Biddle ranged up alongside, and the two ill-matched ships exchanged fierce broadsides for about twenty minutes, until *Randolph* suddenly blew up, killing her captain and all but four of her crew, 311 men gone in the wink of an eye.

Of the thirteen Continental frigates, none survived the war. *Hancock, Boston, Providence, Delaware, Raleigh, Trumbull,* and *Virginia* were all captured; *Warren, Montgomery, Congress, Washington* and *Effingham* were burned to prevent their loss, some as they were still fitting out in Philadelphia or up the Hudson. And *Randolph* blew up in battle. This was fairly typical; the same sort of fates befell later vessels authorized by Congress, and illustrated that the small American navy simply could not stand the strain. Meanwhile the British, all the time losing ships in action, or by storm or accident, nearly doubled their numbers, so that by the end of the war they had gone from 270 to 468 ships, not counting the two hundred the Americans took during the course of the war. The Royal Navy could afford to lose ships and keep on going; the Continental Navy could not.

It was against this overall losing record that the single-ship victories shone out like stars on a dark night. John Paul Jones took sixteen prizes in a cruise in his first command, the *Providence*; promoted to the new sloop of war *Ranger,* and based in France, he harried the British coasts and even made some slightly discreditable raids ashore. He made up for these by taking H.M.S. *Drake* in a brilliant fight in the Irish Sea. Then, taking command of an old French East Indiaman converted into a frigate and named the *Bonhomme Richard,* a French compliment to Benjamin Franklin, he achieved his greatest fame by taking the British frigate *Serapis* in September 1779. The terrific battle against heavy odds, and Jones's immortal retort to a request for surrender—"I have not yet begun to fight!"—transformed him into America's first enduring naval hero. His subsequent treatment by the republic he helped found was pretty shabby—once home, he never again sailed under the American flag—but that could be said for most of the men who won American independence.

*   *   *

The French entry into the war naturally changed the over-all dimensions of the conflict. Britain was now involved in one of her classic wars, similar to those she had been waging against France ever since 1689. What was different about the naval aspect of it was that, for the first time since the 1690's, the French were prepared for a naval war, and were indeed in better shape for one than the British were.

A surprising aspect of the Anglo-French naval struggles is that in many respects the French were usually ahead of the British. Their central administration was at least as efficient; their means of procuring seamen, and providing for them between campaigns, were far more advanced; and their ship-building and design was infinitely superior to the British— who avidly sought French captures for their own navy. Their basic problem was that France was first and foremost a land power, and naval affairs therefore always took secondary importance with them. The result was a tradition of defeat. The French were better than the British in every respect but the most important: the British always won.

It happened that the French had taken a severe beating, both by land and by sea, during the Seven Years' War. Their performance had been so bad that it gave rise to a vigorous spirit of reform, and in the sixties and early seventies the French armed forces were startlingly transformed. In the army the theories and systems were developed that ultimately produced Napoleon. In the navy, the reforms of the Duc de Choiseul resulted in a force that, in numbers and equipment, was better than anything the French had had for years. There were four major arsenals, eighty ships of the line ready for action, 67,000 seamen, and a highly trained corps of "seamen gunners." There was an advanced signal code, and for the last several years the French had been able to practice squadron maneuvers, something they had seldom managed before when at war with Britain. Their only real deficiency was an officer corps that was still too class-conscious to put seamanlike duties first, but they were going to present Britain with a truly formidable adversary.

Eventually, Spain and the Netherlands declared war on Britain as well, and the Baltic powers, Russia, Denmark, and

Sweden, combined in the "Armed Neutrality," a coalition to protest British highhandedness, which was about as close to a declaration of war as they could get without actually doing so. None of these were particularly active, however, and what little intervention they did offer had more effect on the peace process at the end of the war, than on the fighting itself. The situation in the Baltic, for example, made it even more difficult than usual for the British to obtain naval stores. Many of these had come from the American colonies, and deprived both of that source, and the alternative market in the Baltic, the British were pressured heavily to make peace.

The belligerence of the European powers entailed a shifting of British strategic perceptions. Until France declared war, the British could concentrate their efforts on dominating American waters, blockading the coast, and snapping up privateers and naval vessels as close to the eastern seaboard as possible. The French before Saratoga were willing to provide surreptitious assistance to the odd American privateer, but would do little officially. After 1777, however, things changed radically. French ports were thrown open to the Americans, with results such as Jones's cruises around the British Isles, and Americans operating out of French and then even Dutch Channel bases were a serious annoyance.

On a larger scale, the British had to worry about French battle fleets, not only in the West Indies and off the American coast, but also in the Mediterranean and in home waters. The near doubling of British ships in service was more than matched by the extension of their areas of responsibility. Their ships of the line, for example, were not of much use in America; they were expensive to man and maintain, and they were relatively unhandy for chasing privateers or even frigates. But when the French had eighty of the line, and the Spanish several dozen more, and all of them were out roaming the seas in heavy squadrons, then the British had to be in a position to match them. From a naval point of view, once France came in, America became very much a secondary matter. In fact, the navy virtually conceded that the American war was lost, and concentrated instead on the larger issue, the old line of beating the French.

Naturally America remained one of the scenes of action, and what the French might do in aid of the rebels, and what the Royal Navy must do to offset that, continued to be of consequence. But from 1779 on, more traditional strategies asserted themselves, and attention focused on the West Indies; the Mediterranean, where Gibraltar was besieged for nearly four years; India, where the French sought to recoup losses from the last war; and home waters, where control of the Channel was the be-all and end-all of British strategic thought.

Of these five theaters of war, the British lost in only one. The culminating naval action of the war was fought at Les Saintes, in the West Indies. Gibraltar survived its siege. A mediocre Admiral, Sir Edward Hughes, held the Indian Ocean against a brilliant French Admiral, Pierre-André de Suffren de Saint-Tropez. The Channel was never seriously threatened. Only in America did Britain lose local command of the sea, in a joint Franco-American campaign that was one of the truly great strategic combinations of the eighteenth century. It meant everything to the Americans. To the British navy, it was but one point out of five. By their standards, winning four to one was not bad at all. It was all a matter of where the observer stood when looking at the picture, whether he saw the whole of it or just a part.

As 1777 drew to a close and France moved toward war, therefore, the Royal Navy girded its loins to do that which it had always done before. The Americans, on land or on sea, were immensely heartened by receiving foreign recognition, and inevitably in its train, overt foreign aid. American ships, both naval and privateers, were at sea and inflicting losses on the enemy. Gates had just won Saratoga, and the defeated British northern army, known after its surrender as the "Convention Army," was wending its weary way toward Boston. General Washington had lost Philadelphia—Franklin in Paris, told that Howe had captured Philadelphia, had replied knowingly, "No, Philadelphia has captured Howe ..."—but his army had recovered quickly and he had maneuvered it creditably at Germantown, before going into winter quarters around Valley Forge. All still hung in the balance. For both sides, the new year would bring new problems and new prospects.

CHAPTER ELEVEN

Progression
and Regression

THE CHRISTMAS season of 1777 featured joyous news from the north, where General Burgoyne's army was on its way to captivity; and good news from overseas, where the French were moving closer and closer to an open declaration of alliance and war. Meanwhile, Sir William Howe and his army settled in Philadelphia, being welcomed, dined and feted by the prosperous, peace-loving, and ostensibly loyal element of the population. Outside the city, a mere twenty miles away, General Washington and his army had taken up winter quarters at Valley Forge, among the rolling hills and hollows of the Pennsylvania countryside.

Valley Forge is etched on the American mind, alongside the bloody footprints in the snow outside Trenton. School-children and tourists by the thousand visit the historic site— in summer, when the grass is green and the winds warm, to watch college students in period rags putter around outdoor fires. As usual, past reality was a little different from present recollection.

The Continental Army remained six months in the campsite, and of some ten thousand soldiers who wintered there, one in four died. Many men did no more for the American cause than report to their regiments, fall ill, and die miserably. It was a strange, paradoxical time, for the winter almost destroyed the Americans, but the remnant that marched forth in the spring was a better army than it had been half a year earlier.

The ruin was not caused by the British. They were quite happy where they were; the rigors of winter movement held no charm for them, and except for the occasional harassing patrol, they stayed in the city, concentrating on army politics and amateur theatricals. Nor, oddly enough, was it particularly caused by the weather. It was actually a fairly mild winter, though the term "mild" often depends upon whether the speaker is from Massachusetts or North Carolina. And of course for soldiers living in the field, a solid frost and snow may be infinitely preferable to recurrent rain and mud.

What threatened to ruin the army, rather, was the near-complete breakdown of its supply system, the bankruptcy of the Continental treasury, and the preference of local suppliers for British cash over American promises. The first of these resulted from odd events in the Quartermaster General's Department. Its chief, Major General Thomas Mifflin, was in some respects a very able officer. He and Washington got along nicely, and at one point he had been an aide-de-camp to the commander in chief. During the winter of 1776 he had performed very well indeed, but for some reason he had fallen out with his chief during the 1777 campaign. Washington's reluctance to relieve him, combined with his increasing preference for military politics instead of his duty, led the always tenuous supply system to fall apart.

Mifflin actually resigned as Quartermaster General in November, but by then the damage was done. There simply were no stores for the soldiers as they went into their encampments. Washington replaced Mifflin with Nathanael Greene—who cordially disliked his predecessor—and Greene set to work with a will, but he had to do it all from a standing start. Meanwhile the miserable soldiers hunkered among the hills, foraged as they could, built huts and lean-tos, and tried to stay alive on the little straggle of food that came in. Several times the army ran out of meat altogether, once for six successive days, and there was a constant shortage of clothing. Washington complained to Congress at one point that nearly half his army was naked, and men had to exchange clothing so that squads could turn out of their huts. Disease was rampant, and medical supplies were nonexistent. Camp sanitation was poor, though the area was fairly high and well-drained. This last was of course standard; it was more noteworthy in the eighteenth century when sanitation was good for an encamped force, because that so seldom happened.

The larger problem was bankruptcy. Congress might harangue Washington about operating more effectively, and he might complain bitterly that he could not operate if he were not given the wherewithal to do it, but the simple fact remained that the young United States had no money. Neither troops nor officers could be paid—there was no money; supplies could not be purchased—there was no money; uniforms could not be made up—there was no money. War is a tremendously expensive process, wasteful of both men and resources, and only under certain rare conditions can it be made to show a profit. Those conditions did not exist in the American Revolution. Congress could not tax, and the states, which could, all insisted they were broke already. The value of currency had depreciated to the point of invisibility, hard money had practically disappeared among the Patriots, and paper money was not worth the paper. The national government had no credit; it had all been exhausted long ago. So the Americans limped from one expedient to another, cadging little loans from France, and Spain, and Dutch banking houses, and hoping for a windfall, such as they got when France finally declared war.

The real tragedy here lay in the fact that there was plenty of money about, and plenty of supplies: it was just that the American government, and its starving and freezing army, had neither of them. The British did not run short during the winter; they paid hard cash for their goods, and they always found plenty of sellers willing to do business with them. In fact, many items from the immediate Philadelphia area were carted all the way across New Jersey and sold in New York to the British. The state of Connecticut actually took rather better care of its units at Valley Forge than did most states, but it also put a ceiling on the price of beef, and Connecticut farmers refused to sell their cattle to the government purchasing agents. Merchants throughout the states held back uniforms and camp items, kettles and medical supplies and suchlike, waiting for prices to go up, and demanding cash, gold and silver and copper, on the barrelhead. Governments might come, and they might go, but balance sheets went on forever.

Except on rare and absolutely desperate occasions, Washington resisted the temptation to seize supplies by requisition. He regarded that, correctly, as the beginning of the end. For one thing, that sort of treatment was supposed to be what the Revolution was against. On a more practical level, requisitioning had the effect of ruining relations between the army and the civilian populace whom it presumably existed to protect. A farmer who had his horses or cattle taken by the army without compensation was not apt to be ardent in the Patriot cause. There were times when it had to be done, and was, but not if there were any possible alternative, including letting the troops go hungry. But as long as the army would or could not seize goods it needed, and as long as those who had the goods would not sacrifice them, soldiers starved and froze. Many writers have remarked that Valley Forge was as much a symbol of American greed as of American endurance.

Yet positive things happened there as well. The army learned at last to drill and act as regulars. The American cause had attracted many foreign soldiers, some of them greedy adventurers, such as Coudray; some of them high-principled amateurs, such as Lafayette; and some of them ordinary, competent, professional soldiers, such as Friedrich von Steuben. A German veteran of Frederick the Great's army in the Seven Years' War, Steuben had the invaluable background of both staff and troop service. When the Revolution broke out, he was in the employ of a bankrupt German petty prince, and after trying unsuccessfully to get into several other armies, he borrowed enough money to get to America. Late in February of 1778 he showed up at Valley Forge as a temporarily unpaid volunteer, able to speak little French and less English. Nonetheless, he was put to work revising a contemporary drill manual, simplifying it for American usage. Then he started drilling troops. He began with a company of one hundred, putting them through their paces and cursing in three languages— for some reason, the words most readily acquired in a new language are curse words—and then went on to spread his teachings throughout the army. For the first time, the soldiers all got a standardized system of drill and movement, one that they could actually make sense of. Steuben became very popular, and his characterization of American troops, in a letter to a European friend, is often quoted: "You say to your soldier, 'Do this,' and he does it. I say to my soldier, 'This is why you should do this,' and *then* he does it." Washington soon made him inspector general of the army. He served the American cause well, and his influence was one of the few positive things to come out of Valley Forge.

While the troops suffered, the commander in chief fought, not with the British this time, but with Congress, and for his own position. There was through the winter a constant pulling and hauling with the peripatetic Congress. Returning from Baltimore in March of 1777, then forced by Howe to move to York, almost impotent and very conscious of it, Congress was even more assertive than ever about its prerogatives; the millionaire can afford to exchange pleasantries with the tradesman, while the man on the verge of bankruptcy must preserve his aloofness. A Congressional committee consulted with Washington about army reorganization, the always contentious issue of officers' appointments, and things such as that. But the real problem was whether or not the Virginian should remain in his command, a problem that burst open in the infamous and misnamed Conway Cabal.

The affair is misnamed because Thomas Conway, an Irish Catholic officer from the French service, was both a fool and a useful dupe for those who may or may not have had a real plot to get rid of Washington. The root of the trouble lay in Gates's success against Burgoyne, matched against Washington's defeat by Howe, and the desire of some of the northerners in Congress, especially Sam Adams, and the Pennsylvanians Mifflin and Benjamin Rush, to replace Washington with Gates, or possibly Conway, or someone they liked better and presumably could manipulate more. It all began with a letter whose contents were leaked by Gates's aide-de-camp, James Wilkinson, one of the perpetual troublemakers of the early republic, a letter in which Conway purportedly referred to Washington as incompetent. There followed charge and countercharge, and a barrage of "He said that you said that I said . . ." and "I deny that I said that you said that he said . . ." It was very unedifying. Eventually Washington laid several separate files of correspondence before the Military Committee of Congress, which clearly revealed Gates and Conway to be small-minded schemers, and unsuccessful ones at that. The evidence was so condemnatory that even the civilians had to acknowledge they were on the wrong trail, and the affair blew over. Conway, meanwhile promoted far beyond his real merits—he did have some—was treated so coolly by Washington and his fellow officers that he offered his resignation, only to be dismayed when it was quickly accepted.

So by the spring of 1778, the opening of the campaigning season at last, a tough little American army, well-trained if poorly equipped, led by a seasoned and increasingly secure commander, emerged to do battle with the British. But then, they had their troubles too.

Sir William Howe used the defeat of Burgoyne at Saratoga as an excuse to get out of a war of which he had long been tired. He wrote home, saying the government had not supported him, which was not entirely true, and that it had ignored his advice throughout the war, which was not entirely false. But there was more to it than that. His stock, which had risen with the capture of Philadelphia, had plunged after Germantown, a silly little battle in which neither side did well. One wag in London commented that "Any other General in the world than General Howe would have beaten General Washington, and any other General in the world but General Washington would have beaten General Howe." That may have been a bit unfair, but then quips always are. The government had lost faith in Howe, and he in them. He was just sick of the whole business, and it was time to go.

He left America three years exactly from his arrival in Boston aboard the *Cerberus;* his officers gave him a splendid send-off, but at home he had to face a parliamentary inquiry into his conduct of the war. Such inquiries are seldom concerned with facts, and in this one opponents and supporters of the government's policy ranged widely and concluded nothing. Howe did not come out well—he was even turned out of his parliamentary seat in the next election—but that mattered little. The war went on.

By this time, of course, it was an altogether new war, for France had come in, and the British government faced a completely different constellation of forces. As usual, they faced it disunited and at cross-purposes. Militarily, they decided upon an essentially defensive stance. Howe was succeeded by Sir Henry Clinton, a bride instead of a bridesmaid at last, but one with a basically negative role. Clinton was told he should defeat Washington decisively, an instruction that meant nothing at all; barring that, he should concentrate upon American ports and shipping facilities, and even be prepared to launch attacks against the French West Indies. This meant giving up Philadelphia, which the government was willing to do, and it might also mean giving up everything in America, and the government was willing to do that too, if it had to. In the worst-case scenario, the British would fall back to Halifax in the north and the West Indies in the south, and continue the war from there.

They were also ready once again to talk to the Americans. A peace commission was sent to negotiate with Congress, but it was not told what the soldiers and sailors were planning to do, so it played a hand of whose weakness the commissioners were themselves unaware. They offered in effect to recognize the semi-independence of the United States, as a component within the British Empire, acknowledging Royal authority but taxing themselves, a mishmash of things that bore some resemblance to the later dominion status of British imperial territories in the nineteenth century. But the Americans could read a map as well as the British could, and trying to negotiate while your own army was abandoning Philadelphia and the French were expected any day was a profitless task. The Americans were simply not interested any more.

Neither, as it happened, was Lord North. He was as tired of the war, and the futile parliamentary wrangling, as General

Howe was; the difference between them was that King George would not let North resign. No one else could manage Parliament for him; the possible prime ministers among the opposition openly exulted in American victories, and the King to his credit and sorrow could not tolerate them. The government limped along from expedient to expedient. Oddly enough, popular opinion and support swung in their favor when France declared war. Money was more readily voted, and recruits came forth more eagerly. This was war against the old enemy, and Englishmen understood that; this was a real war, not some poor niggling little thing against fellow Englishmen, where there was a constant stream of minor victories signifying nothing, this suppurating sore in the body of the family. Not that increased popular support seemed to matter much. That was the trouble: nothing they did mattered much. Their policy was no policy; drift and muddle, search for expedients and hope for miracles. Maybe they would get lucky.

But it remained maddening. At the end of 1776, after capturing New York City and winning his campaign, Howe said he needed twenty thousand more troops to win the war; at the end of 1777, after capturing Philadelphia and winning his campaign, he said he needed eighty thousand more troops to win the war. If the British kept winning like this they would soon be as bankrupt as the Americans were.

Sir Henry Clinton was not the man to breathe victory into a dying cause. He was a solid administrator, and a reasonably capable field commander. He had had a strong dose of reality, and had an even stronger appreciation of the difficulties that faced him at every turn. He had been involved in the war ever since the siege of Boston, waiting in the wings for the supreme command, holding a dormant commission in his back pocket. In the British Army of the day, there were substantive ranks, and then there were all sorts of avenues by which a man might achieve command for some particular purpose. There was temporary rank, local rank, and brevet rank; for example, Wolfe at Quebec in 1759 was only a lieutenant colonel, but he held a brevet colonelcy, temporary rank as a brigadier, and local rank as a general. In Howe's army around New York, Clinton was actually a major general, with the local rank of lieutenant general, and the further local rank of full general. This was because he was substantively ranked by the commander of the German forces, General Leopold von Heister, and the British government did not want Howe succeeded by a German should something happen to him. So Clinton was given the dormant commission as commander in America, to become effective if Howe became incapacitated. Now in early 1778, too late to change the course of the war, he had his chance.

Under the new circumstances, with the French in, and in view of the new British plan for continuing the war, vague though it might be, Clinton's first real operation was the abandonment of Philadelphia. His instructions were to go back to New York by sea, and also to send five thousand men to the West Indies for operations there. But Clinton had had enough of being harassed by his own side, and in an unusual show of independence, he decided to do neither.

The West Indies was an obsession with British governments in the eighteenth century. For a hundred years or more it had been the very treasury of empire, pouring sugar into the mother country and making fortunes for slave traders, sugar plantation owners, and merchants. Many of these had seats in Parliament, where the "sugar interest" constituted a formidable force that always had to be assuaged by the ministry. As soon as a war began, the sugar interests screamed for protection of their islands. When the war went well, they intrigued for expeditions to capture the French sugar islands. When the war was won, they intrigued to have the conquests returned to France, because they feared their cheaper competition. They were a constant nuisance, and in every war, at their behest, Britain shoveled troops into the islands, to die by the thousands from malaria and yellow fever. With better sense than most British generals showed, Clinton simply ignored that part of his orders.

He also decided to march overland to New York City. To go by sea was to travel 225 miles, at the mercy of the weather—look what had happened to Howe—and of the French, who were suspected to be lurking about in some force. Not only that, but Clinton did not have sufficient shipping to move his whole army and its equipment, followers, Tories, and all the other junk the British had acquired, in one move. It would have to be done by stages, which was simply not feasible. To go by land meant a seventy-mile march across New Jersey to Sandy Hook or Perth Amboy, just across from Staten Island. That might be a hard march, but it was not at all impracticable; the British had just done forty miles in a couple of days chasing Lafayette and a detachment back to Valley Forge.

So Clinton gathered up his army. The trains, heavy guns and baggage, sick, and about three thousand loyal Philadelphians were sent by ship. Throughout the city there were scenes of anguish and exultation. The King's people had flown high during the occupation, parading their loyalties with their balls and intimate dinner parties for those elegant British officers. Now the biter was bit, and they packed in haste and departed in tears, while the Patriots watched them go with undisguised satisfaction. By late May everyone knew the British were going, and on June 16 the move began. It took them two days to cross the Delaware, but by the 18th they were ready for the march, 10,000 troops and 1,500 wagons, a column that stretched for miles across the New Jersey countryside.

Washington let them go. He knew everything they were doing, of course, but he and his officers in a council had decided to let them get out of the city before moving after them. Spring had brought the usual fleshing out of the American army, and in mid-June the commander in chief had about 13,500 men at his disposal. About 2,000 of them were already over on the New Jersey side, local militia and one brigade of Continentals. On the 18th, as Clinton was completing his crossing of the Delaware, Washington's army began to move. This was quite a different sight from the army that had gone into winter quarters. Uniforms might still be ragged, but now the regiments marched in close formation, arms aligned, intervals kept, ranks regular. These looked like a real army, and it was a heady feeling to think that for once they were chasing the British, and not the other way around. They swung off at a good, steady, ground-eating pace: now, Mr. Clinton, let's see what happens . . .

What happened was an exhausting pursuit across central

New Jersey in the summer heat. The road network in the area was not very good, forcing the British into long and unhandy columns. There was a variety of routes they might take, and Washington had to hang back until he had a pretty good idea where they were going. But he had light forces out, cutting down bridges and making pests of themselves, and the Americans rapidly began gathering in stragglers and deserters. The general soon had intelligence suggesting that Clinton was heading for Sandy Hook, by way of a long southeasterly loop that led away from the Delaware River. Suggesting was still not knowing, and he and Clinton played a game of hide-and-seek through the third week of June, Washington trying to block most routes but at the same time needing to keep his army in sufficient strength to fight, and Clinton trying to keep all his force together, but tremendously encumbered by wagons, guns, carts, and camp followers.

Washington held a council of war on the 24th: should they try to fight? Charles Lee, back with the army after a captivity during which he may well have offered to change sides, said no; the British were tough and good, the Americans were neither. Henry Knox reluctantly agreed. Most of the others, Greene, Wayne, Steuben, Lafayette, wanted to fight. In the end they made the worst possible decision: to harass the British with a force large enough to get in serious trouble, but not large enough to survive it.

The harassing force was rightly Charles Lee's; he was second in command. But he ceded it to Lafayette; a detachment of 1,500 was hardly up to his exalted standards. Then when the tactical picture changed, and Washington increased the force to 4,000, Lee decided he wanted it after all. Again Washington hedged; Lafayette could have the command and do what he might with it, but then when Lee came up, he could take over. It was the best, bad, compromise that could be managed, and it had a markedly adverse effect on the operations in the offing.

The British literally staggered into Monmouth on the late afternoon of the 26th, after nineteen miles in heavy, humid heat. They left behind them a long trail of men broken down with sunstroke and heat prostration, many of whom actually died from it. Marching all day in a heavy red wool uniform, with crossbelts constricting your lungs and a sixty-pound pack on your back, and fifteen pounds of musket and bayonet gouging into your shoulder, eating dust and longing for water, in the middle of a New Jersey summer, is not much fun. On the 27th they took up a position that would let them fight, advance, or retreat. Lafayette closed up to them, and late in the afternoon was superseded by Lee. The latter, with orders to attack as soon as the redcoats moved out, sent back word to Washington that he was afraid the British were about to attack him! He therefore did nothing for the remainder of the day.

The stage was now set for one of the more confusing battles of American military history. That stage itself consisted of a crescent-shaped piece of ground, perhaps five miles from one horn of it to the other, with the belly of the crescent sweeping to the south. The Americans were at the western end of this, and the British started from the eastern end. Monmouth Court House itself was a little past the center, bottom, of the crescent, to the east of it. It actually did not figure in the fighting at all, but was merely a convenient name to give the battle. Several roads ran through this area, meeting each other along the perimeter of the crescent, and there were three ravines that were significant terrain features, the East Ravine and the West Ravine, whose names are self-explanatory, and the Middle Ravine, which was actually only a mile or so east of the West Ravine.

Clinton moved early on the morning of the 28th. He sent General von Knyphausen and the baggage train off toward Sandy Hook. His main body he held as a covering force just above the court house, ready to move out at dawn. Besides that he had a rear guard and several flanking parties out to the west, the direction from which he expected he might see Americans. These patrols ran into Americans through the early morning hours, so the battle opened with a number of inconclusive skirmishes. As a result of these, General Philemon Dickinson of the New Jersey militia was able to report to Lee that the British were on the move.

Lee now had almost half of the American army under his command. But he had concocted no plan of what to do with them, and in fact had told his officers at a council the day before that he planned to have no plan, and would let circumstances dictate how they should all act, either collectively or individually. Several hours after Knyphausen had started to move, and indeed several hours after he had been informed of the move, Lee at last sent detachments forward across the chord of the arc or crescent, seeking to come into contact.

There were confused encounters between the American advance elements and British flanking patrols, but eventually the Americans bumped into, not the moving Knyphausen, but the still motionless Clinton and the main British body. Before he did anything else about it, Lee stopped his whole force for close to an hour while he called Dickinson a liar and got into a hot argument with him. He finally ordered his troops forward to a position along the East Ravine, where they overlooked the British line of march. While the Americans made this move, Clinton too got going, so his main body was marching past the arriving Americans. Lee then apparently decided to snap up the British rear guard to the south, to his right, around Monmouth Court House. Without telling anyone what he intended, he began sidling his units off to the right. To the troops and their officers, this looked like a retreat, and that was the character it soon assumed. Without any real fighting, the entire American advance was soon trudging back along the line of the crescent, some units in a near panic, some marching in good order, all the officers asking each other what was going on, and the more assertive of them giving orders that no one else bothered to obey. In the midst of it all, clumping along on his horse, sat Charles Lee, grumbling profanely to himself about everyone's shortcomings but his own, and the unfairness of the world in general.

By the time they crossed the Middle Ravine, actually a boggy area with a causeway through it, the soldiers were hot, tired, and confused, and many of the officers were furious; the temperature was in the nineties, and it was quite humid. Not only that, but Sir Henry Clinton, who though he might not want to fight was not one to throw away a gift, was following them up and ready to do battle.

Sometime after noon the advancing Washington began to meet the first retreating men from Lee's command. He simply could not figure out what was going on. Then he began to meet formed units, and their officers could provide no ex-

planation either. Finally along came Lee; there was a somewhat heated exchange between the two, accounts of which
vary widely, and Washington sent Lee to the rear, and began
to pull his army back together. With this, the real battle of
Monmouth began.

First the Americans drew up in a line, a temporary de-
laying position which was probably between the West and
Middle Ravines; reports differ on all of this. General Anthony
Wayne, with several of the regiments that had been under
Lee's command, and had subsequently formed his rear guard,
held this position until driven back by Clinton's advance.
While this was going on, though, Washington had formed his
own troops, plus any of Lee's that he could stop and reform,
in a major position that was probably just behind the West
Ravine. As Wayne's people fell back, the British came on to
meet this main line.

There then developed the heaviest fighting of the day. The
American position was strong, with Stirling's brigades on the
left, Lafayette's in the center, and Greene's on the right. American guns located on a hill to the south enfiladed the British advance. Clinton was determined to force this position, and he
hit it with the best of his army, battalions of the Guards, the
Black Watch, composite formations of grenadiers and light infantry companies, and some of his regular line regiments.

First the Black Watch advanced against Stirling's men on
the American left. The latter wheeled into line, held their
dressing like veterans, and then began firing volleys on command. Washington, watching them, beamed with pride while
Steuben swore happily in his several languages, and the two
sides exchanged volleys at shockingly close range. Then two
New Hampshire regiments and the 1st Virginia flanked the
Highlanders through the woods, and the British went back.

Next the British tried Green's wing, with no better results.
The American guns off to the south took them down in wind-
rows, and when they got close enough for musket fire, the
steady American lines drove them back again. Finally they
came on against Lafayette and Wayne (the latter having fallen
back on the former) in the center. This was the good old stuff,
grenadiers, fusiliers, light infantry, just like Minden and Fontenoy, and the battalions came on with the colors flying, the

sergeants calling the step, and the drums rattling and banging away. Behind the silent American lines the officers urged, "Wait, wait, steady . . . let 'em come . . ." and then, at a mere forty paces, "Present! . . . Fire!" and a leaden hail swept across the field, and the red ranks went down in a tangle of thumps, screams, and curses, broke, and went back. They came a second time, with the same result, and then, after an hour to gather themselves together, they came yet a third time. They got so close that their foremost color-bearer fell and dropped the colors virtually into American hands, but they never reached that steady American line.

That was all they could do. The battle degenerated into an artillery duel, but as evening came on, the British drew off and camped. Washington's army rested on its arms, and the general hoped to renew the battle the next morning, but when daylight came, the British were gone. Clinton had intended only to fight a rearguard action, and he had let himself get a bit carried away, but he was not going to stay to pursue the issue. During the night he took up his retreat, and two days later his army was at Sandy Hook, and ready to be ferried across to New York City.

Casualty figures are as disputed as everything else about Monmouth. There were the usual killed, wounded, and missing, about 400 for each side. In addition, each side had dozens die from sunstroke and heat prostration; and there was one more significant category: during the retreat the British lost 600 deserters, about 450 of them Germans.

Basically the battle was at best a draw. Clinton had not wanted to fight at all, and had really no more than shaken clear of pursuit; Washington had wanted a victory, and had not got it, except in the qualified sense that his men had shown their ability to stand up to the British on a level field. Had he managed at this point to destroy the main British Army in the north, he might then and there have won the war. As it was, about all he really achieved was to get rid at last of Charles Lee. This latter worthy demanded a court-martial for his unseemly treatment, got it, and was temporarily dismissed from the service. Full of wounded vanity, he then resigned his commission, and the resignation was accepted with relieved haste.

As Clinton moved his army into New York City, Washington marched again over the old route north through New Jersey, and eventually took up positions around White Plains. Gradually the Americans extended their net around the city, building up a distant cordon that hemmed the British in. There was little possibility of doing more than that, at least for the immediate future. But they were not quite back where they had been in 1776; great things were anticipated any day now: the French had arrived!

Just a few days after Admiral Lord Howe's fleet and transports had cleared the Delaware Capes with Clinton's sick and baggage, another fleet raised the same landfall. It was Admiral the Comte d'Estaing, here at last to make war upon the king of France's enemies. The Americans, eagerly, even passionately awaiting the long-promised aid, were delighted. Surely now something decisive would occur.

In fact, very little happened. Naval warfare was always a nice calculation of forces, tempered by conditions of nature, and it was as likely to be indecisive as land operations at the time. D'Estaing, for example, had left Toulon in mid-April. It took him eighty-seven days to make his Atlantic crossing, which meant he had advanced at about two knots, or less than fifty miles a day.

He did have a substantial fleet with him, however, twelve of the line and four frigates, and with that he ought to be able to accomplish something. Having missed Howe at the Capes, he sailed north for New York City, and there was his prey awaiting him, the British admiral with only nine of the line, anchored behind Sandy Hook in Raritan Bay. It was perfect; the French had odds of four to three. There was only one slight catch: the French vessels were bigger than the British, with a deeper draft—they could not get across the bar at the mouth of the bay, to engage the enemy. For eleven days d'Estaing sat there, offering immense rewards to anyone who could pilot him across, but it could not be done. Finally he held a conference with Washington, and the two decided that the French fleet should sail up the coast and take the British base at Newport in Rhode Island.

This, it appeared, would not be much of a problem. Newport was garrisoned by a mere three thousand troops, with some small naval vessels based there. American General John Sullivan was at Providence, with a thousand Continentals, and New England responded so readily to a call for five thousand militiamen that six thousand turned out. Washington then sent not only Lafayette, but three thousand New England Continentals up from New York, so Sullivan had an army of ten thousand men, plus the French, who arrived at the end of July.

Things began well; the French sent heavy ships up the Middle Passage, west of Newport, and trapped the British ships there, so that four 32-gun frigates had to be burned and blown up, and a goodly number of other vessels were scuttled in the harbor. But from there, the affair went downhill. Sullivan and d'Estaing agreed to coordinate their land operations against the town, the French to have the place of honor on the right of the line, but then, when Sullivan seized an opportunity to get his people across early to the island on which Newport is located, d'Estaing conceived that as a slight, and retired to sulk on his flagship. No sooner had that been patched up than the Royal Navy appeared. Howe had been reinforced, and now was ready to fight, with twelve of the line, and six big frigates.

So the French fleet put to sea, and the two antagonists stood off to the southward. For two days they each tried to gain an advantage over the other, until the problem was solved for them by an August gale that scattered ships all over the sea south of New England. Several inconclusive single-ship encounters resulted, but it all ended with d'Estaing back off Newport, and Howe going back to New York to refit.

Meanwhile Sullivan had invested Newport, carefully leaving the right of the line to be filled in, yet again, by the French. And once again, d'Estaing decided that his honor had been offended. Instead of cooperating, he now decided he must sail off to Boston to refit, and in spite of abject American pleas, he soon did so. Sullivan's militiamen responded to this contretemps by deserting in disgust and en masse, and the British came out of their city and drove off the remnants of what had been a most promising expedition.

All this was followed by the usual welter of correspondence, everyone demanding or offering explanations. While the French paraded around Boston, boasting greatly of the little they had done, Washington was soothing both Sullivan's anger and d'Estaing's hurt pride. The former went unfortunately public, but the latter was assuaged by a resolution of Congress thanking him for his great efforts, and eventually he took his troops and his fleet and sailed off to Martinique. There is an old military adage that the only thing worse than fighting a war without allies is fighting a war with them.

CHAPTER TWELVE

The War Moves South

B Y THE second half of 1778, the war had once again achieved a sort of equilibrium; the British were back in New York, and the Americans were ensconced on the hills in a distant ring around the city, observing and loosely confining them. Neither side could do much more; the British held Newport as a naval station, but were incapable of mounting anything substantial out of that port. The Americans, and their allies, demonstrated their inability, or their incompetence, to drive the British out. Both sides now degenerated into a series of diversions, the Americans because that was all they could do, the British because they did not know what else to do.

The initiative appeared to rest with the Americans, given the advent of their new ally, France, but that was largely an illusion. By his insurmountable stupidity, the Comte d'Estaing had demonstrated that one wrong man, if he is in the right place, can undo the work of many, and the frustration of Washington and other American leaders may easily be imagined. In fact, the Americans were somewhat in awe of the French, who had so often proclaimed themselves the masters of warfare and Western culture that most of the world accepted them at their own assessment. Except for the tactless Sullivan, who had an ax to grind anyway, the Americans were not just being diplomatic to the French when they praised them; they also tended to think that this must be how real wars were fought, just because it was the French who were doing it. Only when a French leader of genuine talent arrived would the Americans overcome their feelings of inferiority, and then something effective would actually happen. For the moment, all they could do was hold on.

Fortunately for them, the British were as much at a loss as themselves. The fact was, America was becoming something of a sideshow as yet another round of the great Anglo-French struggle for world mastery developed. Clinton's orders were to do what he could, but not to expect much help doing it. Indeed, in the standard British approach, he was instructed to dispatch several thousand troops off to the West Indies early in 1778. Only the arrival of the French delayed their departure, but they left toward the end of the year. What Clinton could not do with them, he could do even less of without them.

All of this merely typified the divisions of opinion among the ruling class in Britain and in the government. Lord North would have resigned if the King would permit it, but His Majesty would not. Several members of the cabinet did in fact give up office; agreeing with the returned Sir William Howe that America could not be held, they refused to support a policy that sought to hold it. North found them difficult to replace, especially as he himself also agreed with their views.

Minor events exacerbated the squabbles. In July the first full-scale naval battle of the new war had been fought in the waters off Ushant, west of Brittany. British Admiral Augustus Keppel (Viscount Keppel), poorly supported by his second, Sir Hugh Palliser, had engaged in a long-distance cannonade of the French fleet. Neither side had closed, neither had lost a ship, a more or less standard result of the formal tactics of the period. Subsequently, both admirals' supporters, in the navy and the press, had busily slandered the two commanders. Palliser had friends in power, and finally got Keppel court-martialed. It was February of 1779 before he was acquitted,

a verdict taken by the general population as an antigovernment victory. Tumultuous mobs in London celebrated by
wrecking Palliser's house and breaking Lord North's windows,
and for hours the city was out of control. Turnabout was fair
play; if Keppel was right, Palliser must be wrong, so he was
court-martialed, and then he was acquitted too. British papers
were convulsed by the matter for several months, the only
consistent themes in the whole mess being that the government was corrupt, all its policies wrong, and that the ministers
were a pack of idiots, villains, or both.

Only the King remained firm. George's view was that to
give in here was to invite collapse everywhere. He knew the
war was expensive, and it and he were unpopular, but what
could he do? Where would concessions end? Every time he
had offered the Americans an accommodation, they had asked
for more. Now nothing short of independence would satisfy
them. But if he recognized American independence, where
would it stop? The West Indies would be lost too; he did not
see that one could be held without the other. Surely if all those
territories were allowed to break away, Ireland must go as
well; how could one give up Ireland? Britain must either hold
all, or lose all.

This indeed was more emotion than reason, and its parallels to late twentieth-century American experience are painfully obvious. None of that made it any less real to George III,
and since he was the man in Britain whose opinions counted
most, the war was going to continue, until events either forced
him to change his mind, or the cost of sustaining this attitude
became simply overwhelming. They were not at that point yet.
Once again they began exploring the options.

Once France had declared war, the British government,
if not the King, had tacitly conceded the loss of America, and
had assumed that the rebellious American colonies would
have to be abandoned altogether. Now, after several months
of French belligerence, it did not look quite that bad. New
York was firmly in their control, and Newport appeared ten-
able. They also began to look, for the first time since Clinton's
abortive expedition to Charleston back in 1776, toward the
south.

In one sense, this was again the chimera that bedeviled

them throughout the war: the illusion that most American subjects were loyal, and that if they could only tap that loyalty, and deliver the King's subjects from the tyranny of a small disaffected minority, the rebellion would come to an end. So far the Loyalists had always been someplace else, and in the north, this illusion had been contributory to some notable disasters. In another sense, however, there were at least some grounds for believing that the situation in the southern colonies might well be more favorable. The British always felt more akin in attitude and outlook to southern Americans than to northern, a view that brought them close to intervention in the Civil War. The events of the early stages of the Revolution had suggested that there was a good deal of loyal feeling, and even if it had been nipped in the bud back in 1775 and 1776 by poor timing and mishandling, there was no reason to think it had been suppressed forever.

So a shift of operational emphasis to the south might well produce substantial local support. It was even possible to develop a sort of reverse domino theory. If Georgia and the Carolinas could be reclaimed to the Crown, then perhaps Virginia might also be recovered. A look at the map suggested that holding Virginia and the Chesapeake would put a stranglehold on the middle colonies. That, plus the hold on New York, should leave the rebellion pretty well isolated in the north. Even at their most optimistic, British planners by now admitted that the New England colonies were lost, and the more realistic would say that everything as far south as Pennsylvania was gone too. But the British Empire could live with that. It was generally acknowledged in British government that the cantankerous northerners were not much of a loss; this was the area that gave the most trouble for the least reward, the one whose climate and therefore products were most directly in competition with the mother country, and the one which fit most awkwardly into the theory of empire as then understood.

An empire in North America which consisted of Hudson's Bay, Newfoundland, Quebec and Nova Scotia in the north, the Atlantic seaboard from the Chesapeake capes to Florida, and the British West Indian islands in the south, was not to be despised, and would be a reasonable solution to Britain's difficulties. Feeling the birth pangs of the Industrial Revolution, Britain did not really need the irreconcilably rebellious northern colonies, and might well be better off without them. If the north were lost, then so be it; if the south were salvageable, then it should be done soon.

The fact that these arguments made sense, and might even be feasible, does not mean they were immediately, automatically, or even consciously, accepted. The government, and the individual ministers, were deluged by conflicting advice and demands. The opposition would do anything to defeat the government, or at least anything short of sinking their various differences and combining effectively for political victory. The sugar interests wanted to concentrate on the West Indies; residual royal governors wanted their colonies reconquered (indeed, it was such men, as late as mid-1777, who were instrumental in turning Lord George Germain's attention to the south); failed generals and admirals wanted to embarrass the ministry, and recover their stature and their sinecures. Backbench members, who seldom put in an appearance, wanted to do whatever they thought the King desired. There was a perfect bedlam of argument. Only slowly did something approaching a coherent plan settle out.

Sir Henry Clinton, back in New York City after his successful retreat across New Jersey, his forces diminished by the departure of units to the West Indies, was neither in a position nor a frame of mind to do a great deal. There was constant bickering and exchanging of posts around New York; in fact, there were some nasty little surprises, with British or American outposts and garrisons stormed and overrun, and often put to the bayonet, but nothing much was going to come of all that. By late 1778, the British were ready to look to the south.

Not a great deal had happened there since the Charleston expedition of 1776. The various little groups of committed Loyalists had been expelled, taking refuge either on ships or down in Florida; a great many of the less firm had gone underground. On the western frontier of the colonies, the Cherokees had come out for the British, but had been effectively suppressed by converging columns of militia and frontiersmen. By 1777 the area was relatively quiet and under Patriot control, and it continued that way into 1778. In the spring of that year, the Americans decided to move on Florida.

The American commander in the south was Major General Robert Howe, of no relation to the ubiquitous British Howes. A wealthy planter from the Cape Fear region of North Carolina, he had long been a leading radical, or Whig, in his area. His activity in driving out the British during 1776 had won him considerable fame, and he was appointed to command the Southern Department in October 1777. He took up his post in Charleston, unfortunately much resented by the South Carolinians and Georgians who saw no need for an outsider to manage their affairs. Early in 1778, Howe mounted an expedition against the thin British in eastern Florida, at St. Augustine. Everything fell apart. Supplies were lacking, the troops got sick, and the local commanders, including the Patriot governor of Georgia, William Houstoun, refused to obey Howe's orders. Local particularism on the American side matched party and factional strife on the British side, and Howe was soon back in Charleston, where criticism of him became so violent that he fought a duel with Christopher Gadsden, the fiery South Carolina politician who had wanted his job anyway. Fortunately, neither seriously hurt the other and they became good friends. In the fall of 1778, General Benjamin Lincoln superseded Howe in command of the Southern Department, but he did not arrive until almost the end of the year. It was thus Howe who met the British expedition to Savannah.

As early as March 1778, detachments of British troops had been sent from Philadelphia to Florida, but the Savannah attack represented the first real effort to reconquer the south, and to implement the new British ideas. Clinton amassed a force of about 3,500 men, led by Lieutenant Colonel Archibald Campbell, and consisting of the 71st Highlanders, two regiments of Hessians, and four battalions of Loyalists. Escorted south by a Royal Navy squadron, they reached the Georgia coast two days before Christmas, and anchored off the mouth of the Savannah River. Campbell's orders were to cooperate with General Augustine Prevost, who would bring British troops up from Florida, but after looking over the situation

THE
SOUTHERN
AREA OF
OPERATIONS

around Savannah, he decided he could take the city by himself.

American General Howe, outnumbered about four to one, nevertheless took up a strong position in front of the little city, his flanks covered by swamps, his front approachable only across a straight causeway; he had a few guns to give his Continentals and militia support, and he thought he was all right. Unhappily, the British discovered a path that led through the swamps around Howe's right. While they noisily demonstrated against his left and front, they sent a column through the swamp. As it broke out on the rebel right rear, the British infantry charged frontally, and the American line broke and collapsed. The rebels, cut off from their only line of retreat, had to fight their way through, and most did not make it. For a mere five men wounded, the British inflicted over 500 casualties, most of them prisoners, and got Savannah, full of ships, guns, and supplies, as well. It was a very neat beginning, and augured well for the success of the campaign.

Meanwhile, General Lincoln had arrived, and was gathering small American forces north of Savannah around Purysburg. Lincoln, a farmer from Massachusetts, a big, florid man in the fashion of the day, was a competent administrator, who had seen a fair bit of fighting; he had been badly wounded in the leg at Saratoga, and been more or less convalescent before being appointed to this southern command. His biggest problem, as Napoleon would have characterized it, was that he was not a lucky general.

Operations over the next six months ran around the triangle formed by Savannah; Augusta, some hundred miles up the Savannah River; and Charleston, South Carolina, about seventy miles up the seacoast from Savannah. Lincoln had between 2,000 and 3,000 men, depending upon the success or failure he was enjoying at any given moment; the better he did, the more the militia came out to support him. Slightly more than a thousand of his troops were reasonably good Continentals; the militia varied from very good to very bad. The British, now under General Prevost, who had taken over from Campbell upon his arrival, had their 3,500 regulars, plus troops brought from Florida, plus a large number of local

Loyalists, who came out for them just as the Patriot militia did for Lincoln; they were as reliable—or as unreliable—as their counterparts on the other side, so both armies had floating populations of support, likely to be there only when least needed.

The British sent a flying column that took Augusta unopposed, but a small expedition to the island of Port Royal was soundly trounced by South Carolina militia commanded by General William Moultrie, famous for the defense of Charleston in 1776. This little action brought increased support to Lincoln, and a few days later, at Kettle Creek, militiamen commanded by Colonel Andrew Pickens of South Carolina roughly handled a force of several hundred Loyalists.

The fighting in the back country of Georgia and Carolina was very rough, and destined to get worse. The Loyalists who came out for the Crown felt they had long-standing grievances, nursed in silence through the last three years of Patriot-inflicted indignities, and they had scores to settle. As the British marched inland, literally thousands declared their true feelings, and when they came out to fight, did so with little regard for military niceties. The Tories had none of the qualms about requisitioning that hampered Washington, and they freely settled scores, robbing and burning, and often killing, as they went. The Patriots were no better. What the British ministry, sitting in London, regarded as gratifying support meant in fact bitter civil war. After Kettle Creek, five of the captured Tories were quickly hanged. In this type of conflict, families were often divided. Moultrie, for example, was one of four brothers. One was killed in 1780 in the Continental service, another was a militia captain, but the last one was a Loyalist, and served on the other side.

Early in March the British got their own back for their defeats. In a brilliant turning operation, they surprised and pinned several hundred Americans against the south bank of the Savannah River at Briar Creek; about 400 were killed, captured, or drowned; most of those who got away went back home and stayed there, having had enough of soldiering, and what should have been a little check caused American spirits to plummet; virtually all Georgia was lost because of it.

Lincoln then marched north toward Augusta, but Prevost outplayed him and moved up the coast on Charleston. It was only a diversion, but it worked; the Carolinians were so slow to come out that Lincoln was forced to give up his own march, and hurry back across to the coast. Prevost then retreated. By now it was late June, and march and countermarch in the Carolina heat had no charms. Both sides sank exhausted into the hazy summer days.

So far, what had happened in the south was largely a sideshow, encouraging though it might be to the British and to their evolving view of the conflict. What happened next, however, turned it into a major theater—and nearly ruined the Franco-American alliance.

Once again the matter centered around the French fleet and Admiral d'Estaing, who appeared to sail whimsically in and out of the war, like the sprites in one of Shakespeare's comedies, who throw in little twists just to confound the efforts of mere mortals. After his failure at Newport in late 1778, and a refit in Boston, d'Estaing had gone off to the West Indies for the winter, leaving only a promise to return in the spring. Lincoln hoped he might come to Charleston, and help out in the south. Washington wanted him to come north, and move against New York. However, the independent Frenchman decided on a southern campaign, and late in August he approached the Carolina coast, thirty-three ships, two thousand guns, and more than four thousand troops. He quickly swept British ships off the coast, including capturing a paychest on one of them, and American hopes soared.

The French fleet stood on and off, but by the second week of September they began landing troops, and the British in Savannah knew they were in for a siege. Lincoln marched troops south from Charleston, including some small cavalry units led by the Polish officer Casimir Pulaski, but even before they got there, d'Estaing had unilaterally demanded a surrender of the city "to the French." The arriving Americans were not very pleased with this, and relations among the allies continued to deteriorate. Lincoln's 1,500 men, almost two-thirds militia, did not make much of a show, and the French regarded them with a disdain they did not even attempt to hide. When General Moultrie suggested a straight-out assault, he was brushed aside. A siege should be done properly, after all.

It took them three weeks to get ready, dragging heavy guns several miles from the coast, digging parallels, establishing camps, and so on. Meanwhile the French naval officers—d'Estaing was actually a soldier—were worried about hurricanes, the arrival of a possible British fleet, and scurvy, which was decimating their sailors, a sad commentary on the quality of their rations off the coast at that time of year. Before his siege engineers pronounced themselves ready, therefore, d'Estaing decided on a storming attempt on October 9, nearly a month after he had scornfully rejected Moultrie's recommendation for just that.

The British had not wasted their time. They had encircled the entire town with a line of entrenchments, earth and logs which the bombardment had hardly damaged at all. General Prevost decided that the main attack must come against Spring Hill, and there he built a strong redoubt and extra defenses.

He and the French agreed on that point at least, and d'Estaing, in concert with his allies, decided to send five columns simultaneously against this feature. The right three were to be French, the two on the left American. These latter hoped to effect a breach through which Pulaski would lead his mounted legion. The attack was set for dawn, but the rising sun found the columns still floundering through the woods that faced their objective. When they finally got untangled, d'Estaing led the first of them, on the right flank, out into the open. Instead of attacking together, they attacked in succession, across five hundred yards of open ground, with the British mowing them down all the way.

In spite of this they got into the earthworks, French on the right and Americans on the left. The 2nd South Carolina, led by Francis Marion, got its flag onto the parapet of the Spring Hill redoubt, where it was quickly joined by the colors of France, carried by one of d'Estaing's aides. For nearly an hour the battle raged back and forth across ditch and abatis, with volleys at ten paces and bayonets and musket butts as the allied troops tried to scramble up the walls and the British and Tories leaped down into the ditch to drive them out. D'Estaing was carried off wounded. Pulaski's cavalry charged into the battle, even though there was no breach for them to get through, and the screams of terrified horses were added to the frightful din; the Pole was mortally wounded, and the cavalry sullenly went back. Slowly the British prevailed, the assaulting columns were pushed back, their supports were all mixed up, and the attack died down.

The allies had lost nearly a thousand men, about two thirds of them French, all in all very nearly a quarter of their attacking force, which is testimony to how deadly eighteenth-century warfare could be when it really got serious. British losses were only about 150, if that, so the advantages of the defense were obvious.

Though Lincoln wanted to continue, d'Estaing had had more than enough. No glory for French arms here; he was ready to leave. Within a week the French were back aboard ship, ready to sail off the stage yet again. The British were delighted; the Americans were thoroughly disgusted. The militia went home by the hundreds, and the American position in the south all but collapsed. So did the alliance with France.

If the Revolution in the south was buckling under British pressure, in the north it was falling apart simply from inability to sustain its own weight. Clinton sat in New York, thinking up little raids and excuses why he could not do more; Washington moved his army north of the city, to the hills on either side of the Hudson, and longed to do more, but could manage little.

The most ambitious idea that surfaced, or resurfaced, was for the conquest of Canada—yet again. This persistent illusion in American minds paralleled the British fixation about the loyalties of the majority of the population. This time it had been developed by the Board of War, a new committee of Congress charged with developing overall strategy. The idea had come up over the winter of 1777–78, even before the British left Philadelphia, and quite independent of Washington, who immediately branded it as nonsense when finally informed of it. Interestingly enough, one of the reasons he was against it was precisely because of the French alliance;

it would do the United States no good, he thought, to get rid of Great Britain if they were to replace her with a reconstituted French empire in the St. Lawrence Valley; that would merely replace the devil they knew with one they had already gotten rid of several years ago. Nonetheless, Lafayette was appointed to command the prospective expedition, presumably on the idea that a Frenchman might meet with a more favorable welcome than an American. He got as far as Albany, where he found virtually nothing done, no supplies gathered, no militia summoned, just a great void. And even though the Americans had done little, the British knew all about the plan, and scouts reported them ready and waiting at the north end of Lake Champlain. At that, second thoughts won the day, and the whole scheme was eventually discarded.

This left neither side with much to do. In September, Clinton sent a foraging expedition up both sides of the Hudson, but since it was obviously no more than that, Washington made no real move to counter it. There was one small, unfortunate consequence. At Old Tappan, General Grey, the British soldier who had commanded the "Paoli massacre," pulled off the same surprise again, catching asleep and virtually wiping out the 3rd Continental Light Dragoons led by Colonel George Baylor; the British again attacked at night and with the bayonet, killing or taking about two thirds of the small regiment. Witnesses testified that Grey would have killed everyone, had not some of his own officers intervened to save the prisoners.

In October the British struck against Egg Harbor in New Jersey, destroying or taking several privateers. In the same operation they surprised and overran a post occupied by Pulaski's legion of cavalry—this before the Pole went south—and again did nasty work with their bayonets.

However unpleasant such affairs were—and the Americans were quick to dub anything in which they were surprised a massacre—they were still arguably legitimate operations of war. But in the no-man's-land around New York City, between the British and American lines and especially in Westchester County, there was a different situation altogether. Here groups of deserters, runaways, and just plain outlaws operated at will, avoiding bodies of troops from either side and preying on

supply wagons, couriers, and civilians. Here was true brutal-
ity, with plunder, rape, burning, and casual murder for the
unwary. This was one of the garbage dumps of the war, and
men and women unhappy enough to live between the lines
slept lightly and moved very carefully. The bandits, often
called "cowboys" or "skinners," operated in groups, tended
vaguely to support one side or another, but basically were out
for whatever they could get. They were pirates on land, and
it would have done society a service if British and Americans
could have cooperated to get rid of them; instead, thriving on
the basically static situation, they lasted from 1778 to the end
of the war.

In November of 1778, Washington disposed his army in
winter quarters. He now had about 12,000 troops present and
fit for duty, as large an army as he ever commanded, and it
was divided up into several divisions. The troops were distributed in camps along a line that looked like a backward
question mark, from Danbury up in Connecticut across the
Hudson and down to Elizabeth in New Jersey. To start the
winter, they were in pretty good condition. In October they
had actually received uniform coats, as well as boots, from
France. The winter proved mild, though living under canvas
tents or in log huts in winter in this area is a chancy business
at best. Still, it was not as bad as Valley Forge had been—nor
as Morristown would be next year.

The eventual news of the loss of Savannah, and then of
most of Georgia, brought little cheer. There was no money,
or what there was, all paper, was worthless. Washington visited Philadelphia several times during the winter, and discussed with leading politicians and financial people the state
of the country's economy, and the prospects for the future,
both military and in more general terms. But the simple fact
was, the Americans had few remaining initiatives. About all
they could do, or indeed see to do, was to hold on and hope
for the best.

CHAPTER THIRTEEN
By Land and by Sea

B<small>Y THE</small> spring of 1779, the war of the American Revolution had become a world war, similar to the Seven Years' War that preceded it. Instead of fighting an isolated rebellion staged by some of her fractious colonies, Great Britain was involved in a war with both the United States and France, and Spain was about to join in as well. Wherever the two, then three, major colonial empires abutted each other, there was fighting, often inconclusive, but often bloody, and if the Americans were hard-pressed simply to stay in the war, the British were in almost equal difficulties on the larger world scene. At home, in the Mediterranean, in Africa, in India, as well as in the West Indies and North America, Britain was fighting if not for her very survival, at least for her empire, which was almost the same thing.

The common factor in all these disparate areas was sea power, the ability of Britain, or France, or France and Spain, to control access to any of the imperial theaters of war. The Royal Navy became increasingly thinly stretched, as more and more opponents entered the lists. As France had a better navy than at any time in the preceding three quarters of a century, so too the Spanish navy, which was also in better shape than usual. Even more importantly, neither was distracted by any Continental struggle or commitments, so that both were able to concentrate on maritime affairs. Under such pressure, the British bent, and nearly broke.

There was always a hierarchy of importance for Great Britain in her efforts to command the world's oceans. This might fluctuate at its outer edges; in one war or another the Indian Ocean might be more crucial than, say, the South Atlantic. But at the top end of the pinnacle, there was never any question. The Channel came first; followed by the eastern Atlantic, that is, the waters generally around Britain and the coasts of western Europe; then the Mediterranean. After that came the West Indies and the American seaboard, which for practical purposes in the age of sail meant the route to and from both the West Indies and America. Then came the routes to India and the Indian Ocean, and later on, the Antipodes. By 1779, with her major imperial rivals in the war, all of these routes, and all of these imperial hostages, were under threat.

But the Channel was the most vital. Britain never had much of an army, in numerical terms, and in 1779 far the best part of it was in America. A French fleet in command of the Channel could well mean a French army landing on the coast of England, and if that ever happened, then the whole imperial edifice was finished. When Spain declared war, which she did in June, and joined forces with the French Navy, it looked as if invasion were imminent.

They certainly thought so in Britain. All along the southern coast little groups of what in World War II were called local defense volunteers drilled and prepared for the French landing. Orders went out to remove livestock and to be prepared to evacuate the coast. Ships were hurriedly recommissioned and manned by the press gang, often with disastrous results, as many of the ships of the line had lain rotting for fifteen years.

A Franco-Spanish fleet did actually make it into the Channel. The British had not been strong enough to blockade France's coasts; just as d'Estaing had gotten out to sail to America, Admiral the Comte d'Orvilliers got out of Brest with a sizable fleet. He then rendezvoused with the Spanish fleet, several weeks later than planned, and together, sixty-six of the line, they swept north to the Channel. The British could muster but half that number to meet them. The French had 40,000 troops on the coast, waiting for transport. It looked like 1588 and the Spanish Armada all over again.

Fortunately the crisis fizzled. The British ships, divided into two squadrons, kept the strategic advantage over their enemies: allied coordination was not at its best—it seldom was—and although the enemy lay off Plymouth for several days, and even took a couple of British ships caught in the wrong place, they accomplished little more. The winds shifted to easterly, blowing them down Channel and out to sea again, and their efforts tailed off inconsequentially. Still, whether it was or not, the threat had seemed real enough, and helps explain why the American Revolution looked different from England than it did from America. As Voltaire had remarked about the loss of Canada by France in the last war, "Who worries about the barn when the house is burning down?"

Pressure was not confined to the Channel. The Spanish had entered the war largely to recoup losses to Britain in the Seven Years' War. Interestingly enough, the Spanish government would not recognize the independence of the United States. Supporting the Americans in a fight against Great Britain might be useful, but the government of His Most Catholic Majesty Carlos III, ruler of one of the greatest colonial empires in the world, had no desire to set a bad example for its own subjects in the Americas; they acted independently enough already. But the Spanish were quite willing to have a try at regaining East Florida, for example, and especially Gibraltar.

The British hold on Gibraltar had been a standing affront to Spain ever since they had taken it in 1704, during the War of the Spanish Succession. Spain always wanted it back, and indeed still does. Soon after the declaration of war the Spanish began a loose blockade of the fortress, helped by a French squadron, and gradually the siege of Gibraltar became one of the key factors of the war, an epic that lasted until 1783.

Matters heated up in India as well. Here the British were well established in the peninsula, but still faced formidable local enemies, the most dangerous of whom was the ruler of the large state of Mysore, Hyder Ali. He and the British had already fought one war, and then made an uneasy alliance. The British were also involved in an ongoing wrangle with a loose group called the Maratha Confederacy. None of these three was any better than necessary, and when France declared war on Britain, and French agents showed up at Hyder Ali's court at Poona, he began to listen to what they had to say. The British then fouled their own yardarm. There were several French trading posts left along the coast, concessions from the Seven Years' War. These were regarded by Hyder Ali as being under his protection, and when the British peremptorily occupied them, he decided to go to war. How much help he would get from France depended upon sea power. but here once again the British found themselves under serious threat, an added problem they certainly did not need.

Both Gibraltar and India were problems that would peak as the war went along. There were similar bickerings on the west coast of Africa, where either side raided and took the other's slaving posts. But the West Indies, along with the Channel, became a major theater of operations right from the French declaration of war.

Europe had an absolutely insatiable appetite for sugar, and in the eighteenth century, the West Indies, far more than India or America, were the true prize of empire. Spain, Britain, France, even the Dutch, settled, colonized, imported slaves, and fought each other for control of little islands that are nothing more than tourist spots today. Two hundred years ago. every businessman and politician knew where Jamaica and Santo Domingo, the Greater and Lesser Antilles, the Windwards and the Leewards were and who owned what, though it could be a pretty difficult time keeping track of them, they changed hands so fast.

A war on the North American continent meant a different kind of prosperity as well, for these islands were not only desirable in their own right and for their own products, they were also useful entrepôts for trade, illegal or otherwise, with the American seaboard. The European powers wanted them as winter bases for their fleets, the Americans wanted to trade with them or through them. The American Revolution, the War of 1812, and especially the American Civil War all brought

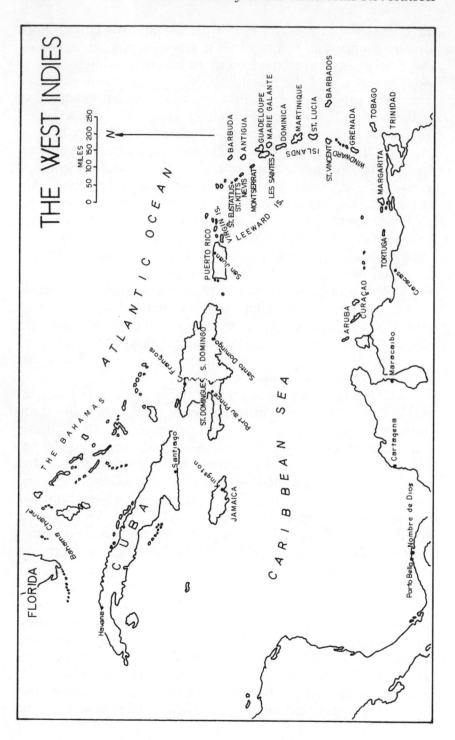

THE WEST INDIES

a secondhand bustle to the islands, as smugglers, blockade runners, privateers, and more legitimate traders sought to capitalize on belligerency. In the age of sail, a bold man with a fast ship could always find something to do.

It was, however, the fleet operations, and the military campaigns associated with them, that were of primary interest. In America, military commanders such as Washington and Clinton quickly became aware that the West Indies were going to prove more than a distraction. Clinton was ordered to send troops there as soon as French belligerency became a fact, and Washington found that his new allies were far more interested in Caribbean matters than they were in him. Unlike many of his more naive or optimistic countrymen, he knew the French were in the war not just from altruistic motives, but for what they could get. Only as long as helping the Americans did not interfere with their other ambitions would the Americans get help.

In fact, as soon as France had declared war, fighting began in the Caribbean. The French governor of Martinique had taken the British island of Dominica, while a small British expedition under Admiral Samuel Barrington, including troops sent down from New York, took the French island of St. Lucia. Here they were attacked in December by d'Estaing, who had sailed south for the winter after his failure at Newport and his refit in Boston. The French general-turned-admiral, figuratively as well as literally all at sea, could not dislodge Barrington's little squadron, which he more than twice outnumbered, so he landed and went sword in hand against the British garrison, and got beat on shore, too.

He then went off to think about it for a couple of months. Both sides were reinforced over the turn of the year, and in early summer, while British Admiral John Byron searched for him, he managed to capture the islands of St. Vincent and Grenada. Byron found him off the latter island early in July, and the two fought another of those inconclusive formal battles in which each side sailed serenely past the other, exchanging broadsides at long range and doing as little damage as possible.

The French then sailed off to Haiti, where their admiral got letters and news that finally led him north again, to the failure at Savannah. After that, he himself went home, sending half his ships back for more operations in the West Indies. His contributions to the American cause were thus hardly very positive. The French presence on the coast had indeed induced the British to evacuate Newport, but in most eyes that did not offset the miserable fiasco at Savannah. But from the French point of view the cruise was far more successful. They had managed to maintain themselves at sea against their old enemy, they had picked up a couple of useful islands, and they believed they had given considerable help to the Americans, whatever the latter might think about it. Just as the view in London, so also the view in Paris was different from the view in America.

Americans were naturally preoccupied with their own difficulties, closer to home, and little aware of these events on the larger world scene. Indeed, given the available communications of the day, they might not hear of such things for weeks or even months. Such matters, too, have been often ignored by American historians of the Revolution, who adopted the same view as the participants; all they could see was a cause floundering through 1779, without much effective happening on either side. In America itself, except for the disaster at Savannah, the war just bumbled along.

Such was certainly still the case in the northern theater. Neither Washington nor Clinton would, or could, come to grips with each other around New York, and the stalemate there just dragged on. Both indulged in small-scale actions which had little effect on the overall scene. They were desperate enough to the people involved in them, though.

In July Clinton decided he was fed up with the activities of Connecticut in Long Island Sound, where the Yankees constantly harassed and ambushed his supply boats and raided across to Long Island. On the 5th he landed detachments on either side of New Haven, and marched on the town. The militia came out, and a body of students from Yale contested the British advance, but the locals were not in sufficient strength to offer more than nuisance resistance. The town was plundered and several prisoners carried off. On the 8th the British and their allies, Germans and Tories, burned Fairfield and the village of Green's Farms, and on the 11th they razed Norwalk. In the whole excursion, several hundred houses, churches, and public buildings were burned, and hundreds of thousands of dollars' worth of supplies and loot were carried off. Perhaps the raid punished the rebels somewhat; but it certainly did not make any new friends for the King in Connecticut.

Meanwhile, there was some activity in the Hudson Valley. Early in June the British had come up the river and seized the little unfinished fort at Stony Point, almost forty miles above New York City and a mere ten below West Point. General Washington was thoroughly annoyed by this presumption, and soon began to think about getting the place back. He gave the job to Anthony Wayne. The Pennsylvanian, in his mid-thirties, had been involved in most of the major actions of the war. He was well-known as a daring and resourceful leader, and had recently been given command of an elite brigade of light infantry. In his own mind, however, he was most conscious of having been surprised and beaten by No-flint Grey at Paoli, and he was determined to erase what he considered the stain on his record.

Wayne had about 1,300 troops, and the British garrison, which had not yet completed its fortifications, numbered just about half that. After very careful reconnaissance the Americans approached the point on the night of July 16. For once all precautions were taken, even to putting down the dogs along the route so they would not bark and give the alarm. Guns were unloaded, except for a small center division that would create a diversion, and at about midnight the storm began. The Americans waded across a deep marsh, up to their necks in some places, and rushed the point. Breaking through at both ends while the British were distracted by the middle diversionary column, they soon surrounded and then overwhelmed the British. The fighting was very heavy for a few minutes; for example, of twenty men leading the forlorn hope of the left-hand column, only three made it into the fort. A French volunteer, Lieutenant Colonel François de Fleury, was the first man in, and he hauled down the British colors himself. As the garrison threw down their arms and surrendered, Wayne, wounded in the head, quickly brought his men under control, and thus the action ended without, as so many of these affairs did, getting out of hand. Both sides suffered about a hundred casualties, but the British had another 475 taken prisoner, virtually the entire garrison.

It was in fact a fairly small matter, and Washington took no strategic advantage from it. On the other hand, it had been very well managed, morale received a major boost, and everyone, even British as well as Americans, was loud in their praise of the troops and the way they had behaved themselves. Anthony Wayne could now lay the ghosts of Paoli to rest.

The Americans did it again, a month later, in a raid on Paulus Hook, on the New Jersey shore opposite New York City. This one, led by the famous Light Horse Harry Lee of Virginia, a twenty-three-year-old beau sabreur of the army, did not work quite as well, though the results were generally satisfactory, and led to another boost of American morale.

If these operations served as small models of how things ought to be done, the infamous Castine expedition at the same time showed how not to do anything. Castine is in what was then the Maine district of Massachusetts, on the eastern shore of Penobscot Bay. Here in June British troops from Halifax started building a small fort, to cover the coast, and to provide a base for timber parties cutting trees for the Royal Navy. The Massachusetts legislature decided to go after them, and mounted a force of about 2,000 men and twenty vessels, several of them Continental ships and some of them state vessels. Commodore Dudley Saltonstall commanded the naval side of the force, and General Solomon Lovell of the Massachusetts militia the land element. When they got to Castine, the sailor favored an immediate assault, but the soldier wanted a proper siege—this of a half-finished log enclosure.

Two weeks into the "siege," a British relief expedition arrived from New York, with 1,600 troops and worse, several ships, including a ship of the line. The Americans fled up the Penobscot River, where they finally burned their blockaded ships, then began a retreat through the wilderness that cost them a quarter of their surviving force. By the time they returned to Massachusetts, there was only sufficient energy left for all the commanders to accuse each other of incompetence, cowardice, peculation, and any other sins they could think of, and the whole sorry mess ended in a series of courts-martial and letters of recrimination between Massachusetts and the Congress. The British held the Penobscot area for the rest of the war.

The matter of frontiers was less easily settled farther west. Along the frontier of western New York and northeastern Pennsylvania, which were then more or less the limits of practical settlement, there was constant irregular warfare. The participants were usually American farmers doubling as militia and part-time soldiers, supported by detachments of Continentals or state troops from the more settled areas, on the one side; and on the other, Tories or Loyalists, occasionally with a few British regulars from Canada, with Indians who had been inexorably drawn into what they initially perceived as the white man's struggle. It was a bitter war, neighbor against neighbor, often brother against brother, of ambushes, burnings, scalping and torturing, a war of little glory and much pain.

One of the peculiarities of this war along the northwest frontier was the dominance, especially on the British side, of several important families. The most notable were the Johnsons and the Butlers, and their names, fathers and sons, appear again and again as leaders of raiding parties. It appears ironic that the Butlers, who seem to have wanted initially to keep the Indians neutral, became the most effective of these partisan leaders, while the Johnsons, great landowners and men of affairs, spurred the Indians on, though preferring themselves to avoid the hot and heavy work of combat. A third name that crops up repeatedly, to make this terrible trilogy, is that of Joseph Brant, but he was a different type; in spite of his European-style name, he was an Indian, the war chief of the Mohawk tribe of the Iroquois Confederacy. A Christian, he had been to England several times, where he was presented at court and painted by the leading portraitists of the day. His sister was the mistress of Sir William Johnson, presenting him with eight children, and though Brant often operated with the Butlers, he was usually allied with the Johnsons in the squabbles between them. Taken as a group, these all made formidable foes.

The American settlers wanted to think, after Burgoyne's defeat and the failure of the St. Leger expedition in 1777, that they were safe, and the frontier would now remain quiet. They were soon disillusioned.

In early July of 1778, the British came down out of Fort Niagara, on Lake Ontario, about a thousand strong, equally divided between Tories and Indians. Their target was not the New York frontier, but rather the lovely Wyoming Valley in northeast Pennsylvania. This is where modern Wilkes-Barre is located—indeed, the name of that city celebrates two famous British Whigs of the day, John Wilkes and Isaac Barré, both regarded as champions of the American cause—and in 1778 it had several thousand settlers spread in little packets for about twenty-five miles. They had a militia of their own and a few stockaded houses to serve less as forts than as places of refuge.

At the first of July, the Tories swept down on the valley, burning and killing as they went. Several hundred militiamen who gathered to stop them were routed, after which prisoners were tortured and scalped by the Indians. In the space of a couple of days, the entire valley was gutted, and a wave of terror swept the northern border as the news spread far and wide.

A month later it was New York's turn, and the Mohawk Valley received the same treatment. Unadilla is now a little village in central New York; in 1778 it was the chief town of the Mohawks; Joseph Brant used it as his headquarters and rallying point, and in July he sallied forth to burn Andrustown. Two months later he wiped out German Flats; though the Patriots knew he was coming, they were little match for the Indians and for the Tories, who were by now skilled professional border warriors, men who had lost everything for their loyalty to the Crown, and who waged vengeful war on their former neighbors.

The Americans retaliated by burning Unadilla in October, but the Indians fled before them, and though they destroyed the town and its substantial buildings, they did not catch many enemies. This was a regular pattern of frontier warfare; the Indians were seldom caught, and it was more the norm to destroy their crops and supplies, and hope winter would do the work the settlers were incapable of achieving.

In November the Tories struck at the isolated settlement of Cherry Valley. The village was garrisoned by Massachusetts troops under a Colonel Ichabod Alden, but they knew nothing of frontier warfare, and Alden seems to have been both arrogant as well as ignorant. He discounted all warnings of Indian activity in the vicinity, refused to let the nervous settlers move into his stockade, and remained himself in a house outside the walls. On the raw, drizzly morning of November 11, Joseph Brant and Walter Butler and several hundred Tories and Indians hit the place. Alden paid with his life for his complacency, and so did Cherry Valley; though the troops in the fort held out, all the houses and barns were burned, several dozen people were massacred, and a number of prisoners carried off, many of whom were later released. To be unwary on the frontier was to be dead.

With all these attacks, the British and their Indian allies were in a fair way to reclaiming the northern border and thereby, access to much of the West as it was then perceived. It was past time for the Americans to take this threat seriously, and early in 1779, they at last did so.

Given the general inactivity on the main northern front around New York City, Washington believed that, as spring came on, he could spare troops to resolve the Indian problem once and for all. The Americans came up with a complicated plan for a regular military expedition: General John Sullivan would advance north from Easton, Pennsylvania, with some 2,500 troops; General James Clinton would lead another 1,500 south from the Mohawk Valley, to link up with Sullivan; once combined, they would advance on Niagara, the fount of all support for the Indians. Meanwhile, Colonel Daniel Brodhead was to move north from Pittsburgh with another 600, also to link up with the main force. Finally, there were also to be operations against Detroit farther west. The aim was simple. Sullivan was going to wipe out the Iroquois Confederacy once and for all.

It did not quite work out that way. The operations were slow, conducted as if they were in Europe against regular-style enemy forces. Sullivan took along several hundred wagons and boats, a huge herd of cattle, and all the other impedimenta of the day. This was not entirely his fault; the kind of troops detailed for the operation needed the amount of logistics support provided, and thus, against enemies as fleet of foot as the Iroquois and Tories, the whole conception was almost self-defeating. Not until August did the main forces even approach enemy territory; there was relatively little fighting, though there were a few nasty ambushes, in which some advance guards were killed, and a few even unluckier ones captured and tortured to death by the Indians.

But for the most part, the enemy fled before the American advance. The march therefore turned into a vast destruction of property and crops, and successive towns were burned, stores destroyed, and even orchards of fruit trees girdled or cut down. Though he killed or caught few Indians, Sullivan virtually wiped out their agricultural economy.

Unfortunately, the advance was so slow, and ultimately so ill-coordinated, that the Americans stopped short of the main target at Niagara. They thus failed to remove the British threat from the frontier; indeed, they had forced the Indians into even greater hostility, and deprived them of any recourse other than war to the death. The expedition was an enormous blow to the Six Nations, and marked the beginning of the end for them as a major force on the northern frontier. But it did not solve the problem of the border; it just made that worse.

At the same time, there was also a series of wide-ranging operations in what was then known as the Old Northwest, the modern states of Ohio, Indiana, Illinois, Kentucky, and southern Michigan and Wisconsin, all of which might loosely be considered the land between the Great Lakes and the Ohio River valley. This whole area had been reserved for the Indians by Britain after the Seven Years' War, but white traders and settlers had seeped in, French from the St. Lawrence area, following their widespread fur-trading networks to the west and south, Spanish coming up the Mississippi from Louisiana, and British/Americans across the Allegheny Mountains from the east.

This was almost but not quite virgin territory, with meadows and huge stands of forest; any serious transportation was by water, and the Ohio and the Mississippi Rivers were both linked with the Great Lakes by a series of smaller rivers and portages between them. For example, one could go up the Maumee from modern Toledo, Ohio, cross to the Wabash, and go down to enter the Ohio below modern Evansville, Indiana; or, from the southern end of Lake Michigan, a short portage led to the Kankakee River, to the Illinois, and ultimately to the Mississippi just above modern St. Louis.

Such infinitely desirable and potentially rich territory was not going to be left to the Indians, no matter how many promises successive generations of white governments had made. Historically, the best claim was French, deriving from the fur trading empire of the St. Lawrence, and inherited by the British after 1763; white traders in the area were largely French, with an admixture of Spanish from down the Mississippi. The American settlement was a fringe of adventuresome, and cantankerous, sorts seeping over the mountains into western Virginia and Kentucky, and west from Pennsylvania in the area known as "the dark and bloody ground" where the Cherokees and Shawnees had tried to stop the flow.

There were a few scattered British posts throughout the entire area, more there to regulate the fur trade than for anything else. As soon as the Revolution broke out, the British governor at Detroit, the infamous Henry Hamilton, did his best to secure the Indians in their fickle allegiance to Britain, and their more determined enmity to the Americans, by encouraging their raids against the mountain frontier. Several Americans had suggested incursions into the area, but nothing much had been done until George Rogers Clark, a twenty-three-year-old frontiersman, approached Governor Patrick Henry of Virginia with a proposal to conquer the territory. Henry persuaded the Virginia Assembly to vote money for an expedition of whose object they remained ignorant, an achievement in itself given the fractious nature of politics at the time, and early in 1778 Clark set out with a force of some 200 men to take an area almost twice the size of Great Britain.

Clark's expedition turned into one of the heroic epics of early America, a story of long marches and water passages, daring, and endurance. There was blessedly little fighting, for the British garrisons had largely been withdrawn, and the

French inhabitants were as willing to be American as British, especially after news of the Franco-American alliance came through. Clark took the main posts, Kaskaskia and Vincennes, with no trouble. While he tried to consolidate his hold, Hamilton advanced from Detroit and retook the latter post. Clark then countermarched, driving his own men and many French volunteers through bad weather and flooded country, and recaptured the post after a short siege. Hamilton went into captivity in Virginia; Clark hoped to move ultimately on Detroit, whose capture would have closed the British out of the Ohio country altogether, and this was the underlying intent behind the coordination of his moves and Sullivan's and Brodhead's. But this was just too much, and the Americans were too thin to do any more than they already had. Indeed, they were lucky, in the remaining years of the Revolution, to hold what Clark's brilliance had won for them.

There were other, smaller successes in 1779, such as John Paul Jones's brilliant fight off the east coast of Britain, when his *Bonhomme Richard* managed to take the British frigate *Serapis*. But these were all around the fringes, even if they were real enough. None of them was sufficient to offset the central fact that little was being done in the main theater of war; certainly none offset the disastrous failure to recapture Savannah, and the ineffectiveness of the French alliance, from which so much had been hoped.

The truth was, the war was stagnating. Both sides seemed bereft of ideas, and the resources with which to put them into practice. At the end of four and a half years of war, neither side was capable of winning it, and both were tired of waging it.

In Great Britain, this state of affairs was personified by the King's First Minister, Lord North himself. The opposition charged that he was corrupt, that the country was collapsing around him, and that there ought to be change, by which of course they meant themselves in power. The King, and much of the country, considered the opposition downright treasonous, and they certainly sounded as if they were. They exulted in American successes, and did their best to move what they still saw as a political and constitutional conflict, rather than a war, closer to home. The best, and most dangerous example of that was Ireland.

The threat of a French invasion had caused an Irish volunteer movement, which attracted thousands of middling and upper-class Irish into its ranks; it was indeed designed to appeal to these classes rather than to the poor, who were too busy just staying alive to worry about an invasion. But the movement got all mixed up in Irish economic and constitutional demands, and soon looked less like protecting Ireland from the French, than it did like raising Ireland against the English. Opposition members of Parliament encouraged the Irish "to fly to arms in order to obtain deliverance . . . ," to "recur to first principles, to the spirit as well as the letter of the constitution." In other words, the Irish might play the American game too, which gave some credence to George III's ideas of the pernicious spread of independence movements.

As if that were not bad enough, the same cries for reform began to be heard from such unlikely places as Yorkshire, in the north of England. There was a Yorkshire Association, dedicated to replacing the King's corrupt servants and ministers with independent-minded and honest politicians, by which members meant, *they* should be out, and *we* should be in. The opposition leaders flirted around the edges of these movements, attracted to them but, in this as in most things, unable to capitalize on them. Lord North tried to steer a course somewhere through the middle, and his attitude is best illustrated by an anecdote of the day. Once as he sat apparently dozing on the front benches, an opposition speaker went on at great length about his shortcomings, ending by pointing his finger at him and shouting, "Look at him! There he sits, sound asleep for all the world!" whereupon North opened one eye and said, "Oh, would to God that were so!"

Unfortunately for him, he could not sleep his way through the war, and the attendant political crises. So he soldiered on, trying to deal with each crisis as it arose, or at least putting it off as long as possible. North was not quite the bulldog breed, not the Elder Pitt nor Winston Churchill, but he was all George III had, and so they kept on.

Had North known how badly off the Americans were, he might have felt better about his own situation. For as 1779

limped toward its close, many Patriots thought the Revolution
was all but finished. It certainly looked that way. For one thing,
the American cause was bankrupt, literally. By September of
1779 Congress, the central government, had issued paper
money to the face value of $200,000,000. It had virtually noth-
ing with which to back this up, however, and as a result, the
money was almost worthless. At that point, Congress decided
simply to stop printing money, a move it should have taken
long before, and would have, except that there was no alternative. Foreign loans and gifts, altogether throughout the war
more than half a million dollars from Spain, and more than
six million from France, were quickly eaten up by the enormous costs of war. By this stage, Congress was reluctantly
concluding that it would have to rely more and more on the
states, in effect to fund its army, and to supply and equip their
own units. This was more of a paper change than anything
else, for that was pretty much what had been happening for
some time now anyway.

But the problem lay not simply in the weakness of the
central government, nor in any other political combination
or lack thereof. The war had by now eaten deeply into the
fabric of colonial society, especially in areas where the war
was actively fought, but even in otherwise quiet areas as well.
Men were away, for longer or shorter periods of time, as regulars or in the militia; a husband or son in the service was a
heavy burden to deal with, particularly in an agricultural society. The men were seldom paid, their families often suffered
real hardship, scarcely alleviated by the efforts of friends,
neighbors, or local patriotic committees. Surviving letters
from wives to husbands tell pathetic tales of bills unpaid and
farms untended; as usual in wartime, it was the women who
were the unsung heroes of the piece. They were massacred
on the frontiers, abused by the passage of armies, and driven
into poverty and despair at home.

Trade was disrupted, especially as colonial America was
so dependent upon waterborne transport. Coastal vessels were
constantly swept up by the Royal Navy, the fishing industry
was ravaged, British hulks in New York Harbor were full of
American sailors who died by the hundreds under scandalous
neglect. There were plenty of markets for colonial industry,

for such products as the output of the iron mines in north-western Connecticut, but all these markets were in the war, and the war itself was nonproductive. Iron went for muskets instead of plows, and the muskets went to kill Englishmen instead of game, and the colonial economy went nearer and nearer to collapse. Some, of course, speculators and contractors, made money out of the war; some always do. But American society as a whole was barely able to sustain the effort it was making.

Consciousness of such difficulties determined Washington's choice of winter quarters at the end of 1779; his army had shrunk again, between detachments, expirations of enlistments, general inactivity, and the inability of first Congress and now the states to sustain their troops. In the rolling and pleasant hills around Morristown, twenty-five miles west of New York City in New Jersey, the army set to work building log huts. They might not have much in the way of clothing or food stocks, but at least by now they knew how to make huts. As they settled down, news came in of the repulse before Savannah. It was not a good augury for the coming year.

CHAPTER FOURTEEN

Seasons of Disaster

Theoretically, in a war, which represents the attempts of either side to impose its will on the other by force of arms, the decline of one should mean the ascendancy of the other, as if the belligerents sat on the ends of a seesaw. Life and history, however, do not lend themselves to the nice balance of forces one derives from mathematics or physics. These are exact sciences, while life and history are messy processes, in which few things ever go as planned, results are seldom those sought after, and consequences almost invariably differ from what they seem to be. The American Revolution by 1780 was less a contest of physical forces than of willpower, or more correctly, staying power. It was likely to prove, as Marshal Foch said of World War I, a matter of who could last fifteen minutes longer.

The Americans' worst enemy over the turn of the year was not the British, but rather their own climate. The troops of the northern army, now ensconced in their winter quarters, encountered an extremely harsh winter, far worse than last year's or the year before at Valley Forge. The 10,000 to 12,000

224

men—numbers varied as they went on outpost duty, fell ill, deserted, or just died—frantically cut trees to keep warm, and soon laid bare the hills around Jockey Hollow. But cutting wood did not answer their pressing needs for food, clothing, and medical supplies. Congress had passed its problems on to the separate states, but they had no more money than the central government did, and the result was the same no matter whose responsibility it was: there were no supplies, and the troops at Morristown suffered.

Some believed they had suffered more than enough for the Patriot cause. There were, as always, numerous desertions. But in late May, when one might have thought the winter crisis pretty well over, two regiments of the Connecticut line came out, formed up without their officers, and got ready to go home. Their officers came running up, there was a scuffle and a bit of a shouting match, and the brigade commander got a punch in the mouth before order was restored, in the form of a Pennsylvania regiment that came in and arrested the ringleaders. The matter then turned into what one authority describes as a New England town meeting. The troops had been on short rations for weeks, and had not been paid for five months, but after they got their grievances out of their system, they returned quietly to their huts, and nothing much was done about it all. Washington, who had once thought mutineers should be summarily punished, took a lenient view; the problem was, he admitted, the troops were right. That made it a little difficult to hang a man.

What they needed, short of supplies or an end to the war, was activity, and fortunately, the campaigning season opened in June. The army was soon on the move, and even if there were only marches and maneuvers that led to little, that was better than sitting starving in the cold. Once again the little army came down out of the hills and took up its vigil around New York City. The equation had not changed much. As long as the British held the sea, they were equally master of New York and its approaches, and that was certainly as true in 1780 as it had been in 1776 when Washington was nearly trapped there. But the soldiers in the line knew little of grand strategy, and as for Washington and his generals, well, they had hopes of something better.

*   *   *

In July it looked as if these hopes might be fulfilled: the French army arrived. This was in some respects a windfall for the Americans arising out of French failures the previous year. In 1779 the government had placed 40,000 troops along the Channel, waiting to invade England. Now, having missed their opportunity to do that, but with their troops mobilized and ready for action, the government agreed to suggestions, in part from Lafayette, that some of these troops be sent as an expeditionary force to America. They decided on a corps of 7,600 men, though in the event they had transport only sufficient for 5,500. They left Brest on the first of May, with an escort of eight of the line, and arrived off Newport and disembarked in the second week of July. The Americans were greatly heartened, and turned out in droves to watch the white coats of famous regiments, Soissonnais, Saintonge, Bourbonnais, and the light blue of Royal Deux-Ponts.

Far more important than the splendid regiments, though, was their commander. After all, d'Estaing had had a splendid fleet, and he had practically ruined the alliance, and the American cause along with it. Fortunately, the French did not make the same mistake a second time. Lafayette had wanted the command, but he was still a young man with far more fame than experience, and the war ministry gave it instead to Jean-Baptiste-Donatien de Vimeur, Comte de Rochambeau, an experienced and well tried—and trusted—brigadier whom they promoted to lieutenant general for the mission. In his fifties, he was a noble and a professional soldier who had fought honorably and well in two wars already, the Austrian Succession and the Seven Years' War. He was tactful enough to handle Lafayette without alienating him, and, most important of all, he and Washington hit it off right from the start.

Both French and Americans would have liked to move against New York City, a project unceasingly advocated by Lafayette; but both generals knew that nothing could be done without command of the sea, and that, for the whole season, was held by the British. Rochambeau's escorting fleet was immediately bottled up in Newport, and though the months brought several shifts of relative strength, it was always that cursed Royal Navy that ended up with a squadron in the right place at the right time. Rochambeau was perfectly willing to act, and he and Washington understood each other well, but the summer, and then the fall, went by, and the French drilled at Newport, and the Americans sat around New York, and nothing happened.

That was not quite correct, for the American cause, beset by mutiny in the spring, was rocked by treason in the fall. It not only came at a very embarrassing time, with the French there, but it was a direct blow to Washington himself, for the traitor was a man he personally trusted and admired, none other than one of the great heroes of the Revolution, Benedict Arnold.

It is ironic that Washington's and Arnold's are arguably the two best-known names in the American Revolution. Few schoolchildren today would recognize such luminaries as Nathanael Greene or Henry Knox, let alone Schuyler or Sullivan, yet almost everyone has heard of Benedict Arnold, whose name, like that of Vidkun Quisling in World War II, has become a synonym for treason.

Life had not gone well for Arnold since the glory days of Saratoga. He was already a man who perpetually felt aggrieved and unappreciated, in large part because he actually was aggrieved and unappreciated; lesser men had repeatedly been promoted over his head, or received the credit for work he had done. This is of course the way of the world, but Arnold, young, ambitious, touchy, overwhelmingly conscious of his own real merits and little disposed to see other men's points of view, grew more and more unhappy. And unfortunately, his personal circumstances combined to reinforce this negative trend of thought.

Convalescent after the great northern victory, Arnold was appointed military governor of Philadelphia, a post he took up in June 1778 after Clinton abandoned the city. He was soon in trouble with almost everyone, for his high living and abrupt manner, and he was finally charged and court-martialed for assorted offenses, some serious, some silly. The eighteenth century was a litigious time, especially when men's honor was concerned, and Arnold's legal affairs dragged on for months, until finally he was cleared of almost everything, receiving on one charge a letter of reprimand from Washington. Though the commander in chief wrote a virtual commendation by way of chastising Arnold, the latter was still furious at not being completely cleared.

Meanwhile, and more to the point, he had married a beautiful young Philadelphia Tory named Peggy Shippen, half his age; less than a month after the wedding, he offered his services to the British. This seems not to have been particularly at his wife's urging, but she certainly knew the people to make contact with, and did more to help than to dissuade. General Clinton's aide-de-camp, John André, became Arnold's handler; for sixteen months, the American hero passed information to the British through a series of Tory intermediaries.

By mid-summer of 1780, Arnold was working to get himself appointed commander of West Point, then perceived as the key fortress on the line of the Hudson, and the vital link between New England and the rest of the rebellion. He was also offering, in effect, to sell it to Clinton, of whom he repeatedly demanded large sums of money. Appointed to West Point, he set about systemically to weaken the garrison by faulty dispositions, to the distress and puzzlement of his subordinates, who of course had no idea what was really going on.

The plot burbled merrily along, Arnold was in regular if surreptitious communication with the British, and on the night of September 21–22 met with Major André to work out some details. When he went back to the British lines, André was picked up by an American militia picket. There was then a near-comedy of errors, as incriminating papers were sent to Washington, who was in the area and about to visit West Point, and notice was also sent to Arnold, who was naturally not suspect at this point. On the morning of the 25th it all came together: Washington arrived, so did irrefutable circumstantial evidence of Arnold's guilt. Arnold fled to a boat which took him downriver to the British, and his wife confused and delayed his pursuers by a brilliant display of histrionics.

André was quickly tried, found guilty, and hanged as a spy, in spite of appeals either for clemency or for death by firing squad. It seemed doubly unfortunate that André, whom everyone regarded as a fine young man of great promise, died an ignominious death while Arnold lived on, commissioned as a brigadier in the British army. But no one on either side ever trusted or liked the Arnolds again, so maybe their fate was ultimately worse than André's.

The whole affair shocked the American cause to the core. Washington was shaken and dismayed, and there was a general feeling that if such men as Arnold could be brought to betray the cause, then matters were serious indeed. Gradually, however, perspective was regained. The treason was Arnold's rather than a general thing, and it was he who was wanting, not the Revolution.

Two supplementary points need to be made. The specific one is that, ever since 1780, a host of writers from serious historians to respected novelists have attempted to rehabilitate Arnold, without any convincing success. His remains a name to stir argument. The more general one is that if honor was more touchy then than now, so principles were more flexible. Private and public business were inextricably mixed; patronage, nepotism, and graft were accepted ways of managing affairs; reasonably honest men might seek accommodation in a family quarrel, and accept rewards for doing so. In other words, the line delineating treason was not very clearly drawn.

None of which obviates the fact that Arnold clearly crossed it.

While Arnold spun his plots, Rochambeau drilled his troops, Washington fretted over keeping his army together, and the Royal Navy held the northern theater in a stranglehold, things happened in the south. The real war had definitively moved to the southern theater. At the end of 1779 the British appeared firmly in possession of Georgia, and in the new year they began to move northward into the Carolinas; modern commentators would call it the "oil slick" method of fighting a war.

At the end of January 1780, Sir Henry Clinton himself, along with Charles, Earl Cornwallis, as his second-in-command, and some 14,000 soldiers, sailors, and marines, arrived off Savannah. They had left New York right after Christmas, against the advice of the naval commanders, and had soon wished they had been more respectful of the weather. There had been heavy storms and head winds all the way; several transports, with most of the horses and many guns, had actually foundered. One ship, carrying a contingent of Hessians, had been blown right across the Atlantic to the Bay of Biscay, then had to turn around and sail back again. Although the original destination of the fleet had been Charleston, in South Carolina, they ended up going first to Savannah just to repair and refit.

At Savannah the British held a council of war, where they began to develop the divergences of view and clashes of personality that were endemic in military politics of the day. Clinton had already requested that he be relieved of command; Cornwallis was his successor-designate, carrying one of the infamous dormant commissions in his pocket. So Clinton, who at the best of times managed to find reasons not to do much, now hemmed and hawed, and consulted and delayed. Finally, after a week of intense but not especially profitable discussions, they moved up the coast and landed near Charleston.

It happened that the Americans at Charleston were in even worse shape than the British about to attack them. Since its heroic defense in 1776, there had been little threat to the city; the fortifications had fallen apart, and so had the militia organization of the area. The major American force available was about 1,600 Continentals, mostly from South Carolina and Virginia, and about 2,000 militiamen from around the state, all under the command of the unlucky General Benjamin Lincoln. Several ships were also in the harbor, trapped by the arrival of the British; most of them were scuttled as blockships, their guns and crews taken to man the land defenses. Lincoln scurried about energetically trying to raise forces and improve fortifications, but it was uphill work.

Meanwhile Clinton moved an inch a day. The troops were gotten quickly ashore—that was the navy's job–but it took a further five weeks before Clinton thought himself ready to begin a formal siege. About the only thing that happened during that period was the arrival of a dispatch from London, telling Clinton his resignation was not accepted. So he had no alternative but to get on with his work.

By April 1 the British were ready to dig, and the siege officially began. The Americans were largely surrounded, though it was possible to get in and out of the city by a circuitous route. After another three weeks, with the British trenches getting ever closer, and the Royal Navy's ships inside the harbor sporadically shelling the town, Lincoln called a council of his own. His officers knew the city was lost, and wanted to get their troops out while they still could, to fight inland. Unfortunately, city and state authorities insisted they stay, and Lincoln was unwise enough to listen to them. After another three weeks, with the British a mere thirty yards from the American defenses and obviously preparing to storm, those same authorities begged Lincoln to ask for terms. Reluctantly he did so, and on the 12th of May surrendered the city, all its stores and supplies, his 2,500 Continental troops, and several hundreds of militiamen. It was in fact the largest American surrender of the war, and a disaster that rivaled the British defeat at Saratoga.

Or at least it should have been. In fact, though it had some obvious influence on the local situation—the Loyalists began to come out in the open again—it had little larger significance at all. The British found once again that when they won, as they usually did, it made little difference. They were the professionals, after all, and no one expected them to do anything but win. It was when the amateur Americans, of whom nobody expected much anyway, won, that fireworks occurred. Saratoga brought France into the war; Charleston was greeted with a yawn, even in Great Britain.

His work done, Clinton went back to New York to shuffle his papers and lament cruel fate. He left Cornwallis with 8,000 troops in Charleston, and ordered him to secure the Carolinas. The noble earl set out to do so with a firm hand. He had in fact several thousand square miles to cover and control; he hoped for assistance from the local Loyalists, and many of them took up arms. He garrisoned a cordon of places facing toward the north, and sent flying columns to pacify the country. The most notable of these was commanded by a young light dragoon named Banastre Tarleton, who soon made a name for himself.

On May 29, at the Waxhaws, Tarleton caught up with a

retreating column of Virginia troops. Although he was badly outnumbered and his men and horses were exhausted after a hard pursuit in killing heat, Tarleton formed his men into line and charged. The Americans held their fire until too late to stop the cavalry, and their line crumpled under the impact. After that it was sabers and bayonets, and a bloody business that the losing Patriots immediately designated a massacre. Troops asking quarter were reportedly cut down viciously; the Americans had more than 100 killed and more than 200 captured, almost all of the latter wounded badly, which indeed suggests a massacre or something very close to it. As a result, Tarleton found himself famous in England and infamous in America, where he became universally known as "Bloody" Tarleton.

The results of such actions were contradictory. Ostensibly, the British and their newly admitted Loyalists were in control of the country. In fact, little bands of outraged Patriots were roaming all over the territory, sniping at redcoats, cutting off couriers, and making nuisances of themselves. The British with their Tarletons were matched by the Americans with their Thomas Sumters and Francis Marions, the latter of whom became famous as "the Swamp Fox." Once again it was civil war, war to the death, with many private as well as public scores settled in the dark of the moon, and men lying face down in the swamps or hanging among the Spanish moss from trees alongside the roads.

What the Americans needed was something to rally around. Guerrillas might cause the British some damage, and become the stuff of legend and schoolboys' tales, but they could not hold territory, and unable to do that, they could not answer for the safety, and thus loyalty, of the population. The Americans needed regular troops who could drive the British back, and eventually out. Washington already recognized this; he was always more disposed toward the creation of and action by regular troops than by militia anyway, and knew that, in addition, the French were demanding more American commitment as return on their investments. He had responded to the southern crisis by starting Continentals south under the command of General Johann Kalb, a Bavarian soldier of fortune who came to America to find a war, and remained to find a country. Kalb had gotten as far as North Carolina with his two brigades of Maryland and Delaware Continentals when Charleston fell, and Congress intervened, without reference to Washington, by appointing Horatio Gates to the command of the Southern Department.

Even after the Conway Cabal, there were those in Congress who were not enamored of Washington, and saw in Gates the means of clipping his wings. The man did have a way with militia, and so he looked as if he might be the one to rally the southerners to the cause; to Washington's detractors, the posting appeared a chance to kill several birds with the same stone. On July 25, Granny Gates arrived to take up his command on the border of the two Carolinas. He immediately designated his 1,300 starvelings the "grand army" and ordered an advance into South Carolina.

The result was a disaster that anyone less vainglorious than Gates might have foreseen. He ignored all local advice about passable routes, availability of supplies, and practically everything else. He commenced his march on July 27, heading his troops straight into the pine barrens of Carolina, where they had nothing to eat themselves, but supplied welcome feasts for hordes of insects. Tarleton's legion before the Waxhaws had covered sixty miles in a day, and done more than a hundred miles in two; it took Gates's pathetic little army two weeks to cover 120 miles, leaving a trail of sick and starved soldiers behind them.

His bombast did have one desired effect, however. The militia began to join in, and by the time he approached Camden he had something around 4,000 men in his command. Of course, his march had not gone unnoticed, so the British concentrated as well. Cornwallis himself had come up, and had a total force of about 2,500 men available. This should not have been enough to fight—the British general did not know the deplorable condition of Gates's troops—but as he had several hundred sick in Camden, and did not want to lose them, Cornwallis chose to stand his ground.

On August 15, Gates called a council to hear his orders. He decided to put his entire army, all disparate units under at least eight different generals, on the move in a night march through unknown country covered with brush and woods, and attack the enemy at dawn. If that were not sufficient folly, he finally found some rations for his troops: green corn and molasses. Half his army got lost during the night, the other half spent the hours running around with their breeches down.

Meanwhile, Cornwallis had decided to do more or less the same thing, and he started his troops north from Camden at about the same time Gates moved south toward it. Advance parties of the two little armies bumped into each other about two in the morning, and a little firefight flared up and then died. Gates called yet another council, which decided they could do nothing but fight where they were, and the Americans spent the rest of the night deploying. Gates put his militia in the front line, on his left and center, with regulars on his right front and in his second, reserve line.

Cornwallis opened the attack on his own right, and the Virginia militia broke at the first sight of the redcoats. They threw down their loaded guns and took off as fast as they could go; the panic infected the North Carolinians in the center, and they broke as well. The Continentals on the American right held on, and the second line, disentangling itself from the fleeing militia, moved up. But the British were all over them, front, flanks, and rear, and the regulars were simply swamped like a rock before a rushing tide. Kalb went down mortally hit after eleven wounds, and the Americans collapsed and scattered.

Horatio Gates has his champions, but even they have been hard-pressed to explain how, on the day of the battle, he himself was the first to reach Charlotte, North Carolina, sixty miles from the scene of his disaster, bringing news of the defeat. Indeed, he barely stopped there; he covered the 120 miles to Hillsboro in the next two days. In three weeks, he had almost ruined the American cause in the south.

There was one happy result of this matter, though. Congress now permitted Washington to appoint a commander of his own choosing to the Southern Department, and his choice was already made. Although Nathanael Greene had recently fallen under a cloud as quartermaster general, largely over disagreements with Congress, Washington unhesitatingly posted him south to salvage the wreck of American hopes there. In the brilliant series of moves that followed, Greene never won a battle, but he completely destroyed British hopes of holding the south.

Cornwallis's fundamental problem, it is worth repeating, was that the British view of the south was incorrect. Their belief that loyalty to the King was sufficiently strong to hold the area, if they provided a rallying point, was simply wrong. There were indeed Loyalists in the south, but they were not strong enough to do what the British expected. From that, Cornwallis's next problem was that he did not have enough men to occupy one territory while he conquered more. Indeed, the more he took, the thinner he got, so that even increased success was ultimately self-defeating. It did little good to beat a rebel force today if another one arose tomorrow, or to take a town today if it reverted to rebel control as soon as the British troops marched out and around the nearest turn in the road. The few towns held by Loyalists were like islands in a sea of Patriots, hostages to British fortune, and as much a liability as a help.

The process of erosion began even before Greene arrived to take up his command. Cornwallis won Camden in mid-August, and he then marched north toward Charlotte, across the line in North Carolina. But in early October came the battle of King's Mountain, a unique event that upset all his plans.

Cornwallis had appointed a Scottish highlander, Major Patrick Ferguson, to command the Loyalist southern militia. Ferguson was known in technical circles as the inventor of an early breech-loading rifle of quite advanced capabilities, and he himself was an active and energetic man. Managing to raise nearly 4,000 Loyalists, he operated generally inland of Cornwallis, in the foothills of the mountain country. But the Patriots were active here too, and there were several forces of their militia as well, including particularly groups known as the "Over-Mountain Men," that is, settlers from across the Blue Ridge in what is now the western part of the state of North Carolina. Such men fiercely resisted regimentation— that was why they lived where they did—but they were hell in a fight. In fact, the Over-Mountain Men made up less than half of the tally of Patriot forces, for when the issue finally came, there were militiamen out from both Carolinas, Virginia, and men from as far away as Tennessee. On October 7, after a great deal of preliminary chasing about, the two sides, Tory and Patriot, met at King's Mountain. Ferguson's entire force consisted of Loyalists of one kind or another, mostly locals but some New York units that by now were as "regular" as anything in either army; of roughly 900 men, he was the only Britisher in the whole group. There were about 1,800 Patriot troops, under a number of separate commanders, most notably Isaac Shelby.

Ferguson took up a position on a low ridge, deciding to make a stand even though he was not cut off and might have retreated. The Americans surrounded him, and scaled the ridge, which is quite steep, with difficulty; several times the Tories launched bayonet charges, which drove the rebels back but were costly in men. Within an hour the Patriots had broken the Tory line and gained the top of the rise, then pushed toward Ferguson's little camp at the northern end of the ridge. The major himself was killed trying to break out, the Tories tried to surrender, and the fighting ended in confusion, in other words, a near-massacre before all the victors were brought under control and induced to stop firing. As usual in affairs such as this, a number of prisoners were summarily tried and hanged. Justice and revenge were hard to distinguish in civil war, and the military formalities were often neglected in the aftermath of battle.

On hearing news of King's Mountain, Cornwallis reluctantly fell back into South Carolina, and spent the next several weeks around Winnsborough. While he did that, guerrillas ate up his supplies and stopped his couriers; at around the same time, Greene arrived, took over command of the wreckage left by Gates, and slowly rebuilt an American army and American confidence. He was faced with a choice of difficulties, but also with a number of opportunities, and his particular virtue as a commander was that he would not allow the former to obscure the latter. In mid-December, with his army only half the size of Cornwallis's 4,000, he boldly split his force. He sent Daniel Morgan, the famed Virginia rifleman, now a brigadier general, west with 600 rifles and light dragoons, to annoy the noble earl on one side, while he moved with the remainder of his men to threaten him on the other.

Cornwallis reacted strongly to such impudence, and he in turn dispatched Banastre Tarleton to cut off and deal with Morgan, while he himself moved north once more. For ten days in early January Tarleton first looked for and then chased Morgan, whom he outnumbered two to one. On January 17 he made the mistake of catching him.

Morgan was a canny old dog, and he took up a position in rolling, more or less open, country, on a rise of ground known as The Cowpens. He put his little army in three lines, a screen of riflemen out front, then the South Carolina militia, and finally his Continentals and some more Virginia riflemen in the main line, keeping his light dragoons in reserve. He told everybody what he wanted: from the first two lines, two good hits, not just shots but hits, then file off and reform behind the main line. This was just about what militia usually could do anyway, and seldom has a battle plan been better suited to the material at hand.

Tarleton came on like the young dandy he was, a fine commander grown careless from poor opposition. He threw his infantry in line, and sent out his light cavalry to develop the enemy position. They came back with a distressing number of empty saddles, but Tarleton did not stop to reflect on that. His infantry now came up the gentle slope against the American second line, to be met by two heavy volleys which cut down several officers and men before the militia, its job done, took off. The British marched on, up to the third line, to be met again. Still they came on, and the Americans fell back under the pressure. Then at the last moment, Morgan got his line stopped and turned around, the Continentals gave a final volley, and came pouring down the hill with bayonets leveled. Morgan's cavalry came in on the flanks, and the British line bunched up. Some shouted for quarter; the 71st Highlanders formed a sort of square and fought desperately on until they were swamped. Tarleton broke clear, and tried to rally his cavalry, which took one good look and fled en masse. Tarleton himself was the last off the field. In an hour's work he had lost more than 900 men, of whom a hundred were killed and the rest wounded or captured or both. Morgan had about seventy casualties, and the American cause in the Carolinas was once again alive and well.

There followed several confused weeks of vigorous marching and countermarching, as both Cornwallis and Greene tried to outmaneuver the other. Both ranged all over the center of North Carolina, and even across the line into Virginia, before they met at last at Guilford Court House on March 15. Here Greene, with about 4,400 troops, tried to do the same thing Morgan had done at the Cowpens. He drew his men up in three lines and let Cornwallis attack him. Cornwallis, who had a mere 1,900 men present, did just that. The British general knew little about the ground, and less about the enemy dispositions, which were rather scattered and difficult to observe on the heavily wooded field. His men were tired and hungry and footsore; they were also sick to death of marching apparently aimlessly about the country, and they were fighting mad.

The British deployed into line and advanced against the first American position, held by North Carolina militia. The militia managed several volleys, then fled before the wicked bayonets as the redcoats drove home. On through the woods the British came until they met the second American line, Virginia militia this time, and again, after several volleys and more losses, they pushed on through. They came up against the main line now, Maryland and Virginia Continentals, some of the best regiments in the American army. The fighting became truly desperate, and at one point, as the Marylanders drove back his grenadiers, Cornwallis opened up with his supporting guns, firing through his own troops, with indiscriminate casualties, to break the American attack.

Greene might have won had he been the gambler his opponent was; but he could not see the whole field, he knew his militia had left already, and he had earlier determined not to lose his army to win a momentary advantage. About the middle of the afternoon, as the fighting reached its crescendo, he began pulling off his units, and he successfully disengaged and got away. The British were too tired to mount any effective pursuit, and Cornwallis was left in possession of the field, to claim a traditional victory and make of it what he could.

Which indeed was not much. If ever there was a useless expenditure of courage, Guilford Court House was it for the British. More than a quarter, perhaps a third, of their forces were casualties, and the desperate bravery of the soldiers won nothing more than the field on which they fought. Cornwallis trailed off to Wilmington, while Greene, still rebuilding and recruiting, was soon on the move again, heading south toward South Carolina and prepared to play the game all over again. But Cornwallis had had enough of trailing his coat through the Carolinas for hard service and no profit. As April of 1781 blossomed into May, he decided to move north into Virginia. It was time to achieve something truly decisive.

CHAPTER FIFTEEN

The Climax of the War

IN THE spring of 1781 the war entered its seventh year. Neither side could see much hope for the future, and both were beset by a war-weariness that, of itself, was becoming a major factor. Neither side asked how long the enemy could last, but rather how long they themselves could last. It seemed as if there was hardly a farm or business in America untouched by the war; ports were blockaded and wharves idle; fields lay fallow while stone walls tumbled slowly back into the ground. The frontier was marked by the charred remains of homesteads and lonely graves; there was no money to turn the wheels of commerce or industry. Even in those places that had not seen much of the actual fighting, say an area such as northeastern Connecticut or central Massachusetts, men were still away, the economy had slowed to a crawl, and people had grown used to the exactions and impositions of a wartime government that was far more demanding than the one they had rebelled against. The whole thing had simply gone on too long. Men desperately wanted it to end, and some flirted with an accommodation, as did the settlers in Vermont. Most, however, wanted it to end only on their terms, and by now that meant independence pure and simple. After six years, these people knew one thing: they were Americans, not Englishmen.

Conditions across the Atlantic, if not as bad economically, were no happier. Lord North's government floundered on. The Netherlands joined the war at the end of 1780, and the Dutch fleet was added to the growing list of enemies. The British tried to find an auxiliary on the Continent who would come in on their behalf and distract their enemies, but no one was interested. In the last war Frederick the Great of Prussia had coined the phrase "perfidious Albion," and it had stuck; none of the European states was willing to pull Britain's chestnuts out of the fire for her this time around. British subsidies were not worth putting up with Britain.

If there was no support abroad for Britain's war effort, there was not much more at home. The government continued to be unpopular. It was universally regarded as corrupt or incompetent or both, though in fact it was neither much better nor much worse than any other government of its period. But every debate was a battle, and Lord North limped from one crisis to the next. In April of 1780, for example, the government lost the Dunning Resolution "that the influence of the crown has increased, is increasing, and ought to be diminished!" That was sufficiently vague to attract all the malcontents, and the resolution passed, 233 votes to 215. In modern parliamentary practice, that would have been a vote of no confidence, and the government would have resigned. But not in 1780. King George would not let him go, and North plodded on.

Even worse happened later in the year, for the summer saw the infamous Gordon Riots in London. This bizarre episode had its roots in the demagoguery of Lord George Gordon, and the ancient British fear and hatred of Catholicism. Lord George was the third son of the duke of Gordon, an ex–naval officer, and a member of Parliament. He was also an erratic and violent anti-Catholic. It happened that in Britain at the time there were still in existence laws against Catholics, which in some cases dated back as far as the sixteenth and seventeenth centuries. Legally, Roman Catholics could not attend university, or hold commissions in the military forces, or do anything else of an official character, because to qualify for any of these things, one had to take an oath to the Crown, and that included acknowledging the sovereign as head of the Church as well as head of the state. Such laws had fallen into abeyance during the last century, and many Catholics had gotten by with the practice of "occasional conformity." For tender consciences, however, this was still a sore point, and in 1778 the government, in an attempt to make recruiting easier among Scottish and Irish Catholic subjects, moved to repeal some of these ancient anti-Catholic laws.

But many Englishmen still hated Catholicism with an atavistic passion. Scottish Presbyterians reacted vigorously to the new acts, and in England itself, Lord George Gordon formed the Protestant Association. Anti-Catholic petitions began to flood into Parliament, and in June, Gordon decided to try more direct pressure. On the 2nd, a crowd of some 50,000 people surrounded Parliament, chanting and singing; though some ministers of the Crown were roughed up getting to their seats, the affair was still more or less amiable.

That night, however, things turned ugly. A mob almost inevitably looks to its lowest elements for leadership, or else it would not be a mob. By dark, the masses of people were moving into the center of London, burning Catholic homes and chapels, breaking windows, and robbing shops. On the 3rd and 4th it got worse, and some observers said that as many as a quarter of a million people were out in the streets, looting, drinking, and burning. There were almost no police in any modern sense; the city authorities were too fearful of the mob to ask for troops, and the national government too afraid to act without a request from the city. On the 6th the mob burned distilleries, which exploded in a fine show, and attacked and opened Newgate prison, letting all the prisoners out to swell the violence. The next day and night, men, women, and even children lay drunk in the streets while the gutters ran with burning alcohol, killing them as they lay.

It was George III himself who finally solved the problem. Overriding the fears of his ministers and the city authorities both, he insisted the troops be called out, and on the night of the 7th, battalions of regular soldiers began herding the mob, and where necessary, firing on them. It took another four days, and almost five hundred dead and wounded, before order was finally restored, ringleaders arrested—several were ultimately hanged, though Gordon's connections got him off, of course —and life returned to what passed for normal in 1780.

Across the Channel in France, things were not as overtly bad as they were in Britain, but there was a great deal of dissatisfaction with the war. The French social and political scene was so markedly different that comparisons are difficult; no French minister had to face a hostile representative assembly—that was in a not-too-distant but still unforeseen future—but the burden of debt was skyrocketing under the demands and necessities of the war, and it was hard even for the responsible ministers to see that they were getting much out of it. Was it worth courting national bankruptcy just to tweak the lion's nose? And were they getting their money's worth anyway? Giving money to the Americans was like trying to fill a bottomless pit with banknotes. General Washington did not even seem to be fighting with his army in the north; no one could figure out what was happening in the south, except that on the face of it the Americans appeared to be losing as usual. There was still a vast enthusiasm for "liberty" among literary and intellectual circles, but the closer one looked at the Americans, the less appealing they were as exemplars of this fascinating principle.

It was therefore possible to agree on one thing as 1781 began: everyone was dissatisfied—with his allies, with himself, with the world in general.

Militarily, the Americans began 1781 as they had 1780— with a mutiny. This time it was much more serious than it had been last year. Anthony Wayne's brigade of the Pennsylvania Line came out, under arms, on January 1, left their encampments at Morristown, and marched off for Philadelphia, trailing their officers behind them, and announcing that they would have redress of their grievances or know the reason why. The men were orderly and well-behaved, treated their officers respectfully though they would not obey them, and as with all American soldiers of the war, had perfectly legitimate complaints, which made it that much more difficult for the officers to deal with them. The troops, more than a thousand strong, marched as far as Princeton, where they were met by Pennsylvania state authorities and officials from Congress.

Negotiations between the two sides were put under added pressure from Henry Clinton; as soon as he heard of the mutiny, he readied his own troops for a move into New Jersey, and sent emissaries to treat with the disaffected troops. The Pennsylvanians were not traitors, however, just angry, and they arrested Clinton's men and threatened to hang them as spies. Meanwhile they agreed with the American negotiators on release of men whose enlistments were up, on back pay, clothing allowances, and such important minutiae of the soldiers' lives. It was the end of the month before order was fully restored. By then the New Jersey Line had mutinied as well, and several of their leaders were actually shot before the affair was settled. Once more it was clear that winter quarters, no pay, poor rations, and most of all inactivity and time to brood, were not good for the troops.

That only underlined the Americans', and General Washington's, strategic problem. Henry Clinton and the British army still sat firmly, and comfortably, in possession of New York City; they did not seem disposed to move out of it on their own accord, and until they did, there was very little that could be done about them. Taking New York became a near obsession with Washington. Eighteenth-century generals seldom realized that the enemy army was a far more important object than the enemy's cities, and Washington was no exception. In this case it made no difference, because taking one meant taking the other. As long as the British held the major city of the United States, they could argue that their war effort was viable. How to deprive them of it constantly haunted Washington's thoughts.

The basic difficulty was sea power, and the Americans' lack of it. Early in May, however, things began to develop. General Rochambeau's son arrived in Boston with the bad news that the second element of the French troops whom his father commanded was not going to arrive; the French government could not provide the transport to get them across the Atlantic. But young Rochambeau brought good news with him as well. A French fleet under Admiral François-Joseph-Paul de Grasse, the Comte de Grasse, was operating in the

West Indies, and the ministry had issued orders that it was to sail north for the summer season and cooperate with the Franco-American forces on the mainland. Armed with this information, Rochambeau met Washington at Wethersfield, near Hartford in Connecticut, on May 22.

There was now an interesting balance of forces. Clinton was in New York City with a garrison of something more than 10,000 men. Cornwallis was in the Carolinas, possibly moving north toward Virginia; there were smaller forces of British and Loyalists operating in that latter state, along Chesapeake Bay. At the moment, the British generally held local command of the sea. On the allied side, Rochambeau had about 4,000 French troops at Newport, and an inferior naval squadron held inside the harbor there. Washington had 3,500 Continental troops, mostly New Englanders, around New York City. More regulars, troops from the middle states under Wayne, were on the verge of moving south to support Lafayette, who was in Virginia with a loose collection of regulars and militiamen, trying to contain the British there. Finally Nathanael Greene was in the Carolinas, skipping back and forth in front of Cornwallis.

The question facing the two generals was where and how to operate, and its resolution depended largely upon two French admirals. What would Vicomte Paul-François Barras, with his ships at Newport, do, and what would de Grasse, coming up from the West Indies, do, and together would they be strong enough to seize command of the sea along the coast from the British? The first thought was that allied troops from the north should be taken south by Barras to the Chesapeake, and the situation in Virginia thus stabilized. Barras was unwilling to do that, for reasons that seemed good enough to him; he did not want to sail, with a relatively weak fleet, encumbered by a convoy of merchantmen and transports, across the flank of the British Navy. The next suggestion was that the French and American land forces march against New York City; they would not be sufficient to take it, but they might well alarm Clinton enough to make him bring home troops from the south. That should mean abandoning Newport, but Barras could take his ships to Boston, so the Rhode Island base would be superfluous anyway. Unfortunately, Barras did not want to do that either. Well what, asked Rochambeau, if de Grasse came north in sufficient strength to alter the whole balance? Washington thought that would be lovely, and something might really be achieved against New York then; however, by now he had sufficient experience of French admirals not to make any plans on the basis of their promises, even though he was too polite to say so to Rochambeau. So they left the conference with the understanding that, if it worked out, they would cooperate during the summer. It was not much of a result, but at least they trusted each other, and recognized mutual good intent.

Because of this situation, the practical initiative passed from the generals to Admiral de Grasse. It was fortunate indeed for the future of the United States that here at last was a sailor worthy of his charge. A member of the old nobility of France, de Grasse had learned his trade sailing with the Knights of St. John of the Hospital, at Malta. Returning to the French Navy in 1740, he had a brilliant career in two wars and fighting against privateers and pirates, and was both a capable seaman and administrator. In March of 1781, now a rear admiral, he sailed from Brest for the West Indies, with twenty of the line, three frigates, and a convoy of 150 merchantmen.

When he reached the Caribbean, he found the British in disarray. Their commander, Admiral Sir George Rodney, had recently captured the newly belligerent Dutch island of St. Eustatius; this coup netted three million pounds in prize money, and Rodney spent the next three months counting his gains. While he did so, de Grasse got safely to his destination, delivered his convoys, and was free to look for trouble. Sitting safely in the French base at Cap François on the north coast of Haiti, he sent letters to Rochambeau and Washington. At long range the three worked out the possibilities. De Grasse was prepared to bring his fleet north; the allies could go either for Clinton in New York, or Cornwallis, now in Virginia on the Chesapeake. De Grasse, as soon as the summer hurricane season ended, was planning to cooperate with a proposed Spanish fleet against Jamaica. He wanted to be able to get back to the West Indies in reasonable time, and also in decent condition. Therefore the waters of the Chesapeake looked better to him than the open ocean around New York Bay. So gradually the idea of a shift south began to germinate in the minds of the allied leaders.

After his costly victory at Guilford Court House, Earl Cornwallis had moved southeast to Wilmington, in March of 1781, near the seacoast on the border of the two Carolinas. Nathanael Greene had followed him part of the way, rebuilding his little army as he went. Greene then turned right and moved down into South Carolina, where he undertook a series of operations that eventually reclaimed the state for the American cause. Cornwallis, after pulling his force together, marched northeast toward Virginia, where there were already numbers of British troops in action.

In the Old Dominion, the British had decided that they might again cut the rebellion in two. In the sheltered waters of Chesapeake Bay, small amphibious expeditions could harass the Patriots, cut their communications between north and south, and perhaps push them back toward the west so far as to overstretch and ultimately break their lines. There was an economic side to this as well, for Virginia was one of the more prosperous states, exporting large quantities especially of tobacco. As early as May 1779, the British raided the ports at the mouth of the Chesapeake, doing two million dollars' worth of damage to shipping, tobacco for export, and military supplies.

In December of 1780 Benedict Arnold showed up, wearing the uniform of a British brigadier general, and with 1,200 troops raided up the James River as far as Richmond. His only opposition was General Steuben and some extremely reluctant Virginia militiamen. The governor of the state, Thomas Jefferson, who was elected in 1779, was better as a political philosopher than as a practical politician, and he began pleading for help. Washington responded by sending down Lafayette and a brigade of Continental light infantry made up of New Englanders and New Jersey troops, and asking the French to dispatch a naval squadron with troops from Newport. When Rochambeau obliged, his naval commanders made a mess of it again, got beaten in a smallish action and went back to Newport, while Clinton sent down 2,000 more troops, under General William Phillips, to support and supersede Arnold.

From this point on, men and events gradually centered in Virginia. Lafayette marched his men south, borrowing money on his own credit to get them supplied; Phillips, Arnold, and other British commanders raided along the Chesapeake and up its rivers; Cornwallis marched north from the Carolinas; Washington sent more troops south to reinforce Lafayette. So it went. In June and July, Cornwallis repeated with Lafayette the same kind of game he had played with Greene, chasing him here and there throughout Virginia, without ever quite catching him. Finally, in late June, totally disgusted with the course of events, Cornwallis gratefully received instructions from Clinton: fall back on the Chesapeake and establish a base. This endless hare-and-hounds game was getting them nowhere, but a British soldier could always be happy and secure within the smell of salt water.

Such a comfortable illusion was soon to be dispelled. As July turned into August, the Americans and their French allies developed one of the few great strategic combinations of the entire eighteenth century. It consisted of essentially five elements: Rochambeau's army, Washington's army, Lafayette's forces in Virginia, Barras's squadron from Newport, and de Grasse from the West Indies. All of these had to come together at just the right time, and miracle of miracles, for once they did. They were not only lucky with wind and weather, but they had as well to outwit their enemy, and they did that too.

All of these forces had to be moved simultaneously to come together in Virginia. First, Rochambeau marched his little army out of Newport and across Connecticut, a glorious march carried out in the second part of June. The French infantry moved through the central part of the state, while a cavalry legion commanded by the Duc de Lauzun took a more southern route. A young staff officer named Alexander Berthier planned the march, and sketched out the routes to be followed; it was the kind of summer frolic a soldier would dream about thirty-some years later, stuck in the snows of Russia. The drums muttered and the fifes tootled, and the Connecticut girls turned out to stare and giggle and the French soldiers twirled their moustaches, rolled their eyes, and strutted proudly along. This was the kind of thing that made young boys join the army.

In early July the French combined with Washington's army north of New York City. A few skirmishes soon confirmed that the city was impregnable, and that the southern operation was the more viable. While the two armies made a lot of noise along the Hudson, their commanders began slipping units south along the New Jersey shore, so that when Henry Clinton noticed what was happening, it might look as if his enemies were planning a move against, say, Staten Island. By late August, the 7,000 men of the allied mobile forces were concentrated around New Brunswick in New Jersey, while militia and a few regulars still held the line of the Hudson. Washington had received letters from de Grasse saying that he was sailing for the Chesapeake with 29 warships and 3,000 troops. The allied army was now in position to jump southward.

Meanwhile, the naval combination was even more complicated. De Grasse left the West Indies in mid-August, sailing north for the mainland. The British squadron there, now commanded by Admiral Sir Samuel Hood—Rodney had gone down sick—chased him north. However, de Grasse, seeking to delude the British as to his final destination, took a roundabout route through the Bahama Channel. As a result, Hood beat him to the mouth of the Chesapeake; he looked in there, satisfied himself that Cornwallis and the British forces in the area were safe, and therefore concluded that de Grasse must be sailing for New York. So he left the Virginia capes and sailed up to New York City. No sooner had he passed over the horizon than de Grasse and the whole French fleet arrived, entered Lynhaven Bay at the mouth of the Chesapeake, and then began off-loading troops and equipment.

When Hood arrived at New York, he was nonplussed to see no French fleet there. Once in New York, he came under the command of the admiral on the North American station, Admiral Thomas Graves. Lacking anything better to do, they sailed up to Newport and had a look in there, only to find that Barras too had disappeared. He had in fact left just ahead of them, taking artillery and supplies to the Chesapeake.

It now dawned on an increasingly horrified Clinton that the allies were closing a trap around Cornwallis, and that if the British were to lose, even temporarily, command of the sea, the result might be disastrous. On the last day of August, Graves and Hood together sailed south from New York, hoping to catch Barras at sea and destroy him before he could reach the Virginia capes and de Grasse.

The allied land element had begun its march south from New Jersey at the end of August, just a few days before Graves sailed. They reached Philadelphia on September 3; the troops were in fact unhappy at marching south, and it took strenuous efforts to find them some pay and provisions and keep them going. Washington himself led the way, in a fever of uncertainty: was Cornwallis still there, would de Grasse actually arrive, would the whole thing work for once? He finally got his answer when he reached Chester, near the top of the Chesapeake. Yes, Cornwallis was in Yorktown, yes, de Grasse was at the mouth of the bay, and was even sending boats and shallow vessels up the bay to transport the soldiers from there and from Baltimore. When Rochambeau and his staff arrived, they were astounded to find the dignified American commander jumping up and down, waving his hat, and grinning like a small boy!

While Washington and Rochambeau were congratulating each other, on September 5, the campaign was actually being decided. Graves and de Grasse were fighting the Battle of the Chesapeake Capes. The British admiral had sailed south with nineteen of the line in pursuit of Barras. When he raised the capes on the morning of the 5th, he expected to find this admiral and his weak squadron and a gaggle of transports. In fact, Barras did not arrive for another five days, so once again the British had sailed faster than their prey. What Graves did find, however, was de Grasse with twenty-four of the line anchored in Lynhaven Bay.

It was a morning of calms and fitful breezes. The French were in complete disarray, unloading material, with working parties ashore, and everything adrift. Hastily they recalled their crews, put themselves in order, and began sallying out past the capes.

Graves could have done either of two things. He might

have sailed in just as he was, devil take the hindmost, and thrashed it out, like Admiral Hawke at Quiberon Bay or Lord Nelson later at the Nile. But Graves was neither of these. Coping with the inadequacies of the British signaling system and the standing *Fighting Instructions*, he struggled to put his own ships in formation, thus giving the far more mixed-up French time to pull themselves together. Then the two fleets, line ahead, sailed off to the southeast, exchanging desultory fire as they came within range of each other.

The actual battle was a total anticlimax. Late in the afternoon Graves, his line finally more or less in order, tried to close with the French; his juniors stubbornly refused to comprehend what he was attempting; Hood never even bothered to try to figure out what his commander wanted, and by nightfall Graves was thoroughly disgusted, and had accomplished nothing.

The fleets remained in sight of each other for five days, with nothing of any substance occurring. Then the wind shifted, and de Grasse, now with the initiative, headed back toward the capes. When he got there, he saw Barras; that raised his force from twenty-four to thirty-six of the line, against Graves's nineteen. Facing odds such as that, the British admiral sailed sullenly off to New York, and left Cornwallis to his own devices. The Chesapeake Capes thus became one of the decisive nonbattles of history.

As the possibility of disaster unfolded before him, Henry Clinton decided to play one more card, albeit a weak one. Benedict Arnold had returned to New York from Virginia, and the British now decided that a strike up the coast from New York might serve to distract the emerging American combination. With Arnold's advice, they fixed on New London, Connecticut, a bothersome nest of privateers and inveterate rebels. A force of about 1,700 men, regulars, Germans, and Tories, sailed up Long Island Sound and appeared off New London on the morning of September 6. Landing on both sides of the Thames River, the troops soon took the town, much of which was subsequently burned, the Americans said deliberately, the British said by accident.

The main defense, however, was at Fort Griswold, a

square earth and stone work on a substantial rise in back of the town. Its garrison of about 160 men, a few state troops and mostly militia, under Colonel William Ledyard, made a good resistance. Twice the British were driven back from the ditch and outerworks, before they came swarming in on the third try. There was some confused bayonet work, and then Ledyard offered to surrender. He turned over his sword to a Tory officer, who then stabbed him with it; an American officer then stabbed the Tory, and the fight swung up again, or in fact became a massacre, as most of the Americans had already thrown down their arms. Within a few minutes eighty men were killed and another fifty shot or bayoneted, before the slaughter stopped.

Arnold was apparently still in the town, clearing out resistance there. Nonetheless the massacre at Fort Griswold was attributed to him, and a hundred years later, the monuments around Fort Griswold, which is still there above New London, testified to Connecticut's bitterness about her most infamous son. The New London raid was in fact the last major operation in the north of the Revolutionary War, no more than a senseless waste of life and property.

By the second week in September, the British options were becoming increasingly unrealistic. The hope of rescue by the navy was gone, as was the thought that minor pinpricks in the north would provide a sufficient distraction. Clinton, with nearly 17,000 troops in New York—he had been reinforced again—surely might have done more against the weak American containing forces, but Henry Clinton was not the man for the desperate move. He was once more busy trying to resign, so he sat shuffling his papers and thinking himself into a frame of mind where everything was someone else's fault, and it served them bloody right, too. That left Cornwallis himself.

With an army that numbered altogether about 9,500 men, Cornwallis had settled in around Yorktown, a little settlement at the very mouth of the York River. He threw up extensive field fortifications, and detached a force across the river to hold Gloucester, on the opposite bank. Having done that, he simply waited for something to happen. It was highly uncharacteristic for the man who had chased Greene all across the Carolinas, who had fired through his own troops to win Guilford Court House, and who would later win fame in India. Some authorities have suggested that he was in the same bloody-minded mood as Clinton, and that the two were at such cross-purposes that they lost the campaign and the war between them. Others have offered the simpler explanation that Cornwallis and his troops both were just exhausted, and therefore succumbed to inertia at this crucial moment.

Whatever chance there might have been for a breakout before the French arrived, or before Washington and Rochambeau arrived, disappeared in the third week of September with the advent of the allied forces from the north. These swelled the besiegers' ranks to a total of 20,000, and left the issue in little doubt. It took the French and Americans ten days to get fully organized, but once they did the outcome was a more or less foregone conclusion.

Yorktown was really not a good choice for defense, as Cornwallis soon found. It was a pretty little place, somewhat decayed from earlier in the century; on a little bluff overlooking the river, it was backed by sloping and rolling ground that offered few advantages of terrain. The British fieldworks were only about three hundred yards deep and a thousand yards long, with some isolated redoubts forward of them. Gloucester Point was also fortified, and several ships guarded the river, eventually being sunk and their crews added to the garrison.

The French and Americans drew up in a long semicircle ringing their prey. The French generously took the left of the line, ceding the place of honor on the right to their allies, perhaps in tacit remembrance of d'Estaing's obstinacy at Newport. Cornwallis abandoned his outposts on the allied approach, giving up some useful ground but saving his men. His fatal correspondence with Clinton had cropped up again, and he had received letters saying another fleet would attempt a rescue early in October, so he concentrated on preserving his army and his last, best, line.

As soon as they had their heavy guns moved up, the allies began a regular siege. On October 6 the French on their side opened a flying sap, that is, a trench providing cover for infantry to approach an enemy work. Meanwhile, on the American side, regular siege lines were begun. The soil made easy digging, and in one night the Americans had a position that would allow a bombardment. They moved their guns up, and the fire was officially opened on the 9th. Within a mere twenty-four hours the British guns were all but submerged, and their return fire faltered. Cornwallis and his staff, and off-duty troops, were driven out of the main part of town and under the bluff, where they took shelter from the din and the crashing cannonballs.

On the night of the 14th, the allies moved to take two strong positions directly to the front of their siege lines. The French attacked Redoubt No. 9 and the Americans Redoubt No. 10. Given that this was a joint operation, there was a good deal of rivalry between the two allies; the French commander suggested condescendingly that he was not sure the Americans were up to real war, while on the American side Lafayette, whose light infantry brigade was to do the job, burned to show up his countrymen. Storming a battery was a potentially desperate business, and these proved the rule. The French ran into heavy fire, had trouble getting through the abatis and ditch, and took serious casualties before overrunning their target, which was defended as gallantly as it was attacked. The Americans, led by a forlorn hope of twenty men of the 4th Connecticut, swept forward against a more lightly manned redoubt, swarmed across the ditch, and took the battery minutes ahead of the French. Lafayette could not resist sending an officer over to ask if any help was needed.

The allies now put guns forward in a second parallel or bombardment position. The siege was now approaching a climax. Early on the morning of the 16th the British mounted a sortie, sending 350 troops out to raid the siege lines and destroy the cannon if possible. The British got into the line, spiked six guns by driving bayonets into the touch holes, and were then driven back by some Americans and a party of French who were nearby.

Even the elements seemed to combine against the British now. The next night Cornwallis decided to ferry his troops across to Gloucester Point and break out from there, but a vicious storm came up, swamped his few available boats, and caused him to cancel the plan. The next day, the 18th, the allies opened a tremendous bombardment from a hundred guns, and the British knew they were doomed. After consulting with his officers—a gloomy meeting indeed—Cornwallis decided there was no alternative to surrender. About midmorning a brave drummer appeared on the British parapet and beat for a parley. This time, unlike a previous example at Bennington, the Americans knew what he meant, and firing slowly ceased.

Cornwallis wanted a twenty-four-hour truce to work out terms; Washington granted two hours for the submission of proposals. In fact it was noon of the 20th before all the details were hashed out; an eighteenth-century siege was as formal as a minuet, and all the niceties of victory and defeat had to be carefully calculated according to the etiquette of the day, including such matters as what marches either side's bands would play, whether units' colors would be flying or cased, guns loaded or unloaded, and a whole host of other points vitally important to soldiers. The twentieth century, which regards itself as above such trivialities, might recall that truce talks for the Korean conflict almost stalled over who should sit at what side of the table, or the long delay in the Vietnam cease-fire talks over the shape of the table at which the negotiators were to meet.

The terms were in fact generous. Arms and military equipment were to be surrendered, and the soldiers to go into captivity. But private property might be retained—a subsequent sore point as much of that "private property" had been liberated from the Carolinians and Virginians. Officers were allowed to keep their sidearms and were paroled, either home or to one of the places still in British hands. Washington carefully provided Cornwallis with a ship to carry dispatches and such people as he might designate, a euphemism for some two hundred American deserters among the British ranks, who thus got away to New York and saved everyone a great deal of embarrassment. Finally the details were all worked out, and at noon on the 20th, American and French detachments occupied portions of the British defenses. The two allied armies then lined up facing each other along the route by which the British would march out to surrender and lay down their arms in a large field some two miles from York-town itself.

The scene was solemn and impressive. The French looked dashing in their white uniforms with light-colored facings, all neat and correct, with the white standards of the Bourbons and the different regimental colors flying. But it was still the Americans who attracted the most attention. Washington, every inch the Virginia gentleman, would dearly have loved to mount an equal show, but his troops were not up to it. Clean and polish as they might, nothing could disguise patched knees in ragged breeches, or jackets cut down until there was little left of them. The commander in chief and his staff had uniforms, and many of the regimental officers did as well, blue or brown faced with buff, red, or white. But the troops looked like what they were, rawboned, hard-used men who had fought a long war on starvation wages. It was just as well; they were far more impressive in their poverty than they would have been in unfamiliar finery.

Finally music was heard and the defeated enemy appeared, marching between the allied lines. These were King George's best soldiers, and they took defeat badly. Many were in tears, a goodly number were drunk; the Germans were correct and very quiet. The British, when they reached the circular field at the end of the march, often threw down their weapons, trying to break them. Returning to town weaponless, they looked less an army than a crowd. Cornwallis himself did not appear. He was taken conveniently ill, and deputized General Charles O'Hara of the Guards to surrender for him. The Irishman gracelessly tried to surrender to Rochambeau, was directed to Washington, and then finally to General Lincoln, a deputy received by a deputy. Sooner than one would have thought, it was all over, and the crowds of civilians who had appeared to watch the ceremony drifted off.

Washington sent off his dispatch: "I have the honor to inform Congress, that a reduction of the British Army under the Command of Lord Cornwallis, is most happily effected. . . ." Meanwhile Cornwallis wrote Clinton, "I have the mortification to inform your Excellency that I have been forced to give up the posts of York and Gloucester, and to surrender the troops under my command. . . ."; he then passed on to explanations of why none of this was his fault.

The British rescue fleet cleared the bar in New York Harbor while surrender terms were being negotiated. They arrived off the Chesapeake a week after the capitulation, and turned around and sailed back to New York.

At the time, great victory though it assuredly was, no one saw exactly what Yorktown meant. There was still a major British force in New York, and smaller but by no means unimportant holdings in the south, at Wilmington, Savannah, and Charleston. There was still plenty of activity along the frontier. And indeed, the larger war still raged.

Only one man immediately recognized what had happened. On November 25 dispatches reached London from America. Lord North, looking them over, broke out with a horrified, "Oh, God! It is all over!" But the unfortunate North was smarter than most men.

CHAPTER SIXTEEN

The World War

T HE BRILLIANT success of Yorktown marked a period to the war, but, to the perplexity of American students, did not mark the end of it. To understand why, when Yorktown was won late in 1781, peace was not signed until almost two years later, and the British maintained their holdings in America even longer than that, it is necessary to look at the larger context of the war. There were military campaigns, of greater or lesser import, all over the world; then, when these had worked their course, it is also necessary to examine the political situation of the three main protagonists, the United States, France, and Great Britain, to see what finally pushed them toward a reluctant and unsatisfactory peace.

Wars more often end with a whimper than with a bang. Even in the twentieth century, which has been called "the century of total war," only World War II ended with the utter collapse of one side and the complete triumph of the other. Most wars end by negotiation, a compound of small advantage and increasing exhaustion or war-weariness. If this is the case now, it was even more so in the eighteenth century, when wars were fought for economic, geostrategic, or dynastic advantages, rather than for consuming ideologies. The American Revolution, though it had much more of ideology to it than other wars of the century, was still no exception to the rule, and indeed, in its conclusion conformed quite closely to the other imperial wars of the time.

Much of that was because the American portion of the war was overshadowed by other events. This was especially true after Yorktown, though it had become obvious even before then. With Cornwallis and his 9,000 troops safely in captivity, Washington had to decide what to do next. It was not an easy decision. The British still held New York in overwhelming numbers, and they had as well posts throughout the south. Eventually he sent some reinforcements to Nathanael Greene, and returned himself to his seemingly endless watch of New York City.

Over the next several months Greene managed to clear the interior of the Carolinas and Georgia, though he maintained his unbroken record of defeat on the battlefield. In April 1781, soon after he had given up his game of chase with Cornwallis, he was beaten by Francis Rawdon at Hobkirk's Hill, just outside Camden. Defeat at Rawdon's hands was no shame, as he went on to a distinguished career in the French Revolutionary Wars and in India. But Greene continued his policy of capitalizing strategically on tactical reverses, and he cleared all of western North Carolina while the victorious but hungry British fell back on the seacoast. The last major action of the war came in September, when Green met another British force at Eutaw Springs. Here he would actually have won a battle, had not his hungry troops broken up to loot the British camp. This allowed the redcoats time to regroup and counterattack, and drive off their victors. But yet again Greene surmounted circumstance, and the maneuvering ended with the British confined to Savannah and Charleston, where they stayed from then on.

Unfortunately that did not end the fighting in the south. Though the British did not try to overrun and hold any more territory, there was another year of guerrilla war, with little bands of Tories and Patriot forces chasing each other about the area. This was very unpleasant for those on the losing end of any particular clash, and though in the long run it did not amount to much, in that the strategic situation was not changed at all, it meant a great deal of pain for those involved.

The south was not the only theater to feel much pain for small gain. Along the frontiers and in the West, skirmish, ambush, and outrage continued. West of a long line that ran from northern New York State all the way down to Kentucky, little columns of Americans on one side, and Indians, Tories, and British on the other, moved silently through the wilderness, falling on isolated posts, ambushing supply parties, and at worst, attacking and murdering settlers foolish enough, or brave enough, to be out on their own on the open frontier. Neither side lacked in courage and endurance, nor was either free of the taint of massacre. In March of 1782 American militia slaughtered about a hundred Indian men, women, and children at the Moravian missionary settlement of Gnaden-hutten in Ohio. This set off a wave of Indian attacks along the whole frontier. An American retaliatory column under Colonel William Crawford was defeated and scattered in June. Crawford and several others were taken prisoner, tortured, and killed by the Indians; Crawford himself was scalped and subsequently roasted alive by his captors, a revolting process that British observers reported took several hours. British officers involved in this frontier warfare were totally powerless—if in fact they were disposed—to control the Indians whom they had incited to war, and on whose favor their success and indeed survival depended.

The same story of raid and counterattack was repeated along the New York frontier. Sullivan's expedition of 1779 had been meant to destroy the Indians, or their ability to sustain operations; instead, it had deprived them of any alternative but war for survival. All through 1780 and 1781 there was bitter, dreadful fighting along the Mohawk Valley and in western New York State. At a couple of points it looked as if the frontier might collapse completely, and at the actual moment when Washington was marching south to Yorktown, several hundreds of the few troops left to contain Clinton were necessarily sent to Albany, Schenectady, and other northern posts. The Johnsons and the Butlers ranged almost at will across the country, until they were eventually met and mastered by American leaders, such as Marinus Willett, as tough and wily as they were themselves. But it was late in 1782 before the raids were contained and slowly began to taper off, with the Tories, their British supporters and their Indian allies grudgingly driven back into Canada.

There have been authorities on the period who have seen in all this a grand strategic design, on the part of American commanders, especially Washington, to affirm the United States' claim to the Old Northwest; or on the part of the British, and men such as Henry Hamilton, to preserve the Ohio Country for Great Britain. In fact, however, it seems that this was less the case than it was a simple response to the desperate exigencies of the moment. There were certainly those of vision, most notably George Rogers Clark, who had a long view of what they were about; but most of the men and women involved were merely caught in the turmoil and upheaval of war, national, civil, or racial, a cruel situation almost beyond anyone's power to direct or contain. It was only in struggling against their fate that they also mastered their future.

George Washington, meanwhile, struggled against a different sort of problem: how to maintain military pressure, indeed, how to maintain an army, when there was little perceived need for either, and when the country was exhausted financially and psychologically. In the immediate flush of victory, Washington tried to persuade de Grasse and the French forces to move south, and to do at Charleston what they had just so successfully done at Yorktown. All his efforts were fruitless; de Grasse stuck firmly to his insistence that he must return to the West Indies, and he soon did so. Rochambeau's expeditionary force went into winter quarters in Virginia, and Washington divided his own command, sending the southern regiments to help Greene, and the northern ones back to New York to their endless watch. He himself took a short furlough, the first since the war began.

With the coming of spring he was back in the Hudson Highlands again, trying to figure out some move that would finish the job. He explored all the available options, and found none promising. New York was just too strong to be forced. For a while he toyed once again with the old dream of conquering Canada, but had to give it up. There was a stir of excitement in May, when news filtered through the lines that Henry Clinton was finally finished; at last he got the relief from command that he had long said he wanted, and he sailed away for home, only to find that Cornwallis had successfully shifted all the blame for Yorktown to his shoulders. His successor was, of all people, Sir Guy Carleton, whose appointment was the product of a change of ministries in Britain. This did little to change the situation around New York; Carleton neither brought reinforcements, nor made any move to evacuate the city. Things went on as before, and a frustrated General Washington sat and fumed in Newburgh, trying to keep his army together.

These were trying times indeed, and relatively small matters assumed great importance. An example was the Huddy-Asgill affair. While the British dampened down their operations, the Loyalists became ever more desperate, and there was a great deal of raiding back and forth between the lines. On one of these, into New Jersey, a Tory officer was shot under cloudy circumstances after being taken prisoner. Loyalists in New York responded by taking an artillery captain named Joshua Huddy out of a prison hulk, and hanging him on the New Jersey shore with a note on his chest: ". . . up goes Huddy for Philip White." The New Jersey Patriots responded in turn by taking a prisoner, nineteen-year-old Captain Charles Asgill of the Guards, chosen by lot, and announcing they would hang him.

This became a matter of state. The British protested, saying the Loyalists had proceeded without proper authorization. Asgill's mother wrote the French minister of war, the Comte de Vergennes; Louis XVI and Marie-Antoinette themselves were said to be in agonies over the fate of this lovely young man, and Vergennes wrote Washington. It was the sort of romantic imbroglio the period loved, full of sighing heroes and swooning heroines, and in the end the British promised to behave and Asgill was let off. The whole provided an interesting comparison with all the other fine, dead young men in the last seven years, but war has a lavish hand in scattering its ironies.

Affairs such as this were of passing importance, but the

overriding and insoluble problem was that of trying to keep the army together. And the bottom line on that issue was the same one that had plagued the country almost since the beginning: bankruptcy. There was no money, and still no money. Soldiers deserted individually and mutinied en masse, and still there was no money. It got even worse through 1782, for now not only were the soldiers' needs neglected, so were the officers'. Congress continually passed its obligations back to the states, and the states, unable to shift the burden elsewhere, just ignored it. The burden therefore came back full circle, to the men who were bearing it in the first place. Washington wrote letter after letter to Congress; he begged, he cajoled, he argued, he pleaded. The result was always the same: no money. During the summer and fall months the army starved in the midst of plenty; no one would advance credit, large or small, and the soldiers went hungry while apples fell from the trees around them, and the beef cattle fattened in the nearby fields.

It was particularly embarrassing when the French came back from Virginia, on their way to New England and embarkation for home. The two allies, fast friends through shared perils, entertained each other; but the French had money, the Americans did not. The former set groaning tables filled with delicacies; the latter could offer only meager return, and American officers were soon declining invitations because they could not afford to return them.

Eventually the officers themselves threatened a sort of mutiny. They set up a committee, drew up a petition, and sent a delegation off to Congress to air their grievances. The gentlemen in Philadelphia heard them out, and made soothing noises, but did—could do—nothing. The officers were not satisfied with noise. They announced ominously that they would not leave the city, but would remain until they got satisfaction.

As usual, there were men prepared to fish in these troubled waters. Not everyone liked the idea of a republic; it was indeed highly radical for the time. The constitution of the new country, called the Articles of Confederation, had not yet been ratified by all the states, and it provided for an excessively weak central authority, with no taxing power—the root of the problem. Some men, such as Alexander Hamilton, who wanted a stronger central government, saw the army as a way to get it, even if it meant a dictatorship by General Washington. The question of keeping the army afloat thus got all tied up with the matter of the kind of country the United States should be, and the whole became so tangled that soldiers, and even officers, could hardly see their way through the mess. And when Congress did manage to get some money, it used it to pay off contractors and debtors, rather than its own soldiers and officers.

Washington himself did not want any such thing as a dictatorship; aristocrat though he was, he had not fought all these years to replace one tyrant with another, even if that other were himself. Hesitant steps to make him some sort of Roman ruler died aborning. But so did grudging attempts to provide sustenance for the army, and until the formal end of the war, the United States stepped from one dubious stopgap to another, issuing paper here and promises there, and skirting between military government on one side and total collapse on the other. It did not put the country in a strong posture from which to negotiate peace with the official enemy; fortunately, while Washington and his dwindling but devoted army kept to their duty, the enemy had other problems in other areas.

If the ultimate fate of the rebellious American colonies was now pretty well conceded, there still remained a great deal to be worked out, and that was still being resolved by force of arms. Britain was now facing much of the Western world, in a war that had gotten completely out of hand.

As early as 1780, British policy had begun to alienate states that might otherwise have left her alone. In her efforts to blockade France and Spain, and to keep supplies from reaching the Americans, Britain had been very high-handed; as one writer has remarked, the British were always very sensitive to violations of maritime rights unless they themselves were doing the violating. A liberally interpreted policy of blockade, search, and seizure gradually infuriated even those states, such as the Baltic ones, whose trade was largely dependent upon Britain. Thus, early in 1780, when Catherine the Great of Russia announced the founding of the Armed Neutrality, she declared that the Russian Navy would be used to enforce freedom of trade for Russian ships and merchants. In fact, the Russian Navy was no great shakes, so this was more of a diplomatic than a military threat, but it was a threat with the power to grow. Denmark adhered to the idea in July, Sweden in August. Before the war ended, Prussia, Portugal, Austria, and the Two Sicilies also joined the alliance, so, if not a structure of great naval power, it was still a strong expression of disapprobation of Britain and her conduct.

With all of these countries passively opposed, and France, Spain, and the Netherlands actively so, the British were at full stretch; and all over the world in 1782, there were actions that had a bearing on the final shaping of the American Revolution. On the surface, there is little connection between American independence and the Indian Ocean; in fact, events on the other side of the world bore strongly on the end of the war.

Late in 1780 the British had decided to reinforce their forces both in India and the Indian Ocean, and they sent out Commodore George Johnstone with five of the line and thirty-five transports on the long sea route to India. He got as far as the Cape Verde Islands, where he stopped for water and supplies. While he was anchored at Porto Praya, a French squadron arrived under Admiral Pierre-André de Suffren. Suffren had sailed with de Grasse, and when the latter went to the West Indies, he detached Suffren for the Dutch colony at the Cape of Good Hope, with orders to hold it against the British. Suffren was arguably the greatest sailor France ever produced, and he believed that the best defense was a good offense; so when he found Johnstone at Porto Praya, he sailed in to the attack, even though this was neutral Portuguese territory. Unfortunately for Suffren, his captains were not as bold as he was, but he still managed to damage the British enough so that they turned back, while he, having thus saved the Cape Colony, sailed on to the Indian Ocean.

Here, through 1782 and into early 1783, he fought five battles with the Royal Navy's Sir Edward Hughes. These were classic fights of the age of sail, and not without some amusement. Suffren was invariably bold, but his captains were not; Hughes was invariably cautious, but his captains were bold.

Had it been a pick-up team, they should have changed sides all around. As it was, Suffren, with no base and no source of supplies or reinforcement, kept himself going by taking what he needed from British bases. In the whole series of battles, neither side lost a ship, but Suffren was a powerful pressure on England's hold over India. He was on the verge of winning command of the Indian Ocean when hostilities ceased and he was ordered home. On the way, he was feted by British admirals and officers at Capetown who vied to honor him, and he received a hero's welcome back in France.

Suffren's threats at sea were matched by events on land in India, where the Second Mysore War kept the subcontinent in an uproar from 1780 to 1783. At one point the Indian leader, Hyder Ali, threatened to drive the British out of Madras, but one of the heroes of the Indian Empire, Eyre Coote, with 8,000 troops destroyed Hyder Ali's army of 60,000 men at the battle of Porto Novo, and restored British dominance in the area. Only when the American war ended, and with it French support, did the Indians subside once again and the march of British conquest resume.

The pressure was equally great in home waters and in the Mediterranean, and from a number of sources. The threat of invasion had passed by now, as the French had committed themselves to the North American–West Indies theater. Nonetheless, there were several squadron-size actions. In August 1781 Sir Hyde Parker was escorting a great British convoy out of the Baltic. Such merchant convoys were the lifeblood of European foreign trade at the time, and could consist of several hundred ships. Sailing vessels then of course carried much less than a single cargo vessel now, so they must have been a glorious sight, with the water literally covered with the different types of rig, often gaily painted, and clouds of sail as far as the eye could see. Parker coming out of the Baltic met a Dutch convoy and escort going in, and the two naval squadrons went at it while the merchantmen scattered like a flock of chickens. The British had the better of it, and fought their convoy through while the Dutch returned to port.

In December there was the Second Battle of Ushant, when the British hit a French squadron sailing for the West Indies, and captured twenty transports, making a welcome bit of prize money for all involved.

The record was mixed in the Mediterranean. Here the Spanish continued their siege of Gibraltar. Early in 1780 Admiral Rodney got a convoy of reinforcements through, fighting a Spanish squadron and taking six of the line in the process. Nearly three years later, when peace negotiations had already begun, the Spanish, assisted by the French, were still at it, and in September of 1782 they mounted a great attack by land and by sea. The sea component featured immense floating batteries, armored with green wood six feet thick. The British employed a new device against these, firing red-hot shot for the first time. By such desperate and dangerous expedients they beat off the attack, and soon after, got another convoy through with supplies. The defense of Gibraltar in this war was the equivalent of the siege of Malta in World War II, and became one of the lesser-known epics of the war.

Britain was less successful with her other Mediterranean base, the island of Minorca. This had been taken by her in 1704, during the War of the Spanish Succession, and held ever since. Spain was determined to get it back, and in late 1780 a joint French and Spanish force landed on the island and invested the British garrison in Fort St. Philip. For almost six months the garrison held out, until they had been so wasted by scurvy they could no longer man their defenses. The allies never even bothered to assault, letting disease do their work for them, and in February 1782 the exhausted survivors gave up and surrendered.

In addition to all these conventional operations, successes or failures, there was as well the ongoing nuisance of privateering. Even with the British blockading much of the American coast, scores of privateers still crept out and annoyed British trade. By 1781 the American navy was virtually gone, and only one ship, the *Alliance*, made a useful cruise in that year. But with all the coasts of Europe open to them, the privateers snapped up ships even on England's doorstep. It was necessary to convoy through coastal waters, trade was still disrupted, and insurance rates rose, causing the business interests to press for peace.

What Britain really needed was a victory with which to go to the negotiating table, and she was given it by Admiral Rodney in the West Indies. Here the fighting had seesawed back and forth, British, French, Spanish and Dutch, all trading islands with each other, and the ascendancy at any moment depending largely upon who had the bigger or better squadron in the area. After Yorktown Admiral de Grasse had returned to southern waters, and for several months he and Admiral Rodney sparred inconclusively around the islands. Given the difficulties of maneuvering squadrons and fleets, it took unusual luck or mutual consent to bring about a major engagement, but on April 12, 1782, Rodney got his chance. De Grasse did not want to fight even then, as he was intent upon preserving his fleet for the long-planned descent on Jamaica; but after several days of inconclusive sparring, with a number of his ships crippled, he accepted battle off a little group of islets called Les Saintes.

It all started out well, with the French having the weather gauge, that is, the wind in their favor. Though numbers vary in different sources, the French are generally given twenty-nine of the line, the British thirty-five. More important than numbers was the fact that the British ships were clean-bottomed and therefore faster sailers than the French, which had been at sea for two years now, and the British had introduced a number of gunnery reforms that enabled them to fire twice as fast as their enemies.

The two fleets approached in the standard line ahead, and sailed past each other, each ship firing as it went. So far it was the traditional pattern, and if continued would allow de Grasse to have a relatively harmless exchange, and then get away about his business. But just as the two lines were fully opposite each other, the wind veered, throwing the French into confusion and giving the British the advantage. For once they seized it. Swinging about, British captains darted forward and broke the French line at several places. It was an unprecedented move, for which the French had made no provision. Their line collapsed, and Rodney, happily joining in the melee, gave the signal for a general chase, independent action by his captains.

Every military man knows that it is in a pursuit that the

real damage is inflicted on a fleeing enemy, and the British took up the chase joyfully. The French went from bad to worse, and their ships simply took off as best they could, all formation, and therefore all chance of real resistance, falling apart. Between flight and hard fighting by those the British caught, including de Grasse himself, the British managed to take only five ships, but the French fleet was completely scattered. A few more ships were snapped up in the following days, and the result was the destruction of allied naval power in the Caribbean for the rest of the year.

The Battle of Les Saintes made Rodney a hero at home, and began a new era in naval tactics. It had another effect as well. By altering the strategic balance of such a major theater as the West Indies, it gave the British the leverage they needed to begin negotiations for the end of the war. Given the conditions all the major participants faced domestically, it was high time someone found a way to bring it all to an end.

CHAPTER SEVENTEEN

Peacemaking

ONCE THEY have been brought to acknowledge its necessity, nations ought to find the process of making peace comparatively easy. All they have to do is sit down at a table, acknowledge who won and who lost, and go home. Since the issue in this war was ostensibly the independence of the United States of America, and since that had been recognized in fact, if not in law, by everyone except Great Britain for at least three years now, and since even the British had long resigned themselves to the fact, all they now had to do was admit it openly. This particular peace process ought therefore to be easier than most.

That, of course, was a commonsense view, but diplomats seldom reason along the same lines as more ordinary people; a diplomat will fight as hard, in his way, for a comma or a phrase as a soldier will in his for a useless hill. Nor is this mere contrariness; it is entirely possible to win a war on the battlefield, and lose it at the peace table, as states have found to their alternate joy or dismay as long as there have been states. Soldiers may despise diplomats, but they also serve who only sit and scribble—or sit and quibble.

The Peace of Paris ended up being as tortured and convoluted as any other, then. Each of the participants sought his own advantage, at the expense of both his enemies and his friends. To understand why it ended as it did, it is necessary to look at the situation of the separate participants, the peculiarities of their negotiators and the manner in which they conducted themselves, and the actual process that they went through.

It is of course a convenience of historians to write as if history had a well-defined set of beginnings and endings, and the process of peacemaking had begun long before the fighting had actually concluded. The United States, for example, had appointed John Adams of Massachusetts to negotiate peace with Great Britain in September of 1779; on the same day it also named John Jay of New York, then President of Congress, as minister to Spain, charged with getting the Spanish to recognize American independence, which they did not do, and to give further assistance to the Americans, which they did. After appointing these two in effect its commissioners, Congress then drew up a list of minimum conditions early in 1780. These included recognition of American independence with certain defined boundaries, British withdrawal from American territories, fishing rights off the coast, and freedom of navigation on the Mississippi River, which was controlled more by Spain than by Britain, and explains why Jay as ambassador to Spain was involved directly in this process.

A year and a half later, they had another try at conditions. By now they were close to the victory at Yorktown, but they did not know that; all they knew was that they and their country and resources were exhausted, so they demanded only independence and sovereignty, two words for the same thing. They also decided they should have a committee to negotiate for them, instead of just Adams, and they named Jay, who was now in Spain; Benjamin Franklin, who was already overseas as ambassador to France; Thomas Jefferson, and Henry Laurens as committee members. Jefferson stayed home, and Laurens's position was quite equivocal. He had earlier been named as American ambassador to the Netherlands, and was captured at sea by the British. Indeed, his capture, together with the incriminating documents he was carrying, was what caused Britain to declare war on the Dutch. He was held in London for several months, became fairly closely associated with leading British politicians, and was finally exchanged in return for Lord Cornwallis. He reached Paris but a couple of days before the peace preliminaries were signed, and was not regarded as wholly trustworthy by his colleagues; nonetheless, he knew the British better than they, and acted as a go-between during the later stages of the process.

So by the time the Americans actually got to Paris, their situation at home was pretty parlous, not because of military reverses, for Yorktown had now been won, but because the war had simply outlasted American ability to sustain it, and this condition is reflected in the instructions to Adams and his fellows: get independence; for the rest, do the best you can. The only real proviso beyond that was that they act in full concert with, and be guided by, the French. Ironically, they soon found it necessary to set that instruction aside, for the French, it appeared, had far different interests from their American brothers-in-arms.

The government of His Most Christian Majesty Louis XVI of France had not gone to war for entirely altruistic reasons. True, the French loved Liberty, whatever that might mean, and they loved, or at least liked, Americans, whom they saw through rose-colored and not too clear glasses as the greatest living champions of liberty. But while such effusions might be all right for the salons of Paris, where ladies in high fashion liked to think of themselves as simple country lasses at heart, the ministers at Versailles, the men who actually issued the orders and handed out the money, were harder-headed than that. And this war had cost France a great deal of money; it had, in fact, quadrupled her national debt, and that, plus the long-established inadequacies of her fiscal system, set her well on the road to national collapse within a decade.

The French were, in fact, as desirous of gaining a peace treaty as the Americans, and to do so, they were quite willing to shortchange their ally. Before Yorktown, for example, they hinted that they might well accept a peace based on the current situation, which would have left the British in possession of both New York City and much of the south. They had little interest in American western boundaries; the more poorly defined they were, the better for France and her friend Spain. They cared nothing about American fishing rights to the northeast, and they were far more concerned about the ongoing Spanish siege of Gibraltar than the Americans were. Under these divergent interests, each partner found itself separately wooing its enemy while treating its ally somewhat disingenuously.

The other allies or benevolent neutrals had little to do with it. The Netherlands was also at war with Britain, but its interest in the United States was peripheral. Adams spent a good deal of his time at The Hague, trying to secure Dutch recognition and a loan, both of which he eventually got. The Spanish provided an annoying complication, for not only were they set on winning Gibraltar back, but they were not at all sure how much of their American position they wished to concede to a pushy new nation, and a republic at that. Spain still had both a much more important empire in the New World than France had, as well as a much more absolutist tradition and government. Eventually Spain had to be nursed along by France, and finally, grudgingly, accepted what it could not avoid.

All of this complication was on just one side of the equation. Fortunately for the other side, the British, they at least did not have to fight with their allies. They only had to fight among themselves. It is easy for the winning side to be willing to end the play; it, after all, has every reason to want to do so. It is the loser who cries, "Play on!" until finally forced to acknowledge his defeat. After Yorktown, the British hoped only for one last victory that would improve their bargaining position, and they got that at Les Saintes. So much for their external situation; internally, though, there was an agonizing process of shifts and readjustments before they were prepared to call a halt.

By the time of Rodney's saving victory, Lord North was already gone. The news of Yorktown, coming in November of 1781, had capped a year of disaster for his government and British arms. In addition to the defeat in America, they had lost Pensacola in Florida, and in the Caribbean Tobago, St. Eustatius, Demerara, St. Kitts, Nevis, and Monserrat. Even more importantly, the government had lost the support of the House of Commons. Several times already they had lost votes, or come close to doing so, but they had kept plugging along, held to their unpleasant duty mostly by the King, and the support of those backbenchers who would go along with what they considered His Majesty's desires, whether they liked them or not.

There were two problems here. One was that King George wanted to continue fighting. George remained a man of strong principle, and even when his principles seemed unattainable or wrongheaded, he still clung to them. In his view, concessions to the Americans would diminish the prerogatives of the Crown, which it was his duty and right to defend and preserve, and he simply would not give up. The other problem, a more practical one, was that the King did not see any real alternative to Lord North as a first minister. Only under extremely rare conditions, such as those that led to the Elder Pitt's ascension as first minister in the Seven Years' War, would the King be forced to accept a minister unpalatable to him. George did not particularly like any of the men who might have enough support in Parliament to replace North; the opposition as a group, or as a series of groups, had certainly behaved neither responsibly, nor even patriotically, nor respectfully to His Majesty. So he had soldiered on, and North had soldiered on for him.

Things changed over the end of 1781 and the beginning of 1782. The most important difference was that the opposition finally coalesced; much as leading members hated each other, they hated being out of office even more, and at last, in March of the new year, North gave up. Facing military and naval defeat, a hostile Europe, a restive country, and an at last unmanageable Parliament, the poor man was finally allowed to resign.

North and his and George's friends and supporters were replaced by an unlikely coalition of two leading opposition groups, those led by the Marquis of Rockingham and by the Earl of Shelburne. The former became first lord of the treasury, the latter secretary of state for home and colonial affairs,

and the ministry as a whole is known as the second Rockingham administration. Neither leader liked the other, and
their followers cordially hated each other, but they were
united by their agreement that the war must end and their
desire for power. The King did not like either of them, but he
disliked Shelburne less, and the two factions were soon at
odds. They were saved from complete breakdown by the sud-
den death of Rockingham in July, after which Shelburne
moved over and up to the treasury. This became the Shelburne
administration, and it was this government that made the
peace.

All of these men had been around for a long time; each
of the leaders had been in government in the sixties, when all
the antagonism began to build up. Both had been favorably
disposed to the American view of things, even if their policies
had often had negative effects, and in opposition they had
consistently been against harsh measures. It was personal an-
imosity more than principle that had kept them from uniting
and gaining power.

Shelburne was little short of genius, and one of the sharp-
est minds on the British political stage. He came out of the
Anglo-Irish aristocracy, though he himself distrusted his fellow aristocrats. A man of enormous intellect, he was considered totally unscrupulous, which was not quite true, and he
was known in politics as "the Jesuit," definitely a left-handed
compliment to his talents. He had a peculiar idea of how he
wanted to make peace. His thought was that he would detach
the Americans from their French allies by a generous settlement; having done so, he would be free to do two things: make
peace with France on a reasonably equitable basis, for he saw
no real reason for ongoing hostility, unlike many Englishmen
of his day; and then, tie the United States back to Britain by
a trade treaty which would bring the two countries into an
economic relationship even closer than they had had before the war. The concept was startlingly new; it was actually
the kind of thing that Britain did in the nineteenth century,
when she was manufacturer to the world, and it was a measure of Shelburne's conceptual brilliance that he could come
up with the idea. In effect, he was going to have his cake
and eat it too.

Unfortunately for Shelburne, the plan had one flaw in it. It had to be carried out in secret. You could hardly tell the Americans you were giving them a generous peace because you hoped subsequently to turn them back into colonies through a trade settlement. And since you could not tell them, you could not tell anyone else either. It was no more possible to carry out secret diplomacy in London in the eighteenth century than it is in Washington in the twentieth. So Shelburne set out quietly, playing his cards very close to his vest, hoping to achieve his ends and square his circles.

Negotiations had already opened. In April the Rockingham ministry had sent Richard Oswald to Paris, and he and Benjamin Franklin had met; Franklin was at that moment the only American commissioner in the French capital. Oswald was a rich London merchant, who had spent many years in America, and who had advanced fifty thousand pounds' bail to Henry Laurens. The two skirted around the various issues. As an earnest of good faith, Henry Laurens was allowed to leave London by the new British government, and he went to see John Adams at The Hague, to keep him apprised of negotiations. Exploratory talks were well begun by the time Rockingham died and Shelburne took over.

For a time the ministry was busy with domestic matters, especially Ireland, which was economically depressed as a result of the war, but in September Shelburne authorized Oswald to treat with the commissioners "of the Thirteen United States"; careful though this wording was, it tacitly conceded American independence, and with that unspoken understanding, the two sides got down to work. The French were left largely in the dark, which they resented when they found out about it, but since they were conducting clandestine negotiations of their own, they had little grounds for complaint. Defeated in the West Indies and India both, France finally got nothing more than a few colonial trading posts. For herself, the whole war and its huge expense proved wasted effort.

Given what Shelburne hoped to accomplish—a "hidden agenda" in modern jargon—the talks went along quite amicably. For example, Britain had an excellent claim, through Canada, to the territory from the Great Lakes as far south as the Ohio, the Old Northwest of George Rogers Clark's activities; had she held to it, the subsequent history of both the United States and Canada would have been far different from what it became. Shelburne just gave it away, perhaps the first but certainly far from the last example of Britain seeking America's friendship at Canada's expense. This epitomized his whole policy: the bigger and more prosperous America became, the better it would be for Britain.

So it went, and the final treaty conceded nearly everything the Americans wanted, and far more than they had initially expected to get. In fact, discussions were couched more in terms of "Whom shall we tell?" than they were arguments over details, and the preliminary terms, which were signed as early as November of 1782, were almost exactly what the Americans got.

There were nine articles to the peace, which can be quickly summarized. Great Britain recognized the independence of the United States of America. Generous boundaries were conceded to the new country, though these left room for later argument with Britain to the northeast and northwest, and with Spain to the south. The Americans got fishing rights off Nova Scotia, Newfoundland, and Labrador, and the right to land and cure fish on shore. Debts from citizens of one country to citizens of the other were to be honored. Congress would "recommend" that the separate states restore rights and property to Loyalists. No person would be punished for actions during the war. Hostilities would cease and the British would evacuate as soon as convenient all posts they held within the area of the new country. Navigation of the Mississippi would be free to citizens of both countries from mouth to source forever. Finally, any conquests either side made between the signing and the receipt of news of the peace would be restored—a reminder that communication was necessarily slow in those days.

The position of France remained something of a problem, and Vergennes, once he found out what was going on, protested that the Americans were negotiating independently of their ally. However, Franklin managed to calm his reservations, and he had to admit the Americans had got a good deal. Fortunately for him, while this was happening the British broke the siege of Gibraltar, which made the Spanish realize they were not going to win, and thus more amenable to a settlement. So France and Spain also signed preliminary articles, early in 1783. That done, there was simply the matter of ratification by the principals. This in fact took another year. The American Congress ratified the provisional treaty on April 15, 1783. The official copy was signed in Paris on September 3, but that was not ratified by Congress until January of 1784, and it was not until May of that year that official, ratified, final copies, signed and sealed by everyone, were at last exchanged.

There remained an enormous number of loose ends. As mentioned, the boundaries of the new United States were so generous that neither Spain nor Britain liked them, and both, in the aftermath, tried to hedge their bets. The arguments with Spain ran on for a decade, involving at one point a half-hearted idea of setting up a pro-Spanish buffer state east of the Mississippi. The issue was finally resolved in 1795.

Things were more complicated with the British, and there were essentially four residual issues here: the boundary question, the Loyalists, the evacuation of the major American ports, and first and foremost, the reception of the treaty in Britain itself, for that dictated much of the subsequent situation.

In Philadelphia there was some complaint that the American commissioners had not consulted sufficiently with France, but that was nothing compared to the storm that broke over London. When the treaty was discussed in Parliament, Shelburne was virtually crushed by the outburst of fury and indignation. The country desperately needed peace, but was resolved to destroy the man who obtained it at such a price. And Shelburne's idea for a greater trading community, with both Americans and British included, was so revolutionary that he did not dare even offer it in defense of his treaty. The great vision that would have tied the United States and Britain together, that would even have brought France into a greater economic community, was simply swept away in the blast. Even bitter personal enemies combined against the minister, and in April 1783 Shelburne fell, replaced by a coalition of Lord North and North's most virulent parliamentary opponent, Charles James Fox. Britain shortly lurched into another constitutional crisis, which one wag summed up by saying, "North lost the war, Shelburne lost the peace, and Fox lost his head." England's troubles were far from over, and there was confusion of parties, policies, and politics until William Pitt the Younger was firmly established later in the eighties.

With Shelburne went the mood of generosity toward the late foe. The residual boundary questions remained to sour relations, and it took years to lever the British out of their posts around the Great Lakes, while the northeastern boundary, between Maine and the British colonies or provinces, was not settled until the 1850's. Nor was mean-spiritedness confined to one side. In the peace treaty Congress had agreed only to recommend that the states be nice to Loyalists, because it lacked power to do anything more than that. The separate states had not the slightest intention of following that recommendation. For the most part, open Loyalists had disappeared long ago, and their property had long been confiscated and sold to new owners, shipping seized, farms taken over, houses moved into. A revolution invariably creates new classes of people, both newly rich and newly poor, and while the latter might earnestly want to regain their old status, the former have no desire to revert to their previous condition—or even to pay fair market price for what they obtained on the cheap. The American Revolution may not have been as bad as most in this sense, but the opinion of most Americans was that the Loyalists had backed the wrong horse and lost, and that was just too damned bad for them. There were, after all, widows along the New York border, and charred homesteads on the Carolina frontier, and orphans in New London, and if not all Loyalists had actively opposed the Patriot cause, they were now all tarred with the same brush.

Ultimately, though several thousands made their peace, or had never declared themselves openly at all, several other thousands left. They went to the West Indies, or home to Britain, but most of them went north, to Nova Scotia or to the west of Quebec. The former meant hard living, and they soon dubbed it "Nova Scarcity," and many moved on to what is now New Brunswick, just past the Maine border. Others, both civilians and disbanded soldiers, settled up the St. Lawrence past Montreal, creating Upper Canada, or what would become Ontario. Eventually they turned the northern country from a French enclave in the British Empire into Canada. Today farmers who wrestle a living from the thin soil of Cumberland County in Nova Scotia trace their ancestors to New York State and the exodus when the British finally left the United States.

Because eventually they did get around to leaving. The peace treaty called for an expeditious departure from the American seaboard posts held by Britain, but they made no haste. Charleston and the southern posts were evacuated in late 1782, but in New York, the British were especially leisurely. Through most of 1783, while his army dwindled away and his officers grew increasingly restive over their unpaid and, it seemed to them, unhonored, condition, Washington sat on guard, patiently writing letters and banking the fires of grievance, waiting and waiting. Finally the news came: the British would leave on November 25.

So, on a late fall day with the clouds scudding across the blue sky, the little army, less than a thousand of them left with the colors now, began what was virtually its last march. Down Manhattan Island, past old Fort Washington, where they had fought and lost, and Harlem Heights, where they had fought and won, and to the little city itself. New York was hardly welcoming; instead it was tattered, run-down, and shabby, all the trees gone for firewood, much of the center still in ashes after the fire of '76, so long ago. The citizens were hangdog, used to expressing British sympathies and accepting British gold. Still, it was the triumph they had all worked and fought and waited for so long. There were the British ships standing down the bay, gone, gone at last. After some fumbling—the British, sullen to the end, had cut the flagstaff ropes and greased the pole—the Stars and Stripes rose up over the Battery to flout the wind and the departing enemy. Few men could have seen that sight without a lump in their throats. It was over at last.

CHAPTER EIGHTEEN

Endings and Beginnings

$\mathbb{A}$ WAR TAKES on a life of its own, especially one which lasts for eight years. It is impossible simply to turn off the habits and attitudes such an experience engenders, and the men and women who pass through wars—even if they are not active participants, but especially if they are—come out on the other side transformed by what they have done. And as the individual goes, so does the parent society or institution. The United States of 1783 was far different from the thirteen colonies of 1775; so was Great Britain.

There are two schools of thought about such upheavals. The older one insisted that they were absolutely traumatic and unique events, and that after them, nothing was ever the same again. The more modern one sees such events more as intense squiggles on a linear graph, suggesting that things are exciting for a while, but that afterward life continues pretty much in the course it was following anyway. The former view ignored the persistence of the norms of human life, the simple facts that people love and hate, are born and die, and have to make a living somehow between the two. The latter view denied the fact of intense experience, preferring to reduce all of human existence to quantifiable matters, in other words, turning life into social science. Both views have some truth, neither is entirely correct.

Life does of course go on; farms have to be tended, and cows milked whether they are colonial cows or American cows. The routines and rhythms of preindustrial society were particularly demanding, and so Americans continued to do what they had done since their distant fathers had first crossed the great ocean. But the difference was that they were Americans now. Men from Massachusetts, who had been accustomed to dislike New Yorkers, had marched side by side with Virginians and Carolinians, and there are few things more conducive to fellow feeling than going hungry together, or sitting up in the rain during an all-night watch. Pennsylvania riflemen had suffered with the Yankees under the walls of Quebec, and Rhode Islanders and Georgians had triumphed at Yorktown, and that made a great deal of difference.

It was fortunate that this was the case, given the enormity of the problems that remained to be worked out. The country was militarily exhausted and financially ruined. The army that had won independence was disbanded with indecent haste, and soldiers and officers were fobbed off with promissory notes that were quickly discounted by speculators, and most of the quarter of a million men who actually fought for American liberty probably did not get more than ten cents of every dollar owed them by their government. Petitions for redress from indigent soldiers were a common feature in Congress for the next generation.

There was of course no money for them, and that lay in the fact that the federal system of the United States simply did not work. The Articles of Confederation lacked the power to create a truly stable central government, and all of that had to be worked out in the coming years. The hidden bright spot in all this, however, lay in the fact that, the war won, the Americans were now free to create a government that *did* work. The stifling hand of imperial control was gone. What was far more important than government, then, was the basic wealth of the land, the intelligence and industry of the people, and their eagerness to capitalize on opportunities. These were a people who believed they were God's chosen, and looking about them, there was every reason that they should so believe. Their waters teemed with fish and their forests with game; there was absolutely nothing to prevent them fulfilling their vision of a new Jerusalem, and they set out with immense vitality to do so, and their success for two hundred years has been one of the wonders of the modern world. This in spite of occasional wrong-turning and backsliding, and Americans, no matter how aware some of them are—and some of them are not—of their own shortcomings, remain the envy of the rest of the world.

The actual military experience of the Revolution taught Americans little, and the lessons they did learn were arguably the wrong ones. The conditions of the war were so peculiar in time and place that they were likely to have little relevance to later events. Within a generation, the art of war was very substantially transformed by the French Revolution and the reaction to it, and even more after that by the Industrial Revolution, two upheavals that taken together brought modern mass society into existence. Americans, isolated by two great oceans, with few and weak enemies anywhere near them, fell into a military lassitude from which they were scarcely rescued by the War of 1812, the Mexican War, or assorted Indian problems. Only in 1861 did they again have to create an army out of virtually nothing, and do it while actually fighting a war. But that became a railroad war, of large armies, one quite foreign to the revolutionary experience of small columns and poor communications. Militarily, Americans could largely ignore their armed forces and, when they did think of them, concentrate on abstruse arguments about the values of a regular standing military establishment versus a militia army of citizen soldiers. Ironically, American military men have always, naturally, preferred the former, but America's big wars, of the last century and a half, have always been fought by the latter.

The lesson of the naval side of the war was almost equally ignored. The new country simply could not afford the kind of money needed to provide an adequate navy; in spite of its fine frigates, the United States Navy in the War of 1812 went the same way as its predecessor, the Continental Navy, did in the

Revolution; in the Civil War a navy had to be almost totally improvised, and not until the twentieth century and the propagandizing of Alfred Thayer Mahan did the country become naval-minded.

But all of these things were marginal to the mainstream of American development, to a country absorbed in creating a workable national system, filling up the ever-advancing frontier, accepting the masses of Europeans fleeing hunger, misery, and oppression. Americans drew from the Revolution the one overriding lesson, the simple, ultimate fact that they were Americans.

Ironically, at the end of the twentieth century, with much of the rest of the world in political or economic turmoil or both, what the British did as losers may be of as much relevance as what the Americans did as winners. For the British situation in the late 1780's through the 1790's bears a remarkable similarity to the situation of the United States in the post–Vietnam War era.

There were of course all the painfully obvious similarities of the actual war itself. It was a situation in which, with the best of intentions, the British usually did the wrong thing, and made conditions worse instead of better. They blundered unwittingly into a struggle at the end of a long and difficult line of communications; they fought over inhospitable terrain against a population that was usually hostile, actively or passively, and at best apathetic. They found that they could hold only those areas that they could actively garrison, or the ground they were actually operating on at any given moment, or territories so distant that the enemy could not effectively mount an attack against them. They never learned successfully to adapt their tactics to those of the enemy; they always deluded themselves that the enemy was a small minority, and that they had a great deal more support than they actually did. And they gradually alienated and lost whatever support they might have enjoyed among the other nations of the day, who, indeed, preferred to support their enemies rather than them. It is often remarked that the American Revolution is the only war of the entire imperial period that Britain fought without allies to help relieve the pressure, and it was the only war she lost.

The domestic situation bears even closer parallels. Here was a war that a substantial proportion, perhaps even a majority, of those who counted in England did not support. The government, having blundered into it, continued to fight it for lack of any vision as to what better to do. One of the major failings of the British at the time, indeed, was their regarding the war as a sideshow and an inconvenience, an item on which opposing politicians might score points off each other, rather than a major problem in its own right. Whoever was right or wrong, it was surely despicable for British public figures to rejoice in defeats in which British soldiers were killed and captured, and the parallels between that and the United States at a later date are surely too painful to need pointing out.

When the war at last ended, British politicians claimed that they had gained at the peace table what they had lost on the battlefield, though that, given Shelburne's half-peace, was somewhat disingenuous. It took them another decade to get over the factional fighting and residual political bitterness the war had unleashed. And by the time they had resolved that, they were involved in the great struggle with Revolutionary France and Napoleon, an epic that monopolized their attention for the next generation, and retarded constitutional development for the same period.

For a while they were totally downcast, and Little Englandism became the vogue. Why have an empire? the writers said. Why pour out money and treasure to pick up foreign territory and settle it with Englishmen? The ungrateful wretches will only grow up to slap Mother England in the face and become independent. Who needs it anyway?—a question that was indeed not answered until Canada and Australia and New Zealand poured out their blood for the mother country on the beaches of Gallipoli and among the clay of Flanders, or, a generation later, sent their young men to fight in the sky over England itself and on the beaches of Normandy.

But the mood of inward-turning isolation did not last, and could not. The world was still there, with all its pressing problems and opportunities. Britons still wanted to trade, and the newly built mills kept turning out Sheffield steel and Manchester cotton, and the Scots and Irish and Welsh kept going overseas and looking back over their shoulders. Fighting France through the French Revolutionary and Napoleonic wars, and then most of Europe, Britain could not help but build up a new, greater empire than the one she had just lost; this second time, the British got it right. Prodded by the Loyalists in the settlements of British North America, the British began slowly to feel their way toward a concept of imperial government. There was a Constitution Act in the Canadas in the 1790's and within a half century, the provinces of British North America had responsible government, which was a legal name for what the Americans had wanted in the 1760's. The newly settled Australia and New Zealand rapidly followed. So out of the ashes of the old First British Empire arose a phoenix, a new, greater Second British Empire. The postwar pessimism of the late eighteenth century gave way to a confident and assertive optimism of the nineteenth century. The truth was, that the politics and the passing mood did not mean that much. Here too, it was people, and resources both human and natural, that made the real difference.

Britain then was a momentary but not ultimate loser by the Revolution, even if, on the other side, the Americans were ultimate winners. Most children, it is said, have to go through a period of conflict with their parents to emerge as adults at the end of it. For some it is more painful than for others; if the parent is tolerant and the children reasonable, then the transition can be fairly smooth. If the children are fractious, and the parent strict or confused or preoccupied, then there is likely to be trouble.

Though such analogies between societies and individuals should not be pushed too far, there is some validity to them. The American colonies were emerging from adolescence, and chafing under the restrictions imposed upon them by a Britain absorbed in her own problems. Both sides worked at cross-purposes until they actually started fighting, and once they did, there was little possibility of going back. From the first hesitant assertion at daybreak on the green at Lexington, all the way to the drama of Saratoga, the classic victory at Yorktown, and the final triumphant raising of the American flag on the Battery in New York City, Americans were asserting a belief, new to the world at the time, in the right of every man to choose his own form of government and make his own way.

The belief that every human being was autonomous was in fact inherent in the western and Christian tradition, but never before had it received such clear expression or been advanced so vigorously. It was this that brought Frenchmen, and Germans such as Steuben and Kalb, and Poles such as Pulaski and Kosciusko, to fight and die in a country of which they knew little but sensed much; what they sensed was that Mister Washington and his embattled militia and dogged Continentals were fighting for an idea that applied not to people of a certain class, or a certain place, but to all people for all time.

Thomas Jefferson once remarked that every man has two countries, his own and France; he might better have said that every man has two countries, his own and the United States of America. For in Europe, the ideals that inspired his remark were perverted by the Terror and by a military dictatorship, and the Continent was condemned to at least another century of government by and for the few. But in the New World, blessed both by nature, by geography, and by history, the vision of a free society was not lost. It would take a long time to work out its implications; indeed, they are still being expanded and developed, but even now, two centuries later, much of the rest of the world still hopes to achieve the ideals to which those ragged revolutionary gentlemen of 1776 pledged their lives, their fortunes, and their sacred honor.

SUGGESTIONS FOR
FURTHER READING

SCHOLARS HAVE been at work on the American Revolution for a long time, and there is an enormous amount of material available for the interested student. This ranges from the early, hagiographic, work, such as Parson Weems's biography of George Washington, which set the pattern that the Americans could do no wrong, through a period, most notably in the early to mid-twentieth century, of debunking, in which no American could do anything right. Putting aside such effusions, however, there is a solid corpus of work by highly respected scholars and writers. A most useful place to start looking is with Richard L. Blanco, *The War of the American Revolution: A Selected Annotated Bibliography of Published Sources* (New York: Garland, 1984). The author lists some 3,700 entries, and offers short notes on many of them, so that a reader may pick and choose as he goes. Far more exhaustive is the compilation by Ronald M. Gephart, *Revolutionary America: 1763–1789: A Bibliography*, 2 vols. (Washington, D.C.: Library of Congress, 1984), listing almost 15,000 titles.

The following suggestions are grouped according to general studies or surveys, including some selections on causes; campaigns and battles; biographies; and some special topics. As will be immediately apparent, no pretense is made that this list is exhaustive.

An atlas is useful to anyone trying to follow operations in detail, and the best is Lester J. Cappon, ed., *Atlas of Early American History: The Revolutionary Era, 1760–1790* (Princeton, N.J.: Princeton University Press, 1976). General studies are John R. Alden, *A History of the American Revolution* (New York: Knopf, 1969), and *The American Revolution, 1775–1783* (New York: Harper, 1954), both excellent surveys; Robert Middlekauf, *The Glorious Cause: The American Revolution, 1763–1789*, vol. 2 of *The Oxford History of the United States* (New York: Oxford University Press, 1982); Edward Countryman, *The American Revolution* (New York: Hill and Wang, 1985); Don Higginbotham, *The War of American Independence* (New York: Macmillan, 1971), from the Macmillan Wars of the United States series. More specifically military surveys are the short book by Howard Peckham, *The War for Independence* (Chicago: University of Chicago Press, 1958); Willard M. Wallace, *Appeal to Arms: A Military History of the American Revolution* (New York: Harper, 1951); and Christopher Ward, *The War of the Revolution* (2 vols.; New York: Macmillan, 1951).

The British political background is covered generally in Stephen Watson, *The Reign of George III, 1760–1815*, vol. XI of *The Oxford History of England* (Oxford, Eng.: Clarendon Press, 1960). There has been a great deal of study of the prerevolutionary British Empire. The most massive of these is Lawrence H. Gipson, *The British Empire Before the American Revolution* (vols. 4–15; New York: Knopf, 1939–1970); the later volumes are the more relevant here. The author summarized his work in *The Coming of the Revolution, 1763–1775* (New York: Harper, 1954). Merrill Jensen's *The Founding of a Nation: A History of the American Revolution* (New York: Oxford University Press, 1968) develops the argument that the Revolution was accomplished before the war was fought; the same period is covered in Bernhard Knollenberg, *Origins of the American Revolution, 1759–1776* (New York: Macmillan, 1960). American radicalism is explored in Pauline Maier, *From Resistance to Revolution: Colonial Radicals and the Development of American Opposition to Britain, 1765–1776* (New York: Knopf, 1972). Rhys Isaac provided a study of one of the crucial areas of development in *The Transformation of Virginia, 1740–1790* (New York: Norton, 1988). A classic study of the development of American ideas is Clinton L. Rossiter, *Seedtime of the Republic: The Origins of the American Tradition of Political*

Liberty (New York: Harcourt Brace, 1953); followed by Bernard Bailyn, *The Ideological Origins of the American Revolution* (Cambridge, Mass.: Harvard U.P., 1967). The British view, and Britain's attempts to restructure its imperial system, is covered in Charles R. Ritcheson, *British Policies and the American Revolution* (Norman, Okla.: U. of Oklahoma P., 1954). A host of eminent British scholars has dealt with Britain's imperial problems, and the constitutional crises that beset the country in the early years of George III; the most famous of these was Sir Lewis Namier, whose *Structure of Politics at the Accession of George III* (London: Macmillan, 1929) and *England in the Age of the American Revolution* (London: Macmillan, 1930) became the starting point for a whole generation of revisionist studies. A general overview is provided in Richard Pares, *King George III and the Politicians* (Oxford, Eng.: Clarendon Press, 1953). Many scholars see the Stamp Act crisis as the turning point on the road to revolution, and the best study of this is Edmund S. and Helen M. Morgan, *The Stamp Act Crisis: Prologue to Revolution* (Chapel Hill, N.C.: University of North Carolina Press, 1953). A more general treatment of causes is in Oliver M. Dickerson, *The Navigation Acts and the American Revolution* (Philadelphia: U. of Pennsylvania P., 1951). An exhaustive specific study is Benjamin Larabee, *The Boston Tea Party* (New York: Oxford University Press, 1964), and Robert Gross, *The Minutemen and Their World* (New York: Hill and Wang, 1976), also covers this area.

Turning to more specific military matters, practically every battle of the war has at least one monograph, and often a full library, about it. The best work on Lexington and Concord is Arthur B. Tourtellot, *William Diamond's Drum: The Beginning of the War of the American Revolution* (New York: Doubleday, 1959); the early period is also covered in John R. Alden, *General Gage in America* (Baton Rouge, La.: Louisiana State University Press, 1948). The best treatment of Bunker Hill is Thomas J. Fleming, *Now We Are Enemies* (New York: St. Martin's, 1960), closely matched by Richard M. Ketchum, *Decisive Day: The Battle of Bunker Hill* (New York: Doubleday, 1974). On Ticonderoga there is the old but interesting Allen French, *The Taking of Ticonderoga in 1775: The British Story: A Military Story of Capture and Captives* (Cambridge, Mass.: Harvard University Press, 1928). The American attempt on Canada is covered in Robert McC. Hatch, *Thrust for Canada: The American Attempt on Quebec in 1775–1776* (Boston: Houghton Mifflin, 1979), and a Canadian view of this operation is the excellent George F. G. Stanley, *Canada Invaded, 1775–1776* (Toronto: Harrapp, 1967).

A number of books cover the campaigns in New York and across New Jersey in the summer of 1776 and into 1777. An overall treatment is Thomas J. Fleming, *1776: The Year of Illusion* (New York: W.W. Norton, 1975); another is Richard M. Ketchum, *The Winter Soldiers* (New York: Doubleday, 1973). Bruce Bliven wrote *Under the Guns: New York, 1775–1776* (New York: Harper, 1972); a work that covers the Long Island fighting is Eric J. Manders, *The Battle of Long Island* (Monmouth Beach, N.J.: Philip Freneau, 1978). Samuel S. Smith wrote *The Battle of Trenton* (Monmouth Beach, N.J.: Philip Freneau, 1965), and Alfred H. Bill covered *The Campaign of Princeton, 1776–1777* (Princeton, N.J.: Princeton University Press, 1948).

The starting point for studies of Burgoyne's campaign is the now dated but still useful Hoffman Nickerson, *The Turning Point of the Revolution: Or, Burgoyne in America* (Boston: Houghton Mifflin, 1928). More current is John F. Luzader, *Decision on the Hudson: The Saratoga Campaign of 1777* (Washington, D.C.: Dept. of the Interior, 1975). Popular coverages are Rupert Furneaux, *The Battle of Saratoga* (New York: Stein and Day, 1971), and John R. Cuneo, *The Battle of Saratoga: The Turn of the Tide* (New York: Macmillan, 1975).

For Sir William Howe's move to Philadelphia, there is John S. Pancake, *1777: The Year of the Hangman* (University, Ala.: University of Alabama Press, 1977), and John F. Reed, *Campaign to Valley Forge, July 1, 1777–December 19, 1777* (Philadelphia: University of Pennsylvania Press, 1965). Specific episodes are covered in Samuel S. Smith, *The Battle of the Brandywine* (Monmouth Beach, N.J.: Philip Freneau, 1976); the same author's *Fight for the Delaware 1777* (Monmouth Beach, N.J.: Philip Freneau, 1970); and Ray Thompson, *Washington at Germantown* (Fort Washington, Pa.: Bicentennial Press, 1971). Alfred H. Bill wrote *Valley Forge: The Making of an Army* (New York: Harper, 1952). Samuel S. Smith produced an excellent *The Battle of Monmouth* (Monmouth Beach, N.J.: Philip Freneau, 1964), while the title of Theodore G. Thayer, *Washington and Lee at Monmouth: The Making of a Scapegoat* (Port Washington, N.Y.: Kennikat, 1976) is self-explanatory.

Some of the lesser actions in the north are covered in Paul F. Dearden, *The Rhode Island Campaign of 1778: Inauspicious Dawn of Alliance* (Providence: Rhode Island Publications Society, 1980); Henry P. Johnston, *The Storming of Stony Point on the Hudson: Midnight, July 15, 1775* (orig. pub. 1900; repr. New York: Da Capo, 1971); Chester B. Kevitt, *General Solomon Lovell and the Penobscot Expedition, 1779* (Weymouth, Mass.: Weymouth Hist. Comm.,

1976); Alfred H. Bill, *New Jersey and the Revolutionary War* (New York: Van Nostrand, 1964).

The war in the south is covered generally in John R. Alden, *The South in the Revolution, 1762–1789*, vol. 3 of *The History of the South* (Baton Rouge, La.: Louisiana State University Press, 1957). Lawrence A. Alexander wrote *Storm Over Savannah: The Story of Count D'Estaing and the Siege of the Town in 1779* (Athens, Ga.: University of Georgia Press, 1951). Robert S. Davis and Kenneth H. Thomas have covered the obscure *Kettle Creek: The Battle of the Cane Brakes, Wilkes County, Georgia* (Atlanta: Georgia Dept. of Archives and History, 1975), and H. L. Landers did *The Battle of Camden, South Carolina, August 16, 1780* (Washington, D.C.: G.P.O., 1929). A popular account by Burke Davis covers *The Cowpens–Guilford Courthouse Campaign* (Philadelphia: Lippincott, 1962). Greene's whole tenure in the south is covered in N. F. Treacy, *Prelude to Yorktown: The Southern Campaign of Nathanael Greene, 1780–1781* (Chapel Hill, N.C.: University of North Carolina Press, 1963; and Russell Weigley wrote *The Partisan War: The South Carolina Campaign of 1780–1782* (Charleston, S.C.: University of South Carolina, 1970).

There is any number of books about Yorktown; a good general coverage is Thomas J. Fleming, *Beat the Last Drum: The Siege of Yorktown, 1781* (New York: St. Martin's, 1963); another is Harold A. Larabee, *Decision at the Chesapeake* (New York: Clarkson N. Putter, 1964); and another, Burke Davis, *The Campaign That Won America: The Story of Yorktown* (New York: Dial, 1970).

A surprising amount of work is available on the western and frontier campaigns. George M. Waller, *American Revolution in the West* (Chicago: Nelson Hall, 1976), Dale Van Every, *A Company of Heroes: The American Frontier, 1775–1783* (New York: William Morrow, 1962), and Jack M. Sosin, *The Revolutionary Frontier, 1763–1783* (New York: Holt, Rinehart & Winston, 1976) are all readable and useful, as is Lowell H. Harrison, *George Rogers Clark and the War in the West* (Lexington, Ky.: University Press of Kentucky, 1976).

For naval history there are many accounts available. Howard I. Chapelle, *History of the American Sailing Navy* (New York: W.W. Norton, 1949), gives much material on the building and design of early ships; William B. Clark in *George Washington's Navy: Being an Account of His Excellency's Fleet in New England Waters* (Baton Rouge, La.: Louisiana State University Press, 1960) covers Washington's early efforts to establish a naval force. A good general account is William M. Fowler, *Rebels Under Sail: The American Navy During the Revolution* (New York: Scribner's, 1976). Older and broader is Alfred T. Mahan, *Major Operations of the Navies in the War of Independence* (Boston:

Little, Brown, 1913). There are several studies of state navies and of privateering, and of special aspects, such as Charles R. Smith, *Marines in the Revolution: A History of the Continental Marines in the American Revolution, 1775–1783* (Washington, D.C.: U.S. Marine Corps, 1975).

The British Navy has had innumerable studies. A general view in is G. J. Marcus, *A Naval History of England*, vol. 1, *The Formative Centuries* (Boston: Little, Brown, 1961). Older but still useful is William M. James, *The British Navy in Adversity: A Study of the War of American Independence* (London: Longmans Green, 1926); Neil R. Stout, *The Royal Navy in America, 1760–1775: A Study of the Enforcement of British Colonial Policy in the Era of the American Revolution* (Annapolis, Md.: Naval Institute Press, 1973), and David Syrett, *Shipping and the American War, 1775–1783: A Study in British Transport Organization* (New York: Oxford University Press, 1970) are both valuable. Most of the major commanders have also had their papers published by the Navy Records Society (London, Eng.). There are some useful works on the French Navy: Jonathan R. Dull, *The French Navy and American Independence: A Study of Arms and Diplomacy, 1774–1787* (Princeton, N.J.: Princeton University Press, 1975); Charles L. Lewis, *Admiral De Grasse and American Independence* (Annapolis, Md.: Naval Institute Press, 1945); Tom W. McGuffie, *The Siege of Gibraltar, 1779–1783* (Philadelphia: Durfour, 1965); and Alfred T. Patterson, *The Other Armada: The Franco-Spanish Attempt to Invade Britain in 1779* (Manchester, Eng.: Manchester University Press, 1960).

For those who prefer their history through the medium of biography, there is any number of studies available of most of the major characters of the Revolution. On the American side Washington himself has many biographers. The most monumental is still Douglas Southall Freeman's seven-volume *George Washington: A Biography* (New York: Scribner's, 1948–1957), but most readers would probably prefer James T. Flexner, *George Washington in the American Revolution, 1775–1783* (Boston: Little, Brown, 1968), or Marcus Cunliffe, *George Washington: Man and Monument* (Boston: Little, Brown, 1958). John R. Alden wrote *General Charles Lee: Traitor or Patriot?* (Baton Rouge, La.: Louisiana State University Press, 1951), treating fairly that difficult subject. Martin H. Bush is more favorably disposed to his subject in *Revolutionary Enigma: A Reappraisal of General Philip Schuyler of New York* (Port Washington, N.Y.: Friedman, 1969), as is Paul D. Nelson, in *General Horatio Gates: A Biography* (Baton Rouge, La.: Louisiana State University Press,

1976). Theodore Thayer wrote *Nathanael Greene: Strategist of the Revolution* (New York: Twayne, 1960); and Charles P. Whittemore did *A General of the Revolution: John Sullivan of New Hampshire* (New York: Columbia University Press, 1961). North Callahan wrote *Henry Knox: General Washington's General* (New York: Rinehart, 1958). Benedict Arnold has attracted more heat than light, but Willard M. Wallace, *Traitorous Hero: The Life and Fortunes of Benedict Arnold* (New York: Harper, 1954), is readable; James T. Flexner, *The Traitor and the Spy: Benedict Arnold and John André* (New York: Harcourt Brace, 1953) is recommended. Willard S. Randall, *Benedict Arnold: Patriot and Traitor* (New York: William Morrow, 1990) appeared too recently to use here. There are as well biographies of many of the major political figures, and some of the lesser military ones, and a group biography of the American commanders is in George M. Bilias, ed., *George Washington's Generals* (New York: William Morrow, 1964). Many naval figures have biographies as well, the most notable being Samuel Eliot Morison, *John Paul Jones: A Sailor's Biography* (Boston: Little, Brown, 1959). On the Europeans who came to America, there is Louis M. Gottschalk, *Lafayette* (5 vols.; Chicago: University of Chicago Press, 1935–1969), and Arnold Whitbridge, *Rochambeau* (New York: Macmillan, 1965).

For the British, John Brooke, *King George III* (New York: McGraw-Hill, 1972) is an excellent study, as is Stanley Ayling, *George the Third* (New York: Knopf, 1972). William B. Willcox wrote *Portrait of a General: Sir Henry Clinton in the War of Independence* (New York: Knopf, 1964); Frank B. and Mary Wickwire covered *Cornwallis: The American Adventure* (Boston: Houghton Mifflin, 1970); and Paul Lewis did *The Man Who Lost America: A Biography of Gentleman Johnny Burgoyne* (New York: Dial, 1973). Ira D. Gruber, *The Howe Brothers and the American Revolution* (New York: Atheneum, 1972) is a classic study. Another group biography is George M. Bilias, ed., *George Washington's Opponents: British Generals and Admirals in the American Revolution* (New York: William Morrow, 1969).

In other areas, a number of special studies is available. Taking these in no particular order, there is an appraisal of American strategy in Dave R. Palmer, *The Way of the Fox: American Strategy in the War for America, 1775–1783* (Westport, Conn.: Greenwood, 1975); and of British in the excellent Piers Mackesey, *The War for America, 1775–1783* (Cambridge, Eng.: Cambridge University Press, 1965). British army background is covered briefly in Correlli Barnett, *Britain and Her Army, 1509–1970* (New York: William Morrow, 1970), and Peter Young and J. P. Lawford, *History of the British Army* (New York: Putnam's, 1970); and more extensively, though in a manner now somewhat dated, in Sir John Fortescue's classic *A History of the British Army* (13 vols.; London: Macmillan, 1935). More specific is John Shy, *Toward Lexington: The Role of the British Army in the Coming of the Revolution* (Princeton, N.J.: Princeton University Press, 1965). A couple of studies of the logistics of the period are James A. Hutson, *The Sinews of War: Army Logistics, 1775–1953* (Washington, D.C.: Office of the Chief of Military History, 1966), and Victor L. Johnson, *The Administration of the American Commissariat During the Revolutionary War* (Philadelphia: University of Pennsylvania Press, 1941). Interesting material on arms and equipment is in two books by Harold Peterson, *Arms and Armour in Colonial America, 1526–1783* (Harrisburg, Pa.: Stackpole, 1956), and *The Book of the Continental Soldier: Being a Complete Account of the Uniforms, Weapons, and Equipment with Which He Lived and Fought* (Harrisburg, Pa.: Stackpole, 1968). On the darker side, Carl Van Doren wrote *Mutiny in January* (New York: Viking, 1943), and John Bakeless did *Turncoats, Traitors, and Heroes* (Philadelphia: Lippincott, 1959), and there is the excellent work by Ford Corey, *A Peculiar Service* (Boston: Little, Brown, 1965) on the American intelligence service. A larger study is by Charles Royster, *A Revolutionary People at War: The Continental Army and American Character, 1775–1783* (Chapel Hill, N.C.: University of North Carolina Press, 1979). The confusions of American attitudes are detailed in Jackson T. Main, *The Social Struggle of Revolutionary America* (Princeton, N.J.: Princeton University Press, 1965).

On the Loyalists there are several good studies. An older one is A. G. Bradley, *The United Empire Loyalists, Founders of British Canada* (1932; repr. New York: AMS, 1980); Wallace Brown wrote *The Good Americans: The Loyalists in the American Revolution* (New York, William Morrow, 1969), and a more detailed examination, *The King's Friends: The Composition and Motives of the American Loyalist Claimants* (Providence: Brown University Press, 1965); Robert M. Calhoon wrote *The Loyalists in Revolutionary America, 1760–1781* (New York: Harcourt, Brace, Jovanovich, 1973); and North Callahan did *Flight from the Republic: The Tories of the American Revolution* (Indianapolis: Bobbs-Merrill, 1963).

Finally, there is an increasing number of studies of several of the minority groups who have not figured largely in the preceding pages, and such studies are changing perspectives on both the Revolution and American character. Among these are Linda Kerber, *Women of the Republic: Intellectual Ideologies in Revolutionary Amer-*

ica (Chapel Hill, N.C.: University of North Carolina Press, 1980), and Mary Beth Norton, *Liberty's Daughters: The Revolutionary Experience of American Women* (Boston: Little, Brown, 1980). Individual biographies are Charles W. Akers, *Abigail Adams: An American Woman* (Boston: Little, Brown, 1980), and Marvin L. Brown, Jr., *Baroness von Riedesel and the American Revolution: Journal and Correspondence of a Tour of Duty, 1776–1783* (Chapel Hill, N.C.: University of North Carolina Press, 1965). The thorny question of what to do about the slaves in the middle of a revolution claiming universality is discussed in David Brian Davis, *The Problem of Slavery in the Age of Revolution: 1770–1783* (Ithaca, N.Y.: Cornell University Press, 1975), and in Winthrop Jordan, *White over Black: American Attitudes Toward the Negro, 1550–1812* (Chapel Hill, N.C.: University of North Carolina Press, 1968). Barbara Graymont examined *The Iroquois in the American Revolution* (Syracuse, N.Y.: Syracuse University Press, 1972), and James H. O'Donnell, Jr., wrote on *Southern Indians in the Americas in the Revolution* (Knoxville, Tenn.: University of Tennessee Press, 1973). And there are very substantial documentary collections, either of individuals' correspondence or on certain items or topics. This limited list of suggestions, like this book itself, is no more than a viewpoint and an introduction.

Index

297